IN PRAISE OF
WHAT ARE OLD PEOPLE FOR?

"Members of the baby-boom generation, who benefited from Dr. Spock in their childhood and Dr. Lamaze in the childbearing years, now have a new physician activist to help transform their old age . . ."—KORKY VANN, THE HARTFORD COURANT

"A revolutionary resource of ideas . . . a "must-read" in today's era . . . a keenly inspired look into the failings on an individual and cultural level that need to be rectified, as well as speculations upon the meaning of aging itself and practical applications to improve quality of life."—THE MIDWEST BOOK REVIEW

"A seminal work and a call to arms—a struggle will (must) ensue."— ARTHUR RASHAP, JEFFERSON AREA BOARD FOR AGING

"Bill Thomas is a rebel with a cause, a 45-year-old geriatrician who wants to overthrow an empire—the demographic empire of adulthood. That long season of life that has become like a cult, he says, a tyrannical power . . . crushing dissidents by distorting childhood and marginalizing old age in a vain effort to control the world . . . You might wonder: Is William H. Thomas, MD, a little over the top? I don't think so. The redefinition of aging is a social revolution to awaken people—all of us in the thrall of adulthood—to the changes ahead in the life cycle. He takes on the role of abolitionist as he challenges the fundamental orthodoxy of forever-young adulthood . . . 'To deny old age [says Thomas] is to invite anarchy in our lives . . . The liberation of elders and elderhood is not an aging issue . . . It is our last, best hope for saving our world from the all-conquering power of adults.' Them's fighting words."—ABIGAIL TRAFFORD, THE WASHINGTON POST

"For anyone . . . who wants to explore the issues and answers about the years, indeed decades, ahead of them, this is an important book to read."— ALAN CARUBA, BOOKVIEWS

"A brilliant work."—JOHN ZEISEL, PhD, CO-FOUNDER AND PRESIDENT OF HEARTHSTONE ALZHEIMER CARE, LTD.

"[An] eloquent and powerful denunciation of the paradox of our times: We have been able to prolong people's lives and at the same time we marginalize older individuals . . . At times it has been hard to interrupt the reading: The book provides a guide to a travel of self-discovery and self-revelation; it is a form of modern-day prophecy. The book may transform any informed reader . . ."—REVIEW IN *TAMPA TRIBUNE* BY LODOVICO BALDUCCI, PROFESSOR OF ONCOLOGY AND MEDICINE AT THE H. LEE MOFFITT CANCER CENTER & RESEARCH INSTITUTE AND THE UNIVERSITY OF SOUTH FLORIDA

". . . Dr. William H. Thomas [has] airtight street cred as a man of good will."—JOHN GOODSPEED, *THE [EASTON, MD] STAR DEMOCRAT*

"A healthy society, Thomas says, will create neighborhoods that blend people of all ages and capabilities. In his vision, old people become your neighbors, living together in small groups, sharing wisdom and wit with children. To do this, living arrangements for elders must change, Thomas says. Even before boomers get old enough to change attitudes about aging, Thomas is working to bring about elder group homes . . . Elders will discover their purpose, he says, because 'old people are the glue that holds the human community together'."—JANE GLENN HAAS, *THE ORANGE COUNTY REGISTER*

"On target! My head is spinning with where all of this can lead."—DENISE HYDE, EDEN ALTERNATIVE REGIONAL COORDINATOR

First-Place Trade Book Winner—*Medical Book Awards*
Book of the Year (Consumer Health)—*American Journal of Nursing*
Author Recipient of Heinz Award for the Human Condition

Other Books from VanderWyk & Burnham by William H. Thomas, M.D.

IN THE ARMS OF ELDERS
(contains the parable "Learning from Hannah")

LIFE WORTH LIVING
(about the Eden Alternative)

What Are Old People For?

How Elders Will Save the World

William H. Thomas, M.D.

VanderWyk & Burnham

First printing in paperback, 2007
Copyright © 2004 by William H. Thomas, M.D.

Published by VanderWyk & Burnham
P.O. Box 2789, Acton, Massachusetts 01720

www.VandB.com

This book is available for quantity purchases. For information on bulk discounts,
call (800) 789-7916 or write to Special Sales at the above address.

Acknowledgments: Sunburst type ornament cast and letterpress printed by Firefly Press.
Elephant wrinkles photograph © John Sullivan, Ribbit Photography. Human wrinkles
photograph © Mediscan, London.

ISBN-13: 978-1-889242-32-3 (paperback)
ISBN-10: 1-889242-32-2 (paperback)

Library of Congress Cataloging-in-Publication Data
Thomas, William H., M.D.
    What are old people for? : how elders will save the world /
William H. Thomas.
        p. cm.
    ISBN 1-889242-20-9
    1. Aged—Social conditions. 2. Aged—Care. 3. Old age. 4. Longevity—Social
aspects. 5. Intergenerational relations. 6. Social participation. I. Title.

HQ1061.T473 2004
305.26—dc22
                                                                    2004044311

Interior book design by Ruth Lacey Design
Graphs and diagrams by Fran Jarvis, ANCOart

Manufactured in the United States of America
10 9 8 7 6 5 4 3 2

For my mother and father

It has been widely said that whatever many may say about the future, it is ours—not only that it may happen to us, but it is in part made by us.

Dr. Ethel Percy Andrus, Social Activist, 1884–1967

CONTENTS

PREFACE

In 1975 Robert Butler, M.D., asked, "Why survive?" in a book of that title. The book documented the terrible price that an ageist society exacts from older people. My own book is offered as an answer to Dr. Butler's question. The importance of aging and longevity grows daily, and with it the dangers associated with the misuse of old age increase. As time passes, we begin to ask what the future holds for us.

At the beginning of my medical career, I paid little heed to aging and the lives of the aged. That changed in 1991 when I took a part-time job as the medical director of a small nursing home. That was when I first read Wendell Berry's collection of essays What Are People For? His eloquence inspired me to begin keeping a daily journal. His ideas encouraged me to reflect on the moral dimensions of the work I was doing in the nursing home. My book's title, *What Are Old People For?* is meant to be a gesture of respect and gratitude to a man whose writing has influenced the course of my work.

I have come to believe that being a physician involves much more than merely having a license to practice medicine. My training prepared me to make careful observations of the people and scenes that surround me, yet I find that I am inclined to look beyond the realm of clinical practice. I feel compelled to connect my daily observations with the essential moral questions of our time. This commitment has helped me survey much of the terrain that makes up human experience. I have held a newborn girl in my hands as she drew her first breath, and I have sat at the bedside of a hundred-year-old woman when she breathed her last breath. I have seen cowards and saints, fools and heroes up close and without the masks they usually wear.

This book was inspired by many of these experiences. While its central argument draws on biology, mythology, sociology, and philosophy, its heart belongs to the simplest observations of the way we live now. Because we live in an age of specialists, it is important for me to convey that I am not a credentialed expert in some of the fields that I draw from. While I have done everything in my power to be accurate in every particular, I recognize that some experts will find fault with some of the specifics. As a devout generalist, I believe that the truth of an important argument can be sustained even when fault can be found with certain of its specifics, and I hope that you will agree.

It has been said that people are not interested in books about aging, but, in fact, people are always interested in learning more about matters that concern their lives and well-being. The questions that revolve around aging and our longevity increasingly rise to that level. Issues related to aging define some of the most important risks and opportunities that confront our society. We live in an exciting time. There is a new old age waiting to be discovered, ready to be explored. Aging and the aged are not, as so often supposed, the cause of our problems—they are and always have been the source of the answers we need. Our longevity is ready to be freed from the shackles of prejudice and fear. It can and it will save our world.

What Are Old People For?

TRUE
LONGEVITY

Draw your chair up close
to the edge of the precipice
and I'll tell you a story.

F. Scott Fitzgerald, *Notebooks*

A New Wrinkle

A Warning

I opened the morning paper and there it was, a two-column advertisement made to resemble an advice column:

> **Reader Looks Younger . . . Now Dating Again!**
> Dear Patty: You've changed my life. I'm a "Baby Boomer," divorced, wasn't even dating. I even began to see those dreaded facial wrinkles and crow's feet . . . I just felt terrible. Then I read your column about that pharmacist's miracle discovery . . . CF-6 Facial Cream. Well, I bought a jar and amazing things began to happen. It changed my life! I do look younger . . . feel great . . . and I'm dating again, thanks to you!

The advertisement, and its chirpy optimism, would be bizarre if it were not so common. These messages are everywhere. Behind their cheerful facade is a warning: There is danger just over the horizon. Old age lies in wait, eager to steal our youth. There is no need for alarm, though. We can hold the threat at bay; our youthfulness can be protected. There is hope. The "pharmacist's miracle" offers us a shield against old age. Youth, or at least the appearance of youth, can be had for just $24.95 a jar.

Billions of dollars are spent every year on such remedies, and with good reason. We live in a profoundly ageist society. The post–World War II generation, in particular, has lionized youth, making its power, energy, and beauty the standard against which we all are to be measured. Gradually, however, the dark side of that obsession is being revealed. We see, with increasing clarity, the calamities that a youth-obsessed society is willing to impose on the old.

Like MacArthur's old soldiers, the aged among us fade away. Strength and bravery, no matter how plentiful, offer no refuge from the passage of time. The decades gradually reduce the old to shadows of their former selves. At best, this new silhouette can be charming—a twinkling eye or kindly smile taking the place of youth's vital glow. More often, though, old people are exposed to a bigoted ageism that is openly expressed and widely accepted. They are herded into complexes and facilities that are cut off from the rest of the community—and are expected to pay for the privilege. They can be confined to institutions, often for life, and must endure this loss of freedom with little or no hope of release. To be old in contemporary society is to inhabit a ghetto without borders. Rich or poor, man or woman, sage or fool, there is no refuge. The bias against old age infects the elderly as well; many older people actively profess the superiority of youth and the young.

I am a physician and my specialty is working with older people. Most of my patients are very old, so old that they first noticed their own facial wrinkles more than forty years ago. Nostrums like CF-6 hold no attraction for them, but these products do interest me. Antiwrinkle creams form the most visible element of a deep and dangerous fault line that cuts through our society. No matter what ingredients are listed on the label, wrinkle cures always include unspoken threats and hollow promises. The multibillion-dollar antiwrinkle industry stokes and then profits from our fear.

Every morning all across America, people peer into bathroom mirrors, searching for signs of age. No line, no blemish is overlooked. We dread the appearance of those little lines at the corners of our mouths and eyes, and then we console ourselves with the thought that, really, they are hardly noticeable. Still we know the truth. We are getting older—every day one day older. Rarely do we set aside our insecurities long enough to ask, "What are wrinkles? Where do they come from and what do they really mean?" Perhaps if we understood them better, we might fear them less.

Human Pachyderms

Snakes don't get wrinkles. Instead, they shed their old skins and sport shiny new skins in their place. Birds don't get wrinkles. Worn feathers are replaced when the birds molt. Mammals, in contrast, keep the skins in which they are born. While it is true that the outermost layer of any mammal's skin constantly sheds dead cells, our true skin (dermis) remains with us all our lives. The need to be "comfortable in our own skin" is something we mammals need to take seriously; we have no place else to go.

Humans are (nearly) hairless mammals, and that is an important fact when our skin and its wrinkles are being considered. For the first two hundred million years of mammalian evolution, skin was rarely, if ever, exposed to the powerful rays of the sun. Among the proven benefits of being covered with fur, as nearly all mammals are, is that fur protects skin from damage by the ultraviolet rays in sunlight. If you doubt that hair is nature's own sunscreen, look closely at a balding man. Notice how the wrinkled brow, which has been exposed to the sun for decades, gives way to a scalp as smooth as a baby's bottom. Hairlessness, as most middle-aged men would agree, is not the natural state for mammals. Indeed, most of our fellow "naked" mammals live in environments that shelter them from the sun. Hairless burrowing rodents take refuge underground; seals and whales live underwater. Humans, however, bathe in sunlight—with inevitable consequences.

As decades pass, the collagen that holds our skin together becomes less elastic. You can demonstrate this change by grasping a fold of skin on the back of your hand. Pull it outward and then let go. Because their skin is highly elastic, children and young adults will see it snap back into place immediately. Older readers will note that this fold of skin relaxes more gradually. The difference is due to age-related changes in the composition of collagen. Long-term exposure to free radicals (aggressive chemical compounds that can damage other molecules) gradually modifies the way our bodies make and repair the collagen building blocks that hold our skin together. Tobacco smoke is loaded with free radicals, which is why smoking accelerates the loss of our skin's youthful suppleness. The warning label on cigarette packages could easily include premature facial wrinkles as one of the many hazards of smoking.

So, what does it take to make a wrinkle? The essential ingredients include

1. prolonged exposure of hairless skin to sunlight,
2. longevity sufficient to experience age-related changes in skin collagen, and
3. exposure to free radicals that can alter skin proteins.

The ideal candidates for wrinkle formation are long-lived, hairless, terrestrial mammals. Humans share these characteristics with just one other species. We, like elephants, get wrinkles. If you have ever seen an elephant up close, you have surely noticed its elephantine wrinkles. We are the elephant's dermatological first cousins. We are human pachyderms.

Elephant Wrinkles

Human Wrinkles

The Botox Brigade

The surest method of wrinkle prevention is death at a young age. Those who want to live and still be wrinkle-free must take special care to hide from the sun. This could mean adopting a completely nocturnal lifestyle or following the example of the naked mole rat and retreating—permanently—to a deep, dark burrow. Less radical

strategies have been proven to reduce wrinkle formation, such as limiting exposure to sunlight (and remembering to use sunscreen), eating a diet rich in fruits and vegetables, and, for those who smoke,
quitting the tobacco habit. These are good things even for those who
are not afraid of wrinkles: many of the tactics that can delay the
appearance of wrinkles also offer protection against cancer.

When we can look past how they make us feel, it is clear that
wrinkles are the natural result of living into the later decades of a normal human life. The methods we use to eradicate wrinkles, in contrast, are decidedly unnatural.

The cosmetics industry and the medical profession are allies in a
war against facial wrinkles. Dermatologist Nicholas Perricone opens
his *New York Times* best-selling book *The Wrinkle Cure* by claiming,
"Wrinkled, sagging skin is *not* the inevitable result of growing older.
It's a disease and you can fight it." If that is true, wrinkles represent a
most unusual form of illness. Diseases are best known for causing
physical suffering, limiting function, or shortening life span.
Cholera, scurvy, hepatitis, AIDS, and . . . wrinkles? Plenty of murky
reasoning is needed to convert wrinkles, which are a normal, natural
feature of human development, into a pathological disorder. The
motivation to make such a leap, though, is straightforward. Diseases
need treatment and treatments cost money. Aided and abetted by
hundreds of millions of dollars in marketing, the antiwrinkle business
sows fear and reaps a rich financial harvest.

The cosmetics and medical industries are happy to fuel an arms
race that perpetuates our fear of wrinkles. They view (and want you
to view) those little lines at the corners of your eyes as advance scouts
from the evil empire of old age. The first line of defense against this
invasion consists of moisturizing creams that promise to restore the
skin's dewy softness. These preparations are harmless enough and
work through the same benign process that puts wrinkles on your fin-
gertips after a long soak in the tub. The water contained in the lotion
is absorbed by the surface skin cells, causing them to swell. On the
face, especially around the mouth and eyes, this swelling fills in the
wrinkles and makes them less visible. No harm, and possibly some
good, is done, but these lotions provide only temporary relief.

Millions of people move on to complex and questionable pseudomedical compounds loaded with whatever vitamins, minerals, and antioxidants are currently in favor. I am not condemning these products, and I understand well why we buy and use them, but they cannot change the fact that we are, indeed, aging. In time, even the most effective of them fail to provide satisfactory results and newer, more powerful weapons must be brought to bear.

The medical profession has developed a prescription-strength antiwrinkle armamentarium. Skin peels and dermabrasion procedures strip away the outer layer of skin, laying bare the tender pink tissue underneath. The exposure of these immature skin cells creates the appearance of youth, but the effect is temporary. The glow of youth is soon lost and another painful procedure is required to re-create the illusion. More durable wrinkle eradication is available to those who are willing to go under the knife. Face-lifts solve the problem of wrinkles and lost elasticity by stretching aged skin over the face and then trimming off the excess. The surgeon's knife is both sharp and fast, and it is easy to go too far. More than a few movie stars have emerged from a series of cosmetic procedures resembling the body-snatched aliens they may once have played on screen.

At the turn of the twenty-first century, the big new gun in the war on wrinkles was Botox, which is actually a diluted form of the deadly toxin that is produced by the *Clostridium botulinum* Type A bacteria and that causes botulism. In its pure form, a single gram of this substance is so potent that it could kill more than a million people. Early symptoms of botulism include drooling and slurred speech. The toxin is known to spread swiftly through the body. Within just a few hours it can reach and paralyze the muscles responsible for breathing. The result is an agonizing death by asphyxiation. The medicinal form of the toxin is extremely dilute, and even though it is injected directly into the patient, it rarely causes death.

Initially employed to control painful and disfiguring muscle spasms, the medication found a new use when a dermatologist injected it into the forehead of his office receptionist. As if by magic, the drug eliminated her frown line and a revolution was launched. While undeniably effective in eradicating wrinkles, there are side effects.

These include, but are not limited to, droopy eyelids, flu-like symptoms, muscle weakness, facial pain, drooling, and nausea. Not to be forgotten are rare but serious episodes of shock, respiratory failure, and heart attack. For the price of a little poison, we can look younger.

The transient nature of the relief provided by Botox should be emphasized because, in addition to the drug's side effects, its use can lead to a bizarre form of dependency. A 2002 *New York Times* article on the subject reported, "Because Botox wears off, more injections are required to maintain its effects or the patient's face will return to its wrinkly state . . . Dr. Michelle Copeland, a plastic surgeon in New York, said Botox use is already so prevalent among her patients that she has to ask their ages. 'I look at their faces and say, "Remind me, are you 70? 50?" I can't really tell anymore,' she said."

In his book *The Force of Character,* psychologist James Hillman explores what is lost when artificial means are used to alter the age of one's own face. "If you imagine your face as a phenomenon . . . with its own destiny, then all that goes on there, after sixty especially, is a work in progress, building the image, preparing a face that has little to do with the faces that you meet . . . A face is being made, often against your will, as witness to your character." Hillman then quotes the ultimate authority, Marilyn Monroe, who said, "I want to grow old without facelifts. They take the life out of a face, the character. I want to have the courage to be loyal to the face I've made."

The Botox phenomenon exploits our dim and uninformed attitude toward the approach of age, and does so at a profit. *Off the Record Research* (a trade publication for dermatologists) quotes a nameless cosmetic surgeon on the monetary benefits of Botox injections: "When they [dermatologists] have a product they can sell and make a reasonable profit—and the product does not involve dealing with insurance companies—dermatologists will jump on it."

The profit motive, the mass media's love affair with the new, and the anxiety provoked by growing old in a youth-obsessed culture have led millions to surrender their faces to the war on wrinkles. We are being asked to unmake what we have spent a lifetime making. What do we receive in return for this sacrifice? Not youth. Instead, we are given, at best, the facsimile of youth. Expressiveness, passion, and history are pillaged in the pursuit of youth's fresh blankness. People fear wrinkles because of what they seem to say about us. They are the sum of all the days we have lived and will never live again. They tell our story even when we do not want that story told. Even the attempt to erase them becomes part of what is written on our faces. We—the doers, the movers, the shakers, the achievers, the rocks of our families and communities—are being written upon. It shocks us to see ourselves, for the first time, as paper and not the pen we imagine ourselves to be.

Wrinkles are painless and harmless. They are us and we are them.

Beautiful Wrinkles

What would it be like to live in a society that adored wrinkles? The idea may seem laughable at first, but for millennia, living to a ripe old age was an exceptional achievement and was often recognized as such by society. Confucian societies, among many others, have long held that the aged should be treated with special respect.

What if the war on wrinkles were replaced by a crazy new wave of wrinkle-promoting ingenuity? Any desire to *intentionally* age one's face seems bizarre to those reared in a youth-dominated culture. It upsets unspoken assumptions about aging. However, imagine, if just for a moment, that we lived in a world that embraced the arrival of a face with character. Millions would grumble, "If they can put a man on the moon, is it too much to ask for faster, better wrinkles that are both safe and beautiful?" Such a society would swoon over wrinkled artists, actors, and models. Songs and poems would celebrate the arrival of a face with character (even if its arrival was hurried along). Spas and retreats would promise, "You'll look ten years older in just two weeks." It really would be a different world.

Let's look again at the advertisement that opened this chapter. Maybe someday I will unfold my newspaper and read the following words as I eat my breakfast:

Reader Looks Older . . . Now Growing Again!
Dear Patty: You've changed my life. I was a "Baby Boomer," obsessed with youth and divorced from my own aging self.

When I looked in the mirror, all I saw was flat, featureless skin. I just felt terrible. Then I read your column about that pharmacist's miracle discovery . . . CF-6 Facial Cream. Well, I bought a jar and amazing things began to happen. It changed my life! I do look older. I'm growing into a wonderful face: wrinkles, crow's feet, smile lines . . . I have it all! I feel great . . . and I'm growing as a person again, thanks to you!

Ridiculous? Why should it be? Far more ridiculous is a society that panics people into painful injections and disfiguring surgery as a result of the benign lines that appear on their faces. Wrinkles themselves do us no harm. The suffering they bring, the suffering that drives people into the arms of the cosmetics and medical industries, is the product of an overt bigotry toward old age and aging. The pain wrinkles inflict is entirely of our own making.

All the self-induced anguish might serve some purpose if it prodded us toward a reexamination of our longevity. Wrinkles give us a way to begin such a conversation, but it is just a start. Gray hair and facial lines are only the first signs of something much more menacing. Finding a new wrinkle on wrinkles is one thing; plumbing the true nature of our longevity presents a much more exciting and demanding challenge.

The Doctrine of Youth's Perfection

From *Senex* and *Sen*

The United States Senate is full of old men. This should come as no surprise, given that the word *senate* is derived from the Latin word *senex,* which means "old man." *Senex* itself is descended from the Proto-Indo-European *sen,* which means "old." *Senility,* another "old man" word, is not used as often as it used to be. Before it was replaced with the more clinically precise term *dementia,* it was used to refer to the relentless decline in thought, memory, and understanding that seemed to accompany old age. Senility has always been a fearful thing.

Sen also gives us *senior,* with its interesting twofold connotations. A senior in college has reached an apex of achievement, a senior officer is always in command, and senior debt is the first to be paid off. *Senior citizen,* in contrast, is unlikely to bring power and achievement immediately to mind. It is a euphemism for "a person declining into old age."

The schizophrenic nature of age-related words can be seen in the sentence, "Señor Smith may be senile, but he is our state's senior senator." The same clash we see between the negative *senile* and the affirmative *senior senator* exists within a single word, *senescence.* Linguistically, *senescence* is closely related to *adolescence,* the root of which is *adolescere,* "to grow up." Adolescents struggle to grow into adulthood. *Senescence* could, quite easily, be understood as the struggle to grow into old age. In common usage, however, it carries a much more pessimistic meaning. Senescence generally refers to the gradual, painful undoing of the vigor of adulthood. It is a falling apart, the sum of all the unhappy changes that accrue after a brief moment in the full sun of youth.

There is another, equally valid, way of using the word. Botanists employ *senescence* to describe the most fruitful events in a plant's life cycle. The senescent phase of plant growth follows the exuberance of early growth. As the end of the growing season approaches, the metabolism of fruiting plants changes. There is a loss of water weight in the stems and leaves. The metabolism shifts away from growth and toward ripening. Botanical senescence is what prepares grapes for the harvest. There is no reason senescence couldn't be used to refer to the peculiar human ripening that accompanies our advancing years. Consider this *American Heritage Dictionary* entry from the point of view of old age:

> **Ripe 1.** Fully developed; mature: *ripe peaches.* **2.** Resembling matured fruit, as in fullness. **3.** Sufficiently advanced in preparation or aging to be used or eaten: *ripe cheese . . .* **5.** Advanced in years: *the ripe age of 90.* **6.** Fully prepared to do or undergo something; ready. **7.** Sufficiently advanced; opportune: *The time is ripe for great societal changes.*

Imagine growing into an old age defined by full development, maturity, awareness, readiness, and advancement; it would truly be an opportune time. Unfortunately, society has not followed the botanists' lead. We are mired in a highly negative view of aging that envisions a one-way trip down the long road toward disease, dementia, disability, and death. Peaches may ripen, but human beings, it seems, cannot.

Though we are all well aware of the real and often unpleasant changes that come with advancing years, we lack a concept that fully recognizes the positive elements of aging. It is as if our longevity consisted solely of deep, forbidding shadows. This emphasis is perhaps the most damaging consequence of contemporary society's glorification of youth. Those who seek a more complete understanding of longevity, an understanding capable of embracing both light and shadow, conduct their search within a culture that rarely misses an opportunity to emphasize the negative aspects of aging. The positive dimensions of our longevity remain, for now, present but unseen. These virtues are admittedly much more subtle and far less obvious than aching joints and sagging skin. They are, however, essential to both our development as individuals and the direction in which our culture is moving.

Discovering the Obvious

Looking and seeing go together. Medical school professors have long urged their students to study hard because "you see what you look for and you look for what you know." The usefulness of such advice goes far beyond the medical profession. A stroll in the woods with a devoted bird-watcher can illustrate this principle in action. As you amble along, your companion treats you to a running commentary: "Fancy that! Remarkable. This far north in midsummer? Most unusual." You, in contrast, cannot see what your friend sees. Despite looking carefully for the bird that excites your friend, you see only a jumble of bushes, branches, and leaves. Even the musical but anonymous chirping high above means little to the untutored ear. What we see, what we hear, the questions we ask, and how we think are all shaped by what we know and, even more powerfully, by what we believe.

Research into human longevity has been misled in large part by its heavy reliance on a core of unstated but deeply held beliefs that color old age with every negative connotation available. The assumptions inherent in these beliefs, while not wholly false, ignore important dimensions of aging. Hardly a straightforward decline from the apex of youth, growing old is actually a complex, richly detailed phenomenon. The difference between the assumptions we make about old age and the reality of life's last decades is the difference between a pen-and-ink cartoon and an intricate oil portrait.

An old man walks past you on the street. Ordinarily, he might not even catch your attention. Now, imagine that you have a geriatrician by your side. She will show you things you might not see. The man walks slowly, tending to stay close to the fronts of buildings and away from the turbulence near the curb. Seemingly by accident but actually from habit, he occasionally touches the storefronts with his fingers. This gives him useful information about his posture and body position and helps him keep his balance. A friend spies him from a distance and calls his name. He does not hear her. (Some loss of hearing normally accompanies aging.) She shrugs and walks on. The day is hot and the man tires, pausing to look into a store he has no intention of entering. At the corner, the late afternoon sun is in his eyes, making it difficult for him to see the crossing signal clearly. He squints and holds his hand to his brow. (Age-related changes in the lens of the eye scatter light, making glare a significant problem.) Across the intersection, he finds that construction workers have barricaded his usual way home. He stands before the obstacles for a long moment and then, tentatively, retreats, forced to find an alternative route. (Researchers have found that older people adjust to novel situations less quickly than younger people.) Finally, he rounds the corner and disappears out of sight. You probably would not have noticed him, let alone watched him closely for these few minutes, but now you can see. He has lost so much and will lose so much more.

An attentive observer in any public place can confirm the details I have recorded. The science comes straight from the field of geriatrics. The error—and it is a colossal error—lies in the narrowness of the interpretation. Rather than seeing the miraculous adaptations the man has made that allow him to live a satisfying life, we see how much he has lost. A declinist view of old age is embedded in our language. It shapes our opinions; it deceives our eyes and ears. Declinism, a concept that has been used to describe the experience of empires that are past their prime, can also be employed to describe the contemporary equation of aging with loss and surrender.

How did declinism come to be so pervasive? History, culture, tradition, psychology, and biology have contributed to this error, and each of these will be given its due, but we begin with what ought to be the purest and least biased of all perspectives, that of the research scientist. Scientific research, by its nature, aspires to objectivity, but when aging is the subject of investigation, we too often find the results to be riddled with bias, stereotypical thinking, and unquestioned assumptions. Our decades-long scientific examination of human longevity has labored mightily to discover the obvious. We have built and continue to enlarge a massive body of knowledge that equates aging with decline and then confidently declares that we decline as we age.

The Mismeasure of Longevity

One influential study shows the extent to which declinist thinking is woven into aging-related research. In its July 1960 issue, the journal *Science* published a paper entitled "General Theory of Mortality and Aging." Its authors asked and attempted to answer an important question: "Why does the risk of dying increase with age?" Bernard Strehler and Albert Mildvan presented a theory intended to explain the common observation that death favors the old.

They included a graph (redrawn in Notes at the back of this book) showing the quantitative relationship between age and death rate. The death rate starts a steady climb at around age fifty, and this explains why we are rarely surprised to learn that a 104-year-old woman has passed away but are shocked to learn of the death of a 20-year-old. A steep slope of the graphed curve in late life highlights the relationship between old age and death but does nothing to explain why such a correlation exists.

The authors began their examination of death and why it favors the old by presenting, paradoxically, a definition of vitality. They described vitality as "the capacity of an individual organism to stay alive." The rising death rate presented in their graph, combined with the authors' definition of vitality, makes it obvious that the young are more vital than the old. The rising death rate late in life, then, can be understood in terms of a progressive loss of vitality with advancing age. Having kicked the question a little further down the road, the authors then asked, "Why does vitality wane with age?" Here, Strehler and Mildvan assumed that every "organism consists of a number of subsystems, each of which has a certain maximum ability to restore initial conditions after a challenge [from the environment . . . Death occurs when the rate at which the organism does work to restore the original state is less than that demanded to overcome the effects of a given challenge."

In other words, older people are less vital (and more likely to die) because age has robbed them of the ability to tolerate changes in their environment. The older the person, the less reserve capacity remains to fight challenges. Death occurs whenever a person fails to restore internal equilibrium after being stressed. The less reserve capacity an individual possesses, the more likely he or she is, on any given day, to encounter a fatal stressor.

Strehler and Mildvan's theory is easier to understand with the help of the following diagram. The box defined by the dashed line represents the reserve capacity (vitality) remaining at a given age. Not surprisingly, this capacity shrinks as the decades pass. Each of the arrows represents an environmental stress capable of pulling the body away from a healthy equilibrium. The longer the arrow, the greater the stress.

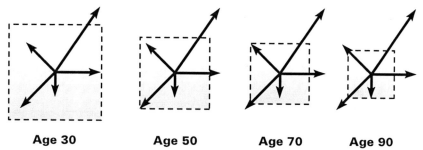

Age 30   **Age 50**   **Age 70**   **Age 90**

As the years pass, there is less capacity to withstand different environmental stressors.

Let's suppose that, from longest to shortest, the arrows represent the following situations:

- Being run over by a bus
- Having a major heart attack
- Contracting influenza
- Falling while climbing out of the bathtub
- Catching a cold

In youth, our bodies have a generous capacity to respond to and absorb changes forced on us by our environment. As we age, our reserve capacity decreases and a stress that we might have tolerated easily in earlier years can, in late life, overwhelm us with fatal consequences. By the time we reach the later decades of life, our vastly reduced reserve capacity increases the chance that, on any given day, we will encounter a fatal stressor.

Strehler and Mildvan approached, from a strictly declinist point of view, the question of why vitality wanes in old age, and that perspective rewarded them with an important new insight into human aging. However, because they employed declinist reasoning to evaluate data that were already tinged with a declinist bias, they missed the chance to develop other, even more useful insights into longevity.

The researchers' bias can be seen in the graph (also in Notes) that formed the centerpiece of their argument. That graph presents measures of body functions such as the heart's ability to pump blood, the kidney's ability to filter blood, and the lung's capacity for gas exchange. When the authors completed their calculations and plotted their data, out popped a graphical representation of what terrifies people about old age. Reserve capacity approached 100 percent among the young and then showed a relentless decline throughout life. When people talk about being "over the hill," this is the hill they are referring to.

The tiny reserve available among the very old was used by Strehler and Mildvan to explain why older people are more likely to die than younger people. Much more interesting, though, is what they did not see. Their declinist perspective limited their ability to fully appreciate the data they cited in their own paper.

Declinism

The data used to make the "over-the-hill" graph were collected by conducting medical tests on thousands of people, recording the results, and then sorting the results by age. This method allows researchers to create a series of snapshots that, when viewed together, are supposed to create a moving picture of aging. This process is attractive because, let's face it, who has the time to spend seventy years collecting serial measurements from the same individuals? The flaw in their work is due to an unacknowledged bias in favor of youth.

The investigators employed measurements of physical characteristics that are at their apex in young adulthood. Such a practice makes sense if and only if you begin with the declinist assumption that aging is best understood as a descent from the summit of youth. The error embedded in this approach becomes plain when we look at what happens when this same strategy is used to evaluate the first half of life. Imagine what would become of scientists who, setting out to better understand men and women in their thirties, chose as their measurements those characteristics that are ideally suited to evaluating the well-being of young children. Three such indicators come immediately to mind and are obtained at every well-child checkup. They are growth in head circumference, growth in height, and weight gain.

For example, there is an enormous (and vitally important) expansion in brain size that defines a healthy child. Adults measured against these childhood standards fail miserably. When a child stops growing, it is considered a "failure to thrive." This is a serious condition that can easily lead to an admission to the hospital. What if an adult visits a doctor and is found to have no increase in head circumference or height? Is this "failure to thrive"? Should an ambulance be called? Of course not.

Adults are not children, and measuring adults by the standards that define a healthy childhood tells us much more about those doing the measuring than about those being measured. By the same token, a declinist bias is inevitable when we insist on measuring old age with the yardsticks of early adulthood—and that is exactly what Strehler and Mildvan did. Their methods and their conclusions owe much to their faith in youth's perfection. In fact, old age is *different from* adulthood, just as adulthood is *different from* childhood. Age changes us. Some of those changes are easily quantifiable; degradation of renal function is an example. But such easily measurable changes tell only one part of the story. Common sense tells us that an adult is not a bloated child who is failing to thrive. Could it be that an older person is something other than an adult in decline?

Continuous Aging

Strehler and Mildvan offer a commonsense, if somewhat dry, description of aging. It is, they write, "a gradual change in . . . physical, chemical, or physiological properties *after reproductive maturity*" (emphasis added). In that context, perhaps an older person is the natural product of an adult's accumulated aging, just as an adult is the natural product of a child's accumulated maturation.

This analogy has its uses but should not be pushed too far. We are accustomed to the phenomenal early growth of the newborn and the "growth spurt" that comes with adolescence. These experiences may help explain why so many people believe that there is an "age spurt," a point late in life at which a person suddenly begins to age. In fact, there is no such thing.

The same data that Strehler and Mildvan used to create the over-the-hill graph can be presented differently, from another perspective. If we let go of the idea that aging must be equivalent to decline, we can create a new graph (also in Notes) with a very different lesson. We can create a graph that shows the *amount of change* in measures of body functions across the years. Decade after decade that amount of change is fairly uniform. There is no sudden upswing, no sudden plunge. It is the very picture of consistency, as if the processes being measured were unfolding in a coordinated fashion. This notion is far from the idea of aging as a chaotic and unpredictable falling apart.

Measurements of normal human physiological functions show a steady decline of between 0.5 and 1.3 percent per year every year after age thirty. Yes, you read that right. The thirty-three-year-old Wall Street bond trader ages *at the same rate* as the ninety-two-year-old retired cop. It turns out that Strehler and Mildvan missed a chance to make headlines back in 1960. Imagine the popular reaction if their findings had dismantled the myth of the "age spurt." Old people and young people age at the same rate.

Growing to maturity is a bumpy, uneven process, with fits and starts. Growing old, in contrast, is smooth as silk, unfolding year after year with clockwork precision. Remember this the next time you stop to watch an old person cross the street. One year from that date, you will both have lost the same percentage of your youthful vitality.

A Ripe Old Age

The most common misunderstanding of old age, and the one to which declinists are most attached, is the idea that the body and its organs break down in the manner of a worn-out machine. This image fits quite comfortably with society's prevailing prejudice. Yet anyone who has experience with very used cars can recognize the limits of such a notion. Old cars break down in haphazard and unpredictable ways. Some parts of the car—the door latches, for example—work as well as they did the day they were made, despite very heavy use. Other components, such as the brakes and muffler, are prone to unpredictable and highly inconvenient failures.

If the human body were a purely mechanical thing, we would expect great variation in the severity and sequence of decline. One last look back at the "over-the-hill" graph shows that this is not the case. What we see is a gradual, orderly unfolding of changes that takes place over a period of decades. It is stable, coordinated, and predictable. Changes in nerve conduction velocity evolve in parallel with changes in cardiac output. Kidney function changes are in accord with changes in the basal metabolic rate. This is not a chaotic breakdown of systems and organs; it is a symphony.

More than anything else, these changes resemble a ripening. Consider the grapes of June: they are tart, juicy, and quite unready for the harvest. As the season advances, a dramatic and entirely predictable sequence of changes unfolds. The doctrine of youth's perfection tells us that the unripe (being younger) is superior to that which has ripened. This is the flaw that lies at the heart of the declinist view of age and aging. The decline that accompanies aging is real and important (it helps explain why we die when we get old), but it is much less than the whole story. The danger is that we allow a thoughtless acceptance of what seems obvious to obscure deeper, more meaningful insights into age and aging. Even though more than half of the normal human life span is spent aging, we understand very little about the potential of the aging process. The powers of old age remain too often devalued or outright hidden from us.

The Hidden Powers of Age

Adaptation

"As Gregor Samsa awoke one morning from uneasy dreams he found himself transformed in his bed into a gigantic insect." Thus begins one of the strangest tales in literature. Franz Kafka was a young man when he wrote *Metamorphosis,* and while I doubt that it was his intention, he created a powerful statement about aging. The story he tells continues to fascinate because it offers us the evil twin of the usual fairy-tale narrative. We are accustomed to the transformation of the ugly duckling into a swan, the frog who is just one kiss away from being a prince. Instead, Kafka chills us with the story of a vigorous young man who is made, in the space of a single night, into an abhorrent, thrashing insect.

The story hints at a fearful question. When will we wake to find ourselves transformed? Though it is rarely admitted in polite company, we all know youth to be a fickle friend and ally. Someday it will betray us. How can we hope to continue living when our skin, our hair, and our lithe and supple limbs are replaced by scales, ugly appendages, and a profound helplessness? We love the beast that becomes a man but abhor the man who becomes a monster.

Gregor Samsa is just such a monster. The body to which he was accustomed, and in which he took great pride, has been snatched from him. He is the innocent victim of an apparently irreversible crime. His overwhelmed mind cannot accept, nor can his body accommodate, what he has become. The easy freedom of youthful vitality is gone, never to return. The doctrine of youth's perfection leaves little room for doubt. We must pity poor Gregor Samsa because something beautiful, something wonderful and altogether good, has been taken from him.

There is another, equally legitimate reason to pity Gregor, but it is rarely considered. His pathetic thrashing may also be lamentable because it reveals youth's most conspicuous defect. It is possible to feel sorry for Gregor not because of what he has lost, which is considerable, but rather for what he has not yet gained. Without a decades-long tutorial in change, accommodation to change, and transcendence within change, the young man is quickly and completely overwhelmed by his suddenly altered circumstances: "[He] swung himself out of bed with all his strength. There was a loud thump, but it was not really a crash. His fall was broken to some extent by the carpet, his back, too, was less stiff than he had thought, and so there was merely a dull thud, not so very startling. Only he had not lifted his head carefully enough and had hit it; he turned it and rubbed it on the carpet in pain and irritation."

Old age may be a time of loss and decline, but it is not only that. There is a countervailing and equally significant increase in the power of adaptation. The development of this capability is one of the most important and least acknowledged virtues of aging. Youth accustoms us to running ever faster and jumping ever higher, and the prospect of change in the opposite direction fills us with a cold dread. The young are utterly unprepared for the experience of aging. Gregor Samsa's rage against his plight actually magnifies his suffering. It is his persistent unwillingness and inability to cope with his vastly changed circumstances that reveals youth's most glaring weaknesses.

An older person wakes up to a new body with new demands and limitations not once but many times. As actor Bette Davis so wisely observed, "Old age is not for sissies." These changes require older people to develop enterprising strategies and subtle adaptations. While it is true that muscles weaken in late life, it is also true that older people are less likely to report symptoms of depression than younger people. Hair may turn white, get thin, and fall out, but, when surveyed, older people often report an enhanced sense of well-being. We grow shorter rather than taller, our toenails turn yellow, and our arches fall, and yet many older people report that their health is good or even very good. These seeming paradoxes are actually the fruits of adaptation. It grows in tandem with and is nourished by the decline in physiological function.

Kafka died young. I wonder how he might have approached *Metamorphosis* if he had lived to experience a ripe old age of his own. He might have changed the story, telling instead of a youth waking to find himself grown old. The effect would be nearly the same. The aged young man would struggle mightily to do that which the octogenarian is master of. Sitting, standing, dressing, and walking would be just as difficult for him as when he woke to find himself an insect. Old age has richness and complexity that, when appreciated, provide a powerful counterweight to the measurable, progressive, steady decline in bodily functions. In old age, the body instructs the mind in patience and forbearance while the mind tutors the body in creativity and flexibility.

Walking the Walk

From an early age, and without ever being expressly told to do so, we come to value the long springy stride and narrow tandem gait of youth. The young trumpet their virtuosity with preposterous shoes, a casual indifference to the terrain underfoot, and arms that swing casually by their sides. Actors and politicians have long understood how we unconsciously judge others by their stride. They lengthen and narrow their stride when they are in public and, in doing so, give the appearance of youth.

Trackers can easily determine a person's age by examining his or her footprints. Compared with the fluid stride of youth, the marks made by an older person can seem tentative and ungainly. This appearance is deceiving. The reality is that older people execute a highly evolved, richly detailed strategy that maintains upright ambulation into the last decades of life. Old people alter their gait in specific ways that account for very real changes in strength, endurance, coordination, sensation, and reaction time. The "shuffling gait" keeps the feet close to the ground and maximizes input from position sensors. The stance is widened to improve balance. The number of steps taken per minute is decreased to accommodate changes in endurance and to allow for increased reaction time. Keeping a human body upright and moving is a spectacular feat of coordination and reaction under any circumstances. Doing so in the ninth decade of life magnifies rather than diminishes the beauty of this achievement.

When the world's best golfers come together to play a tournament, the course is lengthened and the rough deepened so that their skill can be tested fully. Olympic divers challenge themselves with the most difficult dives, not the easiest. The Tour de France includes in its route the most taxing climbs, including some that are rated as "beyond category" in difficulty. When you see an old man or woman walking, you are witnessing a similarly exciting high-level performance. This is a tightly choreographed ballet, the product of decades of refinement. Watch and marvel. Miracles are all around you, once you know where to look.

New Heights

The adaptive strategies employed by older adults are routinely misinterpreted as inferior copies of youth's gold standard. Appreciating the shuffling gait of the older person as a triumph of adaptation takes thought and effort. We have grown so accustomed to our declinist blinkers that we mostly overlook important attributes that improve measurably with age. Old people do not, will not, and cannot run faster and jump higher than when they were twenty years old, but they can and do outperform the young in other areas. These new skills and capacities are subtle, and they are routinely overlooked or dismissed outright even by older people themselves. They are also important, even vital, to our well-being.

Researcher Laura Carstensen has long been interested in the unfolding of human terrain in late life. In her paper "Emotional Experience in Everyday Life across the Adult Life Span," she offers support for the idea that improvements in emotional functioning may continue well into old age. Earlier work had shown that advancing age was associated with a self-reported increase in positive affect and a decrease in negative affect. Dr. Carstensen's paper attempts to define these changes with greater precision.

Carstensen gave 184 people ranging in age from eighteen to ninety-four years a beeper and a journal in which they could record their emotional state. During the following week, she beeped the participants at random intervals. When the beeper went off, the participants recorded how they were feeling at that moment. After collecting the journals and analyzing the data they contained, Carstensen and her team reached several surprising conclusions:

1. Older people were less likely than younger people to experience persistent negative emotional states. "Not even at the oldest ages did the frequency of negative emotions approach that observed in younger adults," Carstensen reported.

2. Older people were found to be better than younger people at regulating their emotional states. Older people "were more likely to maintain highly positive states and were more likely to maintain the absence of negative emotional states" than younger study participants. A careful review of the data showed that emotional regulation improved with age and that increasingly better regulation was found among the oldest participants included in the study.

3. Age was associated with greater complexity of emotional experience. Older people were more able to make subtle discriminations between different emotional states than younger people were. This ability is something like that of the artist who sees tan, beige, taupe, and cocoa where others see only brown.

4. Older people were more able to experience poignancy. *Poignancy* is experiencing positive and negative emotions at the same time. Interestingly, when I have shared these results with students, they have often had difficulty grasping the essence of poignancy. The experience of holding on to a positive emotion (such as happiness, joy, or contentment) while also experienc-

ing a negative emotion (such as anger, sadness, or fear) is something they have trouble understanding. Older people balance conflicting emotions better than young people do.

Simply observing, as many have, that the physiological markers of a healthy young adulthood decline with age leaves other less obvious and more interesting elements of aging unexplored. Carstensen's investigation of the active developmental process that is concealed within old age gives us a refreshing alternative to the morbid declinism of Strehler and Mildvan. She concludes her paper by relating her findings to classical developmental theory:

> Development brings increasing differentiation. We found greater differentiation in emotional experience in older as compared with younger people, and we found that emotional differentiation is related to a positive profile of characteristics, including less neuroticism and better emotional control. Such findings about emotion are especially important given widely documented decrements in cognitive and biological aging . . . At the same time in life when cognitive speed and biological hardiness are on the decline, emotional functioning may continue to improve.

The emotional dimension of old age is vast and remains little understood. By freeing ourselves from the presumption of decline, we can begin to explore new ideas and concepts that can illuminate age and aging in modern society.

Gerotranscendence

Lars Tornstam defended the first thesis in Sweden in the field of gerontological sociology in 1973. Since then, he has built an international reputation, publishing dozens of research papers and leading the Social Gerontology Group at Uppsala University. He is best known, though, as the creator of the theory of gerotranscendence. This model suggests that human longevity includes the potential for a transcendent movement away from the materialistic and rational point of view common in the first half of life. His research suggests that the successful completion of such a shift is accompanied by an increase in life satisfaction.

The theory of gerotranscendence grew from the decades Tornstam spent making careful observations of people living into old age. The papers he has written in support of this theory run into the hundreds of pages, but the essentials of his work are easily grasped. Typical of his work is a paper that presents in-depth interviews with Swedish men and women aged fifty-two to ninety-seven years. The patterns of self-reported change in the subjects' relationships with self, society, and the cosmos are the bedrock of this theory. In his analysis, Tornstam groups these experiences into three categories:

1. **The self**
   - Self-confrontation occurs—a continuing process of discovery that reveals previously hidden aspects of the self, both good and bad.
   - There is a decrease in self-centeredness. With an increasing awareness that the individual is not the center of the universe, there is a change from egoism to altruism.
   - There is a rediscovery of childhood and the pleasure of recalling episodes from one's own childhood.

2. **Relationships**
   - The character and importance of social contacts change in late life. Older people become more selective and less interested in superficial relationships. There is an increased need for solitude.
   - The distinction between one's self and one's role becomes increasingly obvious.
   - Attitudes toward wealth change. There is less acquisitiveness and a greater awareness that possessions can ensnare and confine a person.
   - There is a newfound joy in transcending nonsensical social norms. This developmental trend is behind the popular declaration "When I get old I will wear purple."
   - A deeper appreciation develops for the large gray area separating right and wrong. This is accompanied by an increasing reluctance to give advice to others.

3. Cosmic insights
- Time and space, long thought to be fixed and unchanging, are now seen as possessing blurred boundaries. Past and present sometimes merge, and the immediate presence of long-absent relatives can be sensed.
- There is often a renewed interest in genealogy and one's relationship with past generations.
- The fear of death recedes. A curiosity about "What comes next?" may develop.
- There is a renewed interest in nature and connections with the vast living world that surrounds us all.

Obviously, not all of the people studied by Tornstam have shared all of these experiences. The theory of gerotranscendence is intended to suggest a general pattern of development that can unfold in the late decades of life. It acknowledges the reality of decline in physical and mental processes as we age but places those changes into a broader, more meaningful context. While it is easy to propose and test theories of child (and even adult) development, this task is much more difficult for people nearing the end of life. Young people, especially the youngest, are quite similar to one another. Older people who are of the same age show much more diversity and it is much harder to make general statements about them. Far from being a weakness or defect, this variability is among the gifts that longevity offers to us.

It is the peculiar union of long experience with life, the embrace of culture and community, and the biology of human longevity that creates the potential for gerotranscendence. The reinterpretation of self, society, and even the cosmos itself is work that requires a lifetime of preparation. The existence of a drive to transcend ordinary understandings of life and living is, if Tornstam is to be believed, an important and distinctively human attribute. This perspective provides a useful, if provocative, way of viewing the difficulties that younger people face when they seek transcendent experiences in their daily lives. Their struggles may be due, in part, to the relative immaturity of the adult brain.

Tornstam's research helps us see that the human mind continues to evolve into the last decades of life. But that is not all. Recent developments in neurobiology allow us to connect the experiences of transcendentalists young and old with specific evidence that is more objective than the musings of old Swedes. The millennia-old practice of meditation and the quieting of the mind have, in recent years, been studied carefully by Western medical science. Brain scans performed during meditation have demonstrated that the experience of transcendence is associated with, among other things, a decrease in activity in the prefrontal cortex. Some have called this part of the brain "the monkey mind." It seems to be the seat of the familiar strivings, anxieties, and obsessions that we associate with the ego and its needs. Other seemingly unrelated research has shown an age-related decline in the activity of the prefrontal cortex and the neurons that connect it to the rest of the brain.

Could it be that devotees who spend decades cultivating the patterns of thought and neuronal activity that allow them to overcome the ceaseless chatter and fretfulness of the prefrontal cortex— and thus open the door to transcendence—are actually anticipating some of the changes that can develop normally, as a consequence and benefit of aging? The shift in brain activity away from the prefrontal cortex and a decrease in dopaminergic neurotransmitter activity would, ordinarily, be used as evidence to support the declinist view of age and aging. For example, the human brain shrinks with age and the prefrontal cortex shrinks faster than the rest of the brain. These changes are objective and measurable, and have been verified by numerous investigators. The declinist view of aging interprets these changes solely as a catalogue of losses. This view is and will remain blind to the new capabilities that these changes may be instrumental in unleashing. Being open to the hidden powers of age allows us to ask and then try to answer the question, "Does normal aging include the opening of a shortcut to transcendental experience?" Our brains change in countless ways as we age; perhaps some of those changes carry the currently unappreciated benefit of loosening the grip that the ego has on the self. This, as many world religions attest, may be the greatest of all possible human victories.

There is great power hidden within old age, but we will remain ignorant of the depth and breadth of that power as long as we insist on simply comparing youth to age. A more useful approach would be to chart—in the context of old age itself—the changes in human capacity that aging calls forth. The doctrine of youth's perfection, in addition to simply being wrong, also distorts and misleads. It confines us to a narrow and uninformed perspective on human experience.

Old age is and will always remain difficult. It demands much from us, and on first inspection seems to offer very little in return. Contemporary society, however, compounds every burden by offering us a monstrous old age that bristles with disease, disability, dependence, decline, and ultimately death. It is the fearfulness of this vision that has led us to ignore the old, to deny aging, and to hope that somehow, someday a cure for this malady might be discovered and made available for our personal use. Such a hope, while understandable, ignores the possibility that there is something vital and true to be grasped and then savored within the distinctively human experience of growing old.

MYTHS AND OTHER THEORIES

Zeus on Aging

Eos, the dawn of the day, was the sister of the Sun and the Moon and the mother of the four winds. Arriving ahead of her brother, the Sun, she woke the Earth each day with the morn's soft glow. Like her sister, the Moon, she was also inclined to find love among the mortals. Early one morning as she gazed upon the Earth she saw Tithonus, a prince of Troy. Enthralled by his beauty, she resolved to make him her husband. There was, however, a problem. For an immortal, the whole of a human life is but a brief interlude. Propelled by her desire, Eos went to Zeus and asked him to grant Tithonus eternal life. He turned her away, telling her that it was not right that a man should live forever. Relentless, Eos pleaded until Zeus agreed.

Newly immortal, Tithonus joined Eos in her magnificent palace in the east. Many happy years passed until Eos found, to her horror, that Tithonus was growing old. Belatedly, she understood that in her haste to gain for Tithonus the gift of eternal life, she had forgotten to ask that her lover be granted eternal youth as well. When his hair turned white, she left his company but allowed him to remain in her palace. In time, he lost the power to move his limbs and his voice faded into a faint chirp. Denied the release of death, Tithonus aged as no man ever had before. At last, Eos took pity on him and changed him into a grasshopper.

Interestingly, this is not the only age-related tale of love and loss the ancient Greeks had to offer.

Selene, the Moon, sailed the night sky while the Sun rested. One night her pale white light fell upon the handsome young shepherd Endymion. She fell instantly in love with him and determined to make him her own. Remembering the hard lesson learned by her sister, Eos, Selene was careful to ask Zeus to grant her lover eternal youth as well as eternal life. Once again, Zeus was reluctant to grant such a wish. Selene, who was as stubborn as her sister, pestered Zeus until he agreed to do as she wished. Endymion was made both immortal and forever young.

Great was Selene's grief when she found that Zeus had united the blessings of immortality and eternal youth with another divine gift, perpetual sleep. Bullfinch's *Mythology* notes archly that "of one so gifted we can have but few adventures to record."

The stories of Tithonus and Endymion remind us that only among the divine may immortality be united with the vitality of youth. Along with the ten fingers, the bare skin, the quirky two-legged gait, and our oversized brains, aging is part of what makes us human. To live is to age. To live long is to age much. The eternally young shepherd paid a terrible price for his youth. His power to act was taken from him, leaving only dreams and murmurs. This, the storyteller makes clear, is very close to having no life at all.

Contemporary society shows little evidence of having learned the lessons of Tithonus and Endymion. Now, instead of beseeching Zeus, it is the power of technology that we approach on bended knee. Cryogenic preservation centers submerge cadavers in liquid nitrogen with the hope that someday science might deliver them from age and disease. The bodies floating in those tanks may not be dead, but they are certainly not alive. Zeus knew what science does not: old age is woven into human destiny. The ancient Greeks understood that we are not and never will be gods.

Dueling Theories

Behind the steady stream of books and magazines that obsess over the mechanics of aging is a steadfast denial of the essential humanity of old age. Articles in scientific journals carefully describe the decline and fall of cells, tissues, and organs. They investigate chromosomal changes and oxidative damage. They want to understand how we age so that we might then know how to prevent aging. The field is large, well funded, and growing. Some of the best-known theories concerning age and aging are included in table 1. Each of these approaches is able to claim some supporting evidence, but none of them has been fully validated. It is most likely that aging is the confluence of a wide range of processes.

Like bees on honey, we swarm over the question of *how* we age and what can be done to slow, stop, or even reverse aging. Meanwhile, a much more important question remains unasked and unanswered. *Why* do we grow old? How did our remarkable longevity become so important to human life? What, if any, ends does it serve?

Table 1
How We Age

Theory of Aging	Brief Explanation
Aging Hormone	A hormone, as yet undiscovered, promotes aging.
Codon Restriction	Aging occurs as a result of increasing errors in protein synthesis. (This one comes from our friend B. L. Strehler.)
Epiphenomenalist	Aging is due to general environmental insults, which cannot be avoided or prevented.
Exhaustion	Aging occurs when an as-yet-undetermined nutrient is used up.
Free Radical	Aging is due to deterioration of body cells caused by the damaging reactions of free radical compounds.
Immunologic	Aging is regulated by the immune system, and immunologic problems are responsible for many of the manifestations of aging.
Pacemaker	Aging is an unfolding of events that is orchestrated by the organism's genes.
Rate of Living	Aging occurs as the organism uses up its allotted number of heartbeats.

The Nature of Aging

When we are young, we often look forward to leaving adolescence and entering adulthood. The tempting fruit of adult freedom has led many a teenager to wish away the years until he or she can be independent. There is no similar rush to enter old age, as it is punctuated by death, not the signing of a lease for one's first apartment. Put old age on a ballot and it will lose in a landslide of historic proportions. People want to be young.

The vigorous pursuit of youthfulness includes a healthy diet, physical exercise, and an optimistic attitude. People who are attentive to such things age more gracefully than those who pay little heed to the legitimate needs of body and mind. The development of age-related diseases and disabilities can and should be delayed, but aging itself will not be denied. It may come sooner, it may come later, but come it will.

Human strength, vitality, and reproductive vigor peak before our thirtieth birthday. Even by the conservative historical standard of a life expectation of three score and ten, that leaves another forty or more years of decline to follow the tender blossom of youth. It hardly seems right that the majority of a normal human life should be lived in a state of decline. The data that quantify our declining bodily functions are not all we have to contend with—society's celebration of youth gleefully rubs salt into the wounds of old age.

This book was developed under the working title *The Illumination of Elderhood: Old Age in a New Century.* As I write this, I do not know what title will grace the cover when the book is published. I do know that my publisher is wary of putting the words *elderhood* and *old age* into the title. There is a legitimate fear that seeing these words on the cover would discourage people from buying the book, or even from taking it off the shelf to examine. Reminding people of old age (and their eventual death) always makes a product less attractive to customers. Much more comforting are the multitude of books that actively and energetically deny the inevitability of old age. They preach a new gospel of immortality joined with eternal youth.

Talking about, reading about, or even just thinking about the changes that accompany late life is difficult for most people. This reluctance is the product of the declinism that dominates our culture. The contemporary aversion to old age pervades, as you will see, every aspect of our society but should not be mistaken for a universal human phenomenon. The development of a new perspective on age and aging is both necessary and possible. Given the importance of aging in our lives, and the impact of aging on our families and society, a new openness and even curiosity about human aging would seem more than warranted. The time has come for our wondrous longevity to emerge from the long shadow cast by the vigor and virtues of youth.

Imagine gathering a group of your friends for a fine meal and good conversation. After dessert is served, you linger over tea or coffee. A break in the conversation allows you to make an announcement: "I have discovered an ancient path to human development that is all natural, subtle but transformative, and requires decades to experience fully. Only mature adults may sign on; the young are unprepared to accept what it has to offer." A murmur of general approval is likely to follow. "Tell us more!" And so you tell them about aging:

1. **Aging requires life.** When we speak of the "aging" of machines, buildings, or cities, we are employing a metaphor. Inanimate objects can and will decay, but they cannot age. Aging is an active process that requires the force of life. A building does not live and thus cannot age, though its human occupants must. Being alive is a continuing prerequisite for growing old. The challenges of longevity are insistent; they cannot be set aside by those who find them unpleasant. Given a choice between growing old or remaining young, there is hardly a soul alive who would not choose youth. Life, however, offers us a different set of options. Given a choice between aging and death, we choose to grow old.

2. **Aging is natural.** We do not have to think about breathing in order to breathe, and we age whether or not we wish to do so. Aging is within us, not imposed on us. While environ-

mental conditions can accelerate or retard aging, the process itself is part of the human being. How a species ages is one of its defining characteristics. A mouse lives two years, not two hundred. An oak tree grows to maturity in fifty years, not five. So it is with *Homo sapiens*—when and how we age is written into our very being. It is because illness and injury so often occur along with the process of aging that we so often confuse them as being part of aging. While illness and injury can and do complicate the aging process, they are distinct from it. When a young man breaks his neck in a fall, he is not aged—he is injured. When an old woman falls and breaks her hip, the fracture is unfortunate and fraught with danger but is not itself a manifestation of aging. Orthopedic wards host young and old alike.

3. **Aging is gradual.** Aging is a gradual, rhythmic, and highly choreographed process. It holds no surprises, and in the main its course and consequences are well known to all of us. No one goes to bed at the height of vitality and wakes up old. Like water on stone, this gradual progression is the source of aging's power. Remember Tithonus. In the palace of his lover, Eos, he enjoyed perfect health, was protected from all harm, and feasted upon the nectar of the gods. Still he aged.

4. **Aging requires maturity.** Some movies, CDs, DVDs, and even books are available only to "mature audiences." We label these products out of concern that the ideas and images they contain might overwhelm younger, less mature people. We restrict access to tobacco and alcohol for similar reasons. There are many things best reserved for people with the good judgment that comes with age. Old age gives us access to a collection of experiences and insights that are beyond the ability of the young to understand or fully appreciate.

Scientific theories about how we age nearly all accept, without question, the doctrine of youth's perfection. They focus on decline and pay little heed to the steady emergence of new gifts and capacities. This tunnel vision is the root cause of their failure to fully explain aging. They fail because they are themselves the products of a culture mired in a misunderstanding of age and aging.

If aging is truly a catastrophic prelude to death, an alien rot imposed on an unwilling adult, then it deserves the dread it currently engenders. But what if aging and old age are a normal, natural ripening? Even a brief examination of the world around us would offer support for that optimistic outlook. Aging is everywhere. Far from being some dreadful anomaly, it works its way into the lives of millions of species and hundreds of billions of creatures each and every day. This ubiquity suggests that nature finds aging to be very useful, even essential. If we hope to understand the benefit of aging, we must begin by exploring the origins of the human being's unprecedented longevity.

BECOMING
HUMAN

*Every man bears the whole stamp
of the human condition.*

Michel Eyquem de Montaigne, *Essays*

A Matter of Life and Death

A Primer on Evolution

Like fins, scales, and wings, longevity is an adaptive trait that has evolved over hundreds of millions of years. To understand how aging came into being and why it functions as it does, we will have to revisit some of the guiding principles of evolutionary biology. For some this will seem like a detour. After all, what does the biology of ancient organisms have to do with the daily experience of growing old in today's society? The problem is that declinism is very deeply rooted in our language and culture. Seeing beyond its limited perspective requires us to take a long view—a very, very long view—of aging. We must return to the origins of life on Earth if we are to gain a full appreciation for the immense power and beauty of human longevity.

Charles Darwin's theory of natural selection holds that the success of every species is dependent on its ability to produce highly fit offspring that are themselves capable of producing highly fit offspring. This is a roundabout way of saying that, in the context of evolution, nothing succeeds quite like success. Those species that are best prepared to produce viable offspring become more numerous over time. Species that are less able to produce highly fit offspring dwindle in number and ultimately disappear.

Darwin was led to reflect on the numerous and changing forms of life that surrounded him well before his historic voyage on the *Beagle*. He had long noted the great number and variety of domesticated livestock that populated the English countryside. Indeed, he opens his classic *The Origin of Species* with the observation, "Why, if man can by patience select variations most useful to himself, should nature fail in selecting variations useful, under changing conditions of life, to her living products . . . I can see no limit to this power, in slowly and beautifully adapting each form to the most complex relations of life."

Today we know that the genes contained in the DNA (deoxyribonucleic acid) of each organism are the essential units of information that can and do alter the fitness of the individual organism. Aging, which we usually think of in highly personal terms, is better viewed as the product of complex and little-understood interactions between genes and the environment.

The best place to look for the "why" of human aging is within the long and tangled history of life on Earth. Human genes may have been adapting slowly and beautifully for millions of years, but aging precedes humanity. To understand aging, we have to set aside our preoccupation with pensions and wrinkles and take a long view of aging and longevity. Evolutionary biology provides just the perspective we need.

The story began long before there were fins, scales, or claws. By looking back to the very beginning of life on Earth, we can see that old age is actually an exciting new invention.

Multiplication by Division

From the moment molecules first began to make copies of themselves, a gradual process of genetic refinement and improvement was set into motion. Still, in the billion years after life first appeared on Earth, little changed. Eons passed as the basic building blocks of life were assembled and perfected. The first fully functioning cells of which we have some record were the blue-green algae. Their approach to life was so elegant that very similar organisms continue to live among us even today.

One-celled organisms (e.g., bacteria, algae, protozoa) closely resemble the most ancient forms of life. None of these simple organisms, however, are capable of growing old. Single-celled organisms and all their kin in all the history of life on Earth have had only one age. They are always and only preparing themselves for the act of reproduction. When we place bacteria under a microscope, it is impossible to distinguish young from old. Each of these cells is either dividing or preparing to divide. Every cell is a parent in the making, busily readying itself to become its own offspring.

The algae growing in a swimming pool are immortal in a way that the pool's owner can never hope to be. Human chauvinism can make it hard to appreciate that single-celled organisms live without the necessity of death. Of course, every time we grab that jug of algaecide and pour it into the pool, millions of cells die. Among the many important differences between algae and humans is that death is a certainty for us, but only a possibility for them. Every alga cell has access to a several-billion-year-old escape hatch: it can disappear into its own offspring. For the greatest part of the history of life on Earth, a very real form of immortality was not only present but very nearly ubiquitous. Its secret lay in the strategy of multiplication by division.

Sex and Death

If life had remained confined solely to simple single-celled organisms, aging might never have come into being. The emergence of aging and longevity as adaptive traits in the biology of life had to wait until the emergence of complex new multicellular organisms. These creatures, plants and animals alike, made the most of the dictum *e pluribus unum*, "out of many [cells], one [organism]." The advent of cellular specialization made an explosion in the complexity and variety of life possible. It also brought into the world the blessing of sex and the burden of an inevitable death.

The immediate challenge faced by new, multicellular forms of life related to reproduction. A complex organism (such as, say, a trilobite) could not simply divide itself into two identical offspring. A new approach was required.

Sex provided the answer. The emergence of complex, sexual, multicellular organisms brought with it a completely new approach to the life cycle of living things. Biology no longer required organisms to play out life in one act. Now, instead of the parent disappearing into its own offspring, parents would contribute genetic material to the next generation. The solution meant that, for the first time, parents were not destroyed during the act of reproduction. Life, which for single-celled organisms had consisted of a single age (preparing for division), now had two acts. In the first act, the complex multicellular organism grew to sexual maturity. The second act allowed the parent organisms to contribute their genes to a new generation while continuing to live simultaneously and separate from that new generation, if only for a brief time.

On the plus side, this gave rise to a wondrous variety of new life forms. The possibilities made available by the combination and recombination of DNA were stunning. Sexual reproduction remains life's most potent source of flexibility and creativity. There is a downside, though, and viewed from the individual's perspective, it is the ultimate calamity. Sex slammed the door on the opportunity to become one's own offspring and thereby live forever. Life's second age fueled the rise of millions of new species even as it blocked the exit that continues to serve single-celled organisms. Complex new organisms became parents and found that, after passing on their genes (and even if they never had a child), there was no way out. Death was inevitable. Thus, sex and death have been bound one to the other from the very beginning.

Folklore is well versed in this relationship. The people of Madagascar tell a story in which the creator offers the people a choice. They can have the gift of eternal life but will be denied the potential of having children, or they may choose to have children but, as a consequence, must accept the inevitability of death. Being human, they choose children—and death.

The contribution of genetic material to a new generation is a necessity for all organisms. As evolution shapes the fitness of living organisms, it places the highest priority on this ability to pass genes on to a new generation of viable offspring. From an evolutionary point of view, this makes reproduction the last required action of the adult organism. Once genes are passed to the next generation, the adult becomes the evolutionary equivalent of wrapping paper on a Christmas afternoon.

For many organisms, the very act of reproduction is, indeed, the concluding act of the life cycle. Remember the spider, Charlotte, in *Charlotte's Web*. Like her real-life spider counterparts, Charlotte did not live to see her offspring, nor do many other creatures. The world is crawling with creatures that do not survive the act of reproduction:

- Octopus and squid
- Annual and biennial grasses and flowers
- Bamboo
- Freshwater eels
- Most insects
- Migratory salmon

However, not all organisms die immediately after reproduction. The dinosaurs, for example, reproduced many times, sometimes over a period spanning decades. These creatures were notorious for their casual approach to life and death among their offspring, and so the survival of succeeding generations could not be assured by any one act of reproduction. It was beneficial to the species for dinosaurs to reproduce many times.

Parenthood and Aging

Mammals appeared on the scene about two hundred million years ago and were the first animals to make *intensive* use of the advantages offered by life after reproduction. The mammal took what followed the biological act of reproduction and turned it into the role of a lifetime. Offering ongoing support to one's offspring turned out to be an astonishingly successful survival strategy.

Parenthood is an unprecedented commitment to the well-being of the young that includes the provision of food, shelter, and protection from predators. The fossil record makes clear, this investment has paid off handsomely. The rise of mammals is one of the great evolutionary triumphs in the history of life on Earth.

One theory about this triumph holds that new-fangled mammals hastened the exit of the dinosaurs by eating eggs left unguarded by the nonparenting dinosaurs. (Having eggs for breakfast, it turns out, may be a very old mammalian habit.) Being in competition with the dinosaurs led early mammals to maximize the advantages offered by early and frequent reproduction and—most importantly—by their parenting. The vital importance of parenting is written into all mammals' anatomy. From the sheltered warmth of the womb to the hidden ingenuity of the placenta to the nutritional output of the mammary glands, the mammalian female is built to shelter and nurture her young before and after birth. A mother's commitment to the well-being of her young begins in utero, continues at the breast, and extends through a species-specific period of youthful immaturity.

Parents, formerly expendable leftovers, were transformed from zeros to evolutionary heroes. This heroic stature comes, as it always has, at a price. When we say that our kids are giving us gray hair, we speak a truth deeper than we know. It is the development of parenting that brought aging fully into being. Indeed, mammals experience the most pronounced form of aging of all types of animals. We age because we nurture our young, and we are allowed (in evolutionary terms) to age because we must be able to function effectively as parents.

Aging is the by-product of an ancient and never-to-be-resolved tension between youthful vigor and the longevity necessary to bring offspring to full maturity. The mammalian need to care for the young added a third act to the drama of life on Earth. It delayed (but was never able to eliminate) the arrival of biological obsolescence. As mammals, humans are intimately familiar with the arc of life that stretches from birth to sexual maturity to parenthood. It is the experience of growing old that we have the greatest difficulty appreciating. We live, every day, with the consequences of two hidden genetic mechanisms. Being aware of them can help us understand how and why we age so well.

Antagonistic Pleiotropy

Among mammals, the genetic preference for youthful vigor must be balanced with the need for longevity sufficient to properly parent the young. Nature would swiftly eliminate any mammal that overvalued strength in youth relative to the longevity needed to parent its off-spring properly. Equally, an especially long-lived organism that lacked the vigor and fertility needed to reproduce effectively or in sufficient numbers would fare poorly. Neither situation is optimal. A balance must be struck.

Scientists have long recognized this conflict and, as is their habit, have hung an unfamiliar name around its neck. *Antagonistic pleiotropy* is the term used to describe the tendency of certain genes to generate diverse and even conflicting effects over time. Mammalian evolution favors genes that foster youthful vigor—even when those genes cause problems later in life. The genes that make you shine in your youth can, later in life, produce very different and much less desirable results.

The workings of antagonistic pleiotropy can be seen on the obituary page. Highly successful athletes are less likely than regular people to live to an old age. The lives of these gifted individuals frequently embody the conflict between the genetic traits that let a young person run faster and jump higher than anyone else, and the genetic traits that foster a long, healthful old age.

Consider the life spans of the first ten Olympic gold medalists in the hundred-meter dash (shown in table 2 on the next page). These men were among the best-known athletes of their time, each earning the title of "the world's fastest man." Their superb fitness might have been expected to bring with it the gift of longevity. By and large, it did not.

Of these ten champions, one died in his forties, three in their fifties, two in their sixties, three in their seventies, and only one lived to see his eighties. There were no centenarians. Only five of the ten champions reached sixty-five years of age, despite the fact that in mid-century America 60 percent of men reaching twenty-one years of age were expected to live at least until their sixty-fifth birthday.

Table 2

Losers of the Longevity Olympics

Year	100-Meter Gold Medalist	Born	Died	Life Span
1896	Thomas Burke, USA	1875	1929	54
1900	Frank Jarvis, USA	1878	1933	55
1904	Archie Hahn, USA	1880	1955	75
1908	Reggie Walker, SAF	1889	1951	62
1912	Ralph Craig, USA	1889	1972	83
1920	Charles Paddock, USA	1900	1943	43
1924	Harold Abrahams, GBR	1899	1978	79
1928	Percy Williams, CAN	1908	1982	74
1932	Eddie Tolan, USA	1908	1967	59
1936	Jesse Owens, USA	1913	1980	67
	Average Age at Death			65

The irony is that despite (but actually because of) their genetic endowment, these men lost the Longevity Olympics.

Mammals have a real need for youthful vigor; they need genetic traits that foster stamina and strength while they rear their young. That task accomplished, the delayed but potent negative side of the genes that have fueled this vigor begins to emerge. This dysfunction, expressed as it is in old age, has no detrimental impact on the success of the species, and so evolution does not weed out these genes. A good youth is no guarantee of a healthful old age. Keep that in mind the next time you watch an elite sports competition. Those outstanding athletes may be drenched in glory today, but given enough time you may well beat them in the race for longevity.

Genetic Drift

A similar complication arises from genes that remain silent until late in life. Because they are expressed only in old age, these genes have little or no influence on reproductive success. Freed from the power of natural selection, they tend to drift, and that drift is rarely in the direction of utility and vitality. The consequences of genetic drift can be seen in the experience of fish that became trapped in an inky-dark cave. Over many generations, the genes that had created useful vision began to mutate. These negative mutations would have been penalized in a world populated by sighted predators and prey, but the ability to see offered no advantage in a world that was completely dark. Over time, the sum of these mutations produced a species of fish with sightless eyes.

So it is with the genes that are expressed only in old age. They are a mad collection of the good, the bad, and the ugly. This is an unexplored region that antiaging advocates have failed to appreciate. People who imagine life spans of two centuries or more conveniently overlook the unknown number of quiet genes that may lie coiled within our DNA. They are silent throughout a normal life span but might be expressed in the thirteenth, fourteenth, or fifteenth decade of life. We know little of them because so few people live past 100 years of age. Still, they are there. The havoc they might wreak on a 150-year-old human is unknown and unaccounted for.

Necessity's Virtue

What Is Old Age For?

Success follows any species that is able to identify, explore, and then refine a new survival strategy. Millions of creatures have taken to the sky, braved desert heat, or gone underground or underwater in life's relentless pursuit of competitive advantage. Every species develops and then relies on the distinctive features that give it an advantage. Most people suppose that our large brains and nifty opposable thumbs make us unique. Scientists have often made note of the vibrancy and utility of human language and our unparalleled tool-making skills as defining human characteristics. These traits are remarkable (even if we do say so ourselves), but they are the result of our most important innovation, not the cause.

Humans traveled the long road from obscurity as one of many hominids to our current status as a globe-dominating species because we unlocked the virtue hidden within the necessity of aging. The discovery and exploration of longevity is what best distinguishes us from all other creatures. We reign supreme as the masters of aging. Old age is our greatest invention, and on an even deeper level, it invented us. In truth, we should be known as *Homo geros,* "man the old." Old age and the uses to which old age can be put have been shaping our development for hundreds of thousands of years. Old age transformed the way our most distant ancestors gave birth, reared their young, lived together, and fed themselves. Later it propelled the development of culture, language, and society. This is much more than a hopeful boast. When we discard our declinist blinkers, we can see that we are, as a species, defined by our longevity. The arc of a creature's life is part of what defines it as a species. All animals have a characteristic life cycle, and closely related species can be expected to have similar life cycles. A Norwegian rat does not live fifty-six years while a brown rat lives fifty-six days. Lions and tigers are evolutionary cousins, and that kinship can be seen in their strikingly similar patterns of gestation, fertility, weaning, and life span.

Humans are primates, and among all primates we are most closely related to chimpanzees. We hold 98 percent of our genetic code in common with them. Given this similarity and the relatively recent divergence of the two species, our life cycles should be nearly identical. Instead, a comparison of human and chimp life cycles reveals some unexpected differences. Human beings can live twice as long as their nearest relatives—surprising in itself. Astonishing, however, is that all of this additional longevity *follows* the loss of fertility. Chimp and human females become fertile at nearly the same age and remain fertile for about four decades. The human female possesses a nearly fifty-year longevity bonus that follows the end of fertility. For the aging chimpanzee, death follows hard on the heels of the loss of fertility. Our postreproductive longevity is a remarkable and distinctly human characteristic. It exists because it affords our species a unique and powerful competitive advantage. Hidden within this extraordinary elongation of life is the story of who we are and how we came to be.

The First Grandmother

It is three o'clock in the morning in Dallas, Texas. Inside the master bedroom of a comfortable suburban home, a man and woman sleep peacefully. The phone rings once, then rings again while the man fumbles for the handset. An excited voice comes through the receiver. It is time; the baby is coming. Soon, very soon, they will become grandparents. The bags are already packed. They will be on the first flight out in the morning. Nothing could keep them from being there. Before the sun sets again, they will be a thousand miles from home, cradling the newborn in their arms. Without being asked, they instinctively "help their daughter." Meals are cooked, errands run. They dote. None of the participants marvel at this; no one wonders why. It is as natural as drawing a breath. The grandparents have come to help with the baby. This is how it is meant to be.

One million years ago on the plains of Africa, a hominid child cries out from hunger. Her mother has recently given birth and is distracted by the needs of her helpless infant. The delivery was long and difficult and much blood was lost. The mother barely has the strength to nurse her infant. She can neither feed nor care for her older child. On this day, in this place, a miracle occurs. An older female, the mother of the new mother, the grandmother of the crying child, is moved to act. For the first time in the history of life on Earth, a grandmother intentionally shares food with her grandchild. Thus was the first tentative step taken down the long road that led to the development of the modern human being.

That such a radical innovation came from a mammalian species is not surprising. Mammals are, by definition, food-sharing animals. Mammalian mothers create a placenta that enables them to share freely with their young throughout gestation. They suckle their young with everything that "mother's milk" implies. Even after weaning, many mammals continue to shelter, protect, and feed their young. The mother, and in some cases the father as well, contributes a portion of what has been hunted and gathered. Parents do this because food sharing is one of the secrets of mammalian success (though it is not necessarily limited to mammals). The truly exceptional thing, the thing that may well have set the course for the evolution of the modern human, is the day when food was shared across three generations. This revolutionary act changed the course of life on Earth.

Why the first grandmother sustained her daughter and helped feed her grandchildren is a question to which we will never have the answer. What we do know is that this innovation allowed the hominid line from which we are descended to break the bonds that biology had imposed on species that were very similar to us. It began to make us human. The first grandmother put a virtuous cycle into motion. She created a new pattern of mutual support that increased the reproductive success of her family and, as the innovation spread, of all human families. Food sharing across the generations was a bold strategy that had no apparent antecedent. It was a risky gamble that paid off magnificently. Old age lifted an undistinguished hominid out of obscurity and enabled the remarkable sequence of adaptations that led to the human being.

We are what we are because of the changes that grandparenting made possible. There is reason to believe that our large brains developed in tandem with our exploration of old age. From birth to the teenage years there is a fourfold increase in the volume of the human brain. The greatest difference between human infants and chimpanzee infants is that the human brain continues to grow in size and complexity after birth. Our wealth of learned behaviors is acquired through the delicate interplay of brain development and social environmental stimulation. Not only is humanity's extended and extensive parenting a rarity in the animal kingdom, but the deliberate enlistment of grandparents into the work of rearing the young stands as a defining characteristic of *Homo sapiens*.

The traits that make us human serve us well but also create problems of their own. Bipedalism frees our hands and allows greater specialization of the fingers and thumb but also tilts the female pelvis upward and thus reshapes the birth canal. As a result, human infants most commonly descend headfirst in a corkscrew fashion through a very tight birth canal. A larger, better-positioned pelvis would make

Table 3
The Evolution of Longevity

Type of Life	Innovation	Relationship to Aging
Single-celled organisms	Asexual reproduction	Aging does not exist.
Multicelled organisms	Sexual reproduction	Aging exists.
Mammals	Parenting	Aging is accelerated.
Humans	Grandparenting	Aging is put to use.

birth easier but at the cost of returning human females to a four-legged gait. Giving birth to smaller babies with smaller brains would eliminate the human species' most important advantages. A difficult birth is part of the price we pay for our combination of upright posture and intelligence.

I remember the first time I assisted at a birth. I watched in amazement as the seemingly enormous head descended into the birth canal. My anxiety level rose as I became certain that there was no way this baby was going to make it out alive. I glanced nervously at the obstetrician, who, to my mind, seemed bizarrely unconcerned. Soon afterward, the baby was born. It was the mother's seventh child, and I realized later that there had never been even a shadow of a doubt. Still, it seemed a miracle to me.

We have, as a species, used a variety of tricks and strategies to resolve the conflict between our large heads and narrow pelvises. (The brain of a human newborn is about the same size as that of an adult chimpanzee.) Humans defer a significant amount of brain development until after birth. The technical name for this prolonged period of development is *neoteny*. It lets us have our large brains and an upright posture, too. But this strategy creates problems of its own. Human pregnancies are about one month longer than those of the chimpanzee, yet the human newborn is much less mature than a newborn chimp. Our species lives on the knife-edge between easier births with more helpless offspring and more difficult births with greater fetal development. Human reproduction would cease (outside of the operating room) if human offspring actually completed a program of in utero brain growth equivalent to that of their chimpanzee cousins.

The bill for neoteny comes due in infancy and childhood. As a group, primates have longer periods of dependency than most mammals, and the human infant is dependent for years longer than any other primate. Giving birth to very immature, large-brained offspring is a viable solution only if we can cope effectively with the intense demands created by a prolonged period of dependency. Caring for young humans is made doubly difficult by the exceptional demands imposed by the infant brain. This greedy, fast-growing organ needs a steady supply of high-quality fats and proteins if it is to develop properly. Like all other mammals, young humans rely on their mothers' milk for these nutrients. Primates are especially devoted to breast-feeding and have some of the longest lactation periods of all mammals. Consequently, the burden of providing these nutrients falls heavily and sometimes exclusively on the mother.

A prolonged period of breastfeeding cements the relationship between the mother and her growing infant and provides a reliable source of high-quality nutrients. Closely spaced pregnancies would place an unhealthy burden on a lactating female, so it is not surprising that females are mostly infertile while they are nursing. Because she bears complete responsibility for the well-being of her infant, a female chimpanzee may nurse for up to six years. Given the even more exorbitant demands of the growing human brain, we would expect *Homo sapiens* to nurse even longer. In fact, the opposite is true. Weaning among humans varies (partly due to culture), but around the world, weaning is typically accomplished within two to three years. Two years or six years—how long an infant nurses might not seem to matter, but it does. The human's relatively brief period of lactation (actually shockingly brief relative to adult brain size) vastly increases the reproductive potential of the species.

Today there are about thirty thousand chimps and over six billion humans. How could two species so similar in so many ways diverge this dramatically? The answer lies with the first grandmother. She changed everything. By sharing food with her grandchildren, she shattered seemingly unbreakable limits that had confined species similar to her own. We are the heirs of a simple unrelenting tendency to share food across generational lines. Other primate species may have dabbled in this behavior, but *Homo sapiens* honed this trait until it became the central strategy for the success of the species. When the first grandmother gave food to her daughter's child, she changed everything.

Substantial advantages accrue to offspring who can be cared for by two generations of adults. The extra food and attention significantly improve survival rates. It is estimated, for example, that among chimpanzees in the wild the mortality rate for immature chimps runs between 40 and 50 percent. Human grandparents (especially grand-mothers) have been reducing child mortality for a million years. An international conference of anthropologists, sociologists, and ethnol-ogists—the first ever on the subject of grandmothers—showed how universal this tendency has been. Researchers presented studies from cultures as diverse as eighteenth-century Japan and rural twentieth-century Gambia. All of these studies pointed to the same conclusion.

University College researchers in London found that in Gambia, infant mortality rates dropped by 50 percent if the maternal grand-mother was present in the household (interestingly, no benefit was found when the paternal grandmother was in residence). Ruth Mace, one of the researchers, noted that the presence or absence of the father had no bearing on infant survival: "If the grandmother dies, you notice it; if the father does, you don't."

In India, a beneficial impact on child mortality was also found, as well as an increase in fertility among the mothers if their own mothers (the maternal grandmothers) were living in the household. Research to date has just begun to explore what these matriarchs do that reduces infant and child mortality and increases the fertility of their daughters. Surely their contributions of time, energy, and mate-rial resources across generational lines are important, but that is not all there is to it. Humans, in particular humans living in active multi-generational families and communities, benefit from the intergen-erational transmission of affection. This phenomenon, known as *gentling*, and described in *Encyclopedia Britannica*, has even been observed among lab rats:

> When female rats are handled gently during their infancy and early life, they appear at maturity less emotional, more ready to leave their cages, and less fearful of strange stimuli than do other rats. In fact, the animal is able to respond more effectively when confronted with normal situations; in other words, its emotional response to novel but normal stimuli is not as intense as it is in rats raised in the usual manner. When such rats become mothers, the body weight and readiness to explore of their young are different from those of stan-dard control groups. These effects appear to be mediated through both the prenatal mother-fetus and the postnatal mother-infant rela-tionship. Not only are the young themselves of a different tempera-

ment as the result of the early experiences of their gentled mothers, but, when these young bear babies their patterns of mothering are also different from what they would have been normally. Because the effect of the gentling that their mothers received becomes apparent in their grandchildren, it has been called "the grandmother effect."

The grandmother effect and the related "grandmother hypothesis" can lead us toward a radical reinterpretation of age and aging. Longevity and its specific development of a useful life span after parenthood is what enables the human pattern of helpless newborns, relatively short lactation periods, increased fertility, and improved infant and childhood survival. The human impulse to share food, energy, resources, and risk across the generations (summarized in the grandmother hypothesis) outranks all other human developments in its importance. Humanity would resemble its primate cousins much more closely if mothers had retained sole responsibility for all the emotional and nutritional needs of their helpless children.

A million years ago the first grandmother attended to the cries of a hungry grandchild. In doing so she increased the reproductive success of her own daughter. Over time, those families that were blessed with older females who were inclined to give this kind of assistance grew in number and power. Families that could not master this strategy were overwhelmed. They became evolutionary dead ends. We take the constellation of traits that define our humanity for granted, little realizing that they are, in fact, the gifts of perhaps sixty thousand generations of elders.

There is, it should be noted, another explanation that has been offered as the basis for understanding the physical evolution of the modern human. Some writers credit these changes to the development of coordinated hunting strategies by males. Early males are said to have discovered that by working cooperatively with others they could be predators rather than prey. The kills are thought by some to have provided the protein and fat-rich food needed to nourish the continuing evolution of our large-brained ancestors. While there are legitimate arguments to be made in favor of the "hunter" theory of human development, the theory is surely buttressed by a contemporary reluctance to believe that we are who we are because a million years ago an old woman shared food with her hungry grandchild. The image of a fearless caveman dragging meat home to his dependents seems so much more robust. Our attraction to explanations of this sort is a manifestation of a broader faith in the doctrine of youth's perfection. The bias against age and aging extends, it seems, even to our theories about the dawn of humanity.

When I was in the early stages of writing this book I shared the logic of the grandmother hypothesis with a well-respected and highly credentialed professional in the field of aging. After hearing me out, she confided in an embarrassed way that when she was caring for her infant granddaughter, she would chew the food and then feed it to her. She blushed as she admitted that her mother had done the same for her own grandchildren. "Don't worry," I told her. "It's been done for a million years. You are doing what grandmothers have always done." When the phone rings at night and that woman's next grandchild is born, you can be sure that she will answer that call. This is the thing that makes us human.

The Genius of Human Longevity

The development of menopause and the refinement of grandparenting played a critical role in the physical evolution of the modern human, but the story does not stop there. About forty thousand years ago, another remarkable round of adaptations changed how people lived. *Homo sapiens* generalized the benefits of grandparenthood by linking old age to the work of social evolution. The development of human culture—its refinement, storage, and transmission—was woven into the fabric of old age. This ancient relationship between culture and old age is often lost on those of us who came of age within highly industrialized Western societies. A friend of mine, Bernard Mambo, helped me see this linkage during a long conversation over dinner. Bernard grew up in Ivory Coast and was raised as a Roman Catholic (a brother and an uncle are priests); his family also respected the ways of their ancestral village. As a result, he gained both a fine Western education (he earned his doctorate in educational technology from Kansas State University) and a firsthand understanding of traditional tribal culture. Later, he sent me this letter, summarizing his thoughts on the relationship between culture and old age:

> An African proverb says: "The death of [an] old person is like the loss of a library." In these words are embedded the important role given to older adults in Africa. Every stage of life in traditional Africa is marked by rites of passage. These rites of passage provide social identity and prepare the youth for the responsibilities of adulthood. Before Africa was colonized by Europe, the initiation was one of the most prominent ways education was provided to the young.
>
> I completed that process when I was twenty-eight. After initiation, adults can get married and participate in the continuity of the society (children are considered blessings). In traditional Africa, before the wedding of the young adult, his peers (the people he did the initiation with) build him a house and are with him to support and assist him in everything he needs.
>
> After a person has productively lived his or her life as an adult in the community, he or she is honored by a second initiation (with different ceremonies) into the Elder circle. This usually happens around the age of sixty-five.
>
> These Elders, now masters of the school of life, have the responsibility of facilitating the transition from childhood to adulthood of new generations. They are responsible for and oversee the process of initiation. The idea of Elders as "library" also reveals the fact that only the Elders have full access to the tribe's knowledge base. The Elders safeguard the highest secrets of the tribe and protect its medicine and inner technologies. They incarnate the wisdom of the society, which they happily share often in the form of storytelling.
>
> In this community, the older you are the more respect you receive. One of the reasons for this practice is the fact that age brings you closer to the ancestors who are themselves "canonized" and seen as intermediaries between the divine beings and us.

This is a vision of old age that, frankly, bears little resemblance to contemporary views of age and aging in industrial societies. Declinism has little use for this form of social organization, preferring to place its full faith in the powers of adults and adulthood. The pinnacle of strength is thus enshrined as a cardinal virtue that must be protected and whose inevitable loss is the source of great grief. Strangely, this kind of thinking is actually mirrored much more closely in nature, "red in tooth and claw," than it is in human history. We know the story well, having seen it played out in countless nature documentaries. The old, the sick, and the slow are quickly found by the jaws of the lion and the wolf.

Even folklore, which has always been attuned to life's intractable difficulties, has something to say on this subject. There is a fable that recounts the experience of two men who were walking in a forest when they came upon a lion. As the hungry beast circled the pair, the first man bent down and carefully retied his sandals. "What are you doing?" asked the second man. "You can't outrun that lion." The first man answered, "I don't have to outrun the lion—I only have to outrun you."

Perhaps alone among living creatures, human beings have been able to fashion a longstanding exception to the rule that only the fittest should survive. Our longevity flourished because our survival has most often *not* depended on the retention of a near maximum of strength, endurance, agility, and speed. Instead, the genius of human longevity has found strength in weakness and distilled meaning out of frailty.

Living in a society that equates aging with the tragic loss of youthful vigor makes the idea of aging as a virtue hard to accept. Contemporary culture lulls us with the belief that old age is and always has been a lethal defect that must be avoided for as long as possible. What is so often lost is precisely what Dr. Mambo described so eloquently: a world in which elders are acknowledged as valued contributors to their families and communities. The world we live in today—our language, art, music, literature, drama, and technology—was brought into being by thousands of generations that recognized the true worth of human longevity. We possess culture because our ancestors had the wisdom to distinguish vigor from value. They saw, as we so often do not, beyond mere physical strength and grasped the virtues hidden within the necessity of growing old.

Humans are the only creatures on Earth that specifically and energetically protect, sustain, and even nurture their elders. Although we all like to believe the best about our personal benevolence, the truth is that protecting older people has long served purposes much larger than simple charity. The elder is different from the adult because elderhood offers us a distinctive way of living. It is life beyond adulthood.

While the idea is shocking to those attuned to the doctrine of youth's perfection, our longevity is meant to be savored *because* aging rigorously diminishes the strength, the daring, and the stamina that are emblems of adult power and glory. These changes inspire dread mostly because industrial societies have made them part of a tragic sequence of decline. Anyone in the last half of life can attest to the difficulties, the aching joints, the fading eyesight. What is open to interpretation is the meaning of these changes. What if they are something other than testaments to our decline? In fact, people have long understood aging as a form of preparation (not unlike adolescence) that is capable of grooming one for a new life as an elder of the community.

To grow old is an extraordinary achievement, and around the world and through the ages, people have recognized the value of longevity by creating different social roles for older men and women. Menopause, which might seem to be a purely biological phenomenon, also eases the transition to elderhood by ensuring that older women cease ovulating. No longer in direct competition with the younger women around them, they are able to inhabit distinct new social roles. Likewise, age whittles male strength and aggressiveness and, with time, ensures that the old *cannot* overthrow the young by force. Secure in this knowledge, adults in traditional societies have long allowed those who reach an advanced age to opt out of the relentless maneuvering for prestige and power. Being freed from the struggle for dominance in the adult hierarchy while still receiving the life-sustaining support and protection of the community is the foundation of our longevity.

The genius of human aging transforms an inevitable physical decline into something new, a reinvention of the self, a portal that leads to a new freedom from the burdens of adulthood. Human societies have long understood how to match the body and mind of the older person with an authentic social role. Every tool must be properly fitted to its purpose, and while it is possible to cut a bouquet of flowers with a chainsaw, a pair of shears will do a much better job. Elders have long been granted social shelter in the last decades of life, not as an act of charity but because old people possess notable talents that make them useful to their families and communities. Elderhood came to life when elders became the bearers of human culture. When it comes to retaining, refining, and transmitting culture, elders out-perform adults.

For many people living in industrialized societies, the expectation that older members of the family would teach the young how life is to be lived is more of a memory than a daily reality. For most of human history, however, close daily contact between the young and old was a matter of survival. Being with, watching after, and assisting in the care of young children, while taxing in many ways, does not require the full vigor of youth. The physical decline that comes with aging actually cements the relationship between old and young. Indeed, an old man still capable of stalking, killing, and butchering a mastodon would have little inclination to spend hours doting on grandchildren, telling them stories, and instructing them in the ways of their people. An old woman still capable of producing young of her own would hardly be inclined to pour time, love, and attention into the lives of her grandchildren. The physiological changes that accompany old age, and upon which contemporary society heaps unlimited scorn, are actually essential preconditions for a socially productive old age.

Many other animals employ (and benefit from) a linear transfer of resources from parent to offspring. Humans have evolved a complex, cyclical, three-generation pattern of interdependence. It is this cycle of intergenerational exchange that has propelled the development and ongoing refinement of human language, technology, and culture.

A child who has been taught and nurtured by his or her elders grows into an adult. An adult equipped with this kind of sophisticated cultural and technical training is well prepared for the work of extracting the necessities of life from an often hostile environment. A rich, supple culture helps create the social surplus that is needed if older people are going to be sustained as their vitality wanes. When such persons can no longer fulfill the duties of adulthood, they are allowed to put down those burdens and enter into the old age the culture has prepared for them. Safe within its embrace, the elders are free to transmit the fullness of the people's culture to a new generation. The old people tell the stories that the young people use to understand how their lives are to be lived. Although the particulars have been combined and varied in a myriad of forms, the essential elements of this cycle have propelled the development of human culture for at least forty thousand years.

Without old age, *Homo sapiens* would have been confined to the typical mammalian pattern of a two-generation social structure. We have used our postfertility longevity to enlarge the range of human possibility and create a complex web of relationships that brings unprecedented benefits to the community as a whole. The social role of "elder of the community" is a brilliant extension of the family-

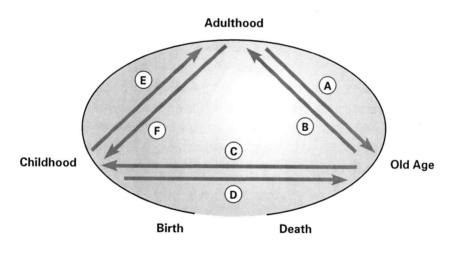

A Support adults provide to elders

B Assistance elders give to adults

C Gentling and acculturation of children by elders

D Assistance and affection given to elders by children

E Participation in work of adults by children

F Food, shelter, clothing, and affection provided to children by adults

The cycle of cultural evolution

specific role of grandparent. Translating the core elements of grand-parenting from the biological to the cultural sphere sparked explosive cultural change. Cross-generational transmission, no longer confined to simple assistance with food and protection, was stretched to include the distinctly human act of communicating meaning.

There is strong (though not universal) support for the idea that human cultures evolve over time and are themselves subject to a form of natural selection. Cultural traits that provide flexibility and adapt-ability are likely to succeed and spread. Old age and elderhood have spread from their origin to every point of the globe because societies that embrace and rely on this innovation are more successful than those that do not. The better a culture becomes at fostering the refinement and expression of its own repository of knowledge, the more complex the strategies it can deploy in pursuit of success.

The discovery of virtue in the necessity of old age is the single greatest achievement in the history of humankind. That we do not understand this as a matter of common sense is the result of the his-torical glare created by the achievements of adults. We remember Caesar, not Caesar's grandmother. But what would Caesar have been if he had been born into a world without elders? Adults and adult-hood obscure but in no way diminish the contributions elders have made to our world. Old age is far from a forgettable vestige trailing after the bloom of youth. It made our world. It is the greatest of all human creations, the mother of all our inventions.

The
RISE
of
ELDERHOOD

Rise like Lions after slumber
In unvanquishable number—
Shake your chain to earth like dew
Which in sleep had fallen on you—
Ye are many—they are few.

Percy Bysshe Shelley, *The Mask of Anarchy*

OLD AGE LONG AGO

Hunter-Gatherer

Although the question can never be settled definitively, current thinking suggests that prehistoric humans migrated out of Africa about two hundred thousand years ago. They traveled in small groups and carried few possessions, preferring to make use of food and materials they found along the way. While genetic evidence allows us to piece together the main thrusts of their migration, their sparse existence and nomadic lifestyle left few physical traces. We know very little about what the lives of these nomadic people were like. We do know, however, that old age came to them early in life. The struggle for survival was mounted with limited and unpredictable access to food, shelter, and safety. The human body, capable of a life span of more than a century, rarely reached the fifth decade.

The lives of our distant ancestors serve as a potent reminder that human longevity is not a purely physiological phenomenon. It is a hybrid, created by the intersection of biology and society. Infirmity, which would seem to be a purely biological phenomenon, actually arrives only when age-related changes begin to interfere with the performance of one's social obligations. The upper limit of longevity may be defined by human genetics, but the experience of living into old age is defined almost exclusively by the customs and mores of one's culture. An individual's ability to live a long and bountiful life depends, most of all, on society's aptitude for making such a life possible.

Ever since our ancestors came out of Africa, nomadic bands of hunter-gatherers have continued to move across the face of the Earth. Before the development of agriculture, survival often depended on the ability to follow the seasons and migrating herds of animals. All the energy required for this relentless movement came from the people themselves, for they lacked pack animals or wheeled vehicles and all but the simplest tools. The dangers imposed by predators made it essential that the group move as one. This solidarity was enforced by the demands imposed by grudging environments.

The constant pursuit of food and fuel often required the group to move faster than the pace of its slowest member. Those who fell behind were exposed to hunger, bad weather, and predators, with lethal consequences. While small children could be carried in their mothers' arms, the older members of the band had to stay with the group or be left behind. There was no other choice. For the bulk of human existence, the energy required to keep pace with one's tribe or band formed the fault line between youth and age.

While archaeological excavations provide little direct evidence of the abandonment of the aged, observation of surviving nomadic bands has created a record of this survival strategy at work. In her masterful book *The Coming of Age*, Simone de Beauvoir presents numerous examples of this behavior. She cites, for example, the notes made by a nineteenth-century observer conveying his experience in the Bolivian rain forest. The Siriono were a nomadic people at the time of their first encounter with Europeans. They lived without ornaments, significant tools, or watercraft, and traveled through the rain forest on foot. Food was very limited and they quarreled ceaselessly over its allocation. Each struggled for his or her share. Old age came early—the tribe members' strength began to fail at thirty and few lived past forty. The early anthropologist cited by de Beauvoir was particularly disturbed by the following incident:

> [The day before the tribe was set to move] he noticed an old woman who was lying sick in a hammock—too ill to speak. 'I asked the chief of the village what they were going to do about her; he told me to ask her husband, who said that they were going to let her die there . . . The next day the whole of the village left without even saying

goodbye to her . . . Three weeks later . . . I found the hammock again, with the remains of the sick woman.'

Even among more settled peoples, the inescapable strain imposed by a subsistence economy worked against one's chances for survival much beyond the apex of youthful vigor. Again from de Beauvoir, the Chukchee of Siberia provide a case in point:

> [Those] who lived on their fishing found it extremely hard to get enough to eat. They used to kill deformed children at birth, as well as those who looked as though they might be difficult to rear. Some few elders managed to carry on trade and to amass a little capital: they were respected. The others were a burden, and they were [leading] such a life that it was easy to persuade them to prefer death. A great feast was held in their honour, a feast in which they took part: the assembly ate seal-meat, drank whiskey, sang and beat upon a drum. The condemned man's son or his younger brother slipped behind him and strangled him with a seal-bone.

Mercifully, examples of this type represent only one part of a wide range of responses to old age developed by nomadic tribal people. The !Kung people of southern Africa have long been known for their respectful approach to the aged members of their community. One of the many ways in which this deference is expressed relates to dietary customs. Among these people it is taboo for adults to eat ostrich eggs. This soft, nutritious food is reserved for the very young and the aged. The Aboriginal people of Australia have displayed a similarly supportive orientation toward their elders, treating them with well-deserved respect: for thousands of years they maintained the vast trove of stories and legends from the Dreamtime.

What are the differences between these societies? Why did some embrace old age while others left the aged to die?

What seems granite-hearted to us today was, in fact, an essential survival strategy. Never far from starvation, rarely out of sight of predators, some tribal peoples simply could not afford to slow down so that the aged could keep pace, let alone to sacrifice the energy required to carry the infirm from place to place. This is where our modern understanding of the biological changes that follow maturity can help explain how aging was experienced among these peoples.

Earlier I reviewed research on "why death favors the old." The authors showed that our biological reserve capacity, or vitality, dwindles with time, making older people more prone to fatal stressors in the environment. What the authors did not say—though they could have—was that the type of environment inhabited by a tribe or people is itself a major determinant of longevity. Demanding environments limit human longevity.

A No doors, windows, heat, air conditioning, or running water   **B** Doors and windows, but no heat, air conditioning, or running water   **C** Doors, windows, heat, air conditioning, and running water

All else being equal, the people living in house C will have greater longevity than the people living in house A or house B, because house C creates an environment that makes few demands on its occupants. Likewise, residents of house B will, on the average, outlive residents of house A.

The more grudgingly the environment gives forth food and shelter, the higher the energy requirement for survival. This increases the risk that, on any given day, an older member of the tribe will encounter a fatal environmental stressor. When we set aside the illusion that the aged are universally beloved and revered as repositories of stories, wisdom, and community lore, we can see that the energy required by the tribe to protect the infirm is a form of social investment. For people engaged in a day-to-day struggle for survival, this protection is a wasteful extravagance. Among these peoples, those who cannot keep pace are left behind, just as a herd of antelope surrenders the weak and the slow to the carnivores that lurk nearby. Nomadic peoples who settled in more congenial environments were more likely to generate surplus food and have a lower energy requirement for daily survival. These conditions promoted increased longevity and made old age a good investment for the community.

Though many nomadic peoples did experience congenial environments, it is tempting for those of us living today to suppose that the lives of nonagrarian tribal people were inherently difficult. We forget, too easily, the massive dislocation that technological societies *imposed* on hunter-gatherers. These people were removed from land that had sustained them for thousands of years and were forced to take up residence in far less enviable habitats. This history is on full display in the United States. Indigenous peoples, who once occupied all of the most fertile and productive land, and some of the continent's most congenial environments, were dispatched to the most barren and unwelcoming territories in all of North America. Their forced relocation disrupted the fabric of their communities and vastly increased the energy required for mere survival, with tragic consequences.

Traditional Aging

The life of the nomadic tribal elder is rarely called to mind when we think of aging in the distant past. Instead, we revere an old age that we suppose existed within agricultural and pastoral societies. When wandering tribes first began cultivating food crops, it wasn't just the plants that put down roots—the people did, too. Fundamental changes in culture and society stimulated technological innovation. Human creativity of all kinds flourished. Cities and villages gave rise to complex new expressions of mythology, religion, and art. The embrace of agriculture also meant that older adults no longer had to keep pace with the young on difficult overland marches. The burden of physical labor was further lightened by the introduction of domesticated animals that were capable of doing work and that gave easy access to meat, milk, and hides.

While food was not necessarily as abundant or as varied as it had been for hunter-gatherer societies, agriculture did foster greater predictability for people of all ages. The insistent rhythmic needs of the land, the animals, and the crops demanded a conservative social order and helped illuminate the full value of longevity. With a new and vital interest in maintaining stability, people sought to maximize the contribution the aged could make to their communities. The dramatic new prominence—and usefulness—of old age and the aged is reflected in the stories of the Old Testament.

The book of Genesis in particular gives considerable attention to the vagaries of age and aging. We are told that Adam lived 930 years, his son Seth lived 912 years, and his grandson Enosh lived 905 years. It wasn't until the time of Noah that the Lord said, "My Spirit will not contend with man forever, for he is mortal; his days will be a hundred and twenty years."

The last half of life developed a reputation as a difficult time. Consider this anonymous rhyme from the early twentieth century:

At 50 stooping we go down a-pace.
At 60 set having run out our short race.
At 70 cloak, staff, and beard we wear.
At 80 upon sticks we are forced to bear.
At 90 without crutches we cannot stand.
And if perchance we reach 100 years,
then bed-rid we forget all anxious care.

Whatever difficulty aging imposed on individuals, our collective longevity was a gift made possible in large part by humanity's increasingly sophisticated ability to harness and use energy. Biblical accounts of life spans approaching a thousand years might be a reflection of a longevity revolution that accompanied the rise of agricultural societies. While advances in food production, tool making, and the domestication of draft animals enabled new perspectives on aging, actually living to an advanced old age remained a considerable achievement. Any person with strength and good fortune enough to survive into the seventh, eighth, or ninth decade of life was rightly regarded as extraordinary. This exceptionalism forms one foundation for the respect of the aged that has found consistent (though not universal) expression throughout history and around the world.

While nomads place a premium on the ability to cope with confusing and unprecedented circumstances, those who lead more settled lives benefit from a deep knowledge of person and place. Agricultural and pastoral societies have a bias in favor of the aged because the ability of the aged to recall and transmit shared memories and beliefs contributes real value to the community. They have long been the bearers of tradition, the keepers of a shared culture. While the aged in traditional societies can and do contribute to their own family's well-being, their most important role lies in their collective contribution to preserving their people's way of life. Within the framework of settled agricultural societies, elders came to be a particularly valuable form of commons.

A commons exists beyond private property. It belongs to everyone and no one. It is a special kind of public property that can also be freely used by individuals and their families. The Boston Commons (now an urban park) takes its name from the time when it was a cow pasture that belonged to all Bostonians. Given this definition, it might seem strange to suggest that elders became a kind of human commons, but for thousands of years, elders of traditional societies served as a storehouse of shared and inherited knowledge, stories, rituals, and beliefs. Their capacity for retaining these cultural treasures made them valuable to the society. Their existence served the community as a whole.

The problem with holding great value in the form of a commons, however, is that it is prone to overuse, abuse, and damaging neglect. Fisheries, pastureland, and hunting grounds have all been misused in this way, often with tragic consequences for the peoples of entire societies. Those who are entitled to a share of the value contained within a commons are motivated to gain the greatest possible advantage from its wealth while personally contributing as little as possible to its care and long-term well-being. This is why the Boston Commons was overgrazed, from first to last.

The danger that this situation creates for older people is easy to see. The community as a whole may derive great benefit from the existence of elders in its midst, but the burden associated with feeding and caring for an elder falls exclusively on the family. The temptation is to give less than full support to an aging relative while supposing that other families will continue to do their part.

Because of the danger this conflict poses to the community (and individual elders), every major religion has issued injunctions against the abuse and neglect of the aged. Societies that openly condone the maltreatment of older people are rare and have few achievements of which to boast. The far more successful strategy for human communities has been to create and maintain an effective social shelter that provides special protection for the aged.

In the Judeo-Christian tradition, the obligation to honor one's mother and father ranks as one of the Ten Commandments. The Torah instructs, "Rise before the aged and show deference to the old; you shall fear your God: I the Lord am your God." The New Testament advises Christians to "never speak harshly to an older man, but appeal to him respectfully as though he were your own father . . . Treat the older women as you would your mother. The church should care for any widow who has no one else to care for her."

Commandments of this kind are cultural guardrails. They are created when the behavior being called for is difficult to maintain and the damage caused by cheating is potentially significant. The greater the temptation, the more necessary the rule to "respect your elders" becomes. Consider this Hassidic story:

> Once there was an old man of considerable means who lived with his son in a fine house on the bank of a river. As years passed, the father grew old and, in time, began to act in peculiar ways. One day the father took a bag of gold from its hiding place and carried it down to the riverbank. There he threw the coins, one by one, into the river. Seeing what his father was doing, the son pleaded with the old man to stop, but the father would not be turned from his unusual purpose. Every day another bag of gold disappeared into the murky water. Desperate for a way to stop this terrible waste, the son went to ask the Rabbi's advice. After hearing the man's story and thinking for a moment, he asked, "The bags of gold, they are heavy, yes?" The son anxiously agreed that they were very heavy indeed. This fact confirmed, the Rabbi announced, "From now on you must carry the gold for him."

The message is clear: the son must treat his father with reverence even in his dotage. To do otherwise would violate God's law. The son's eagerness to take control of his father's affairs before all the gold was gone makes the obligation to honor the father that much more vital. The story can also be seen as a lesson for society as a whole. We are easily convinced that the aged are wasting our rightful inheritance, and just as easily we forget the decades of loving attention that brought us into our own maturity. This bias is universal and it is what makes divine commandments, taboos, customs, and admonishing folklore necessary. If old age were truly and only a boon to all, no such requirements would be needed. A commandment demanding, "Thou shalt eat, drink, sleep, and breathe" would be both very easy to obey and meaningless in the conduct of social life. The drives to eat, drink, sleep, and breathe are built into our beings, whereas the impulse to protect infirm older people is not. Commandments of this kind must be powerful because the lure of momentary advantage is so great. They exist to protect us all from the shadows that haunt old age.

Society has traditionally assigned responsibility for the support and protection of the aged to the family. This ethic grew out of long experience with the high birth rates, stable extended family structures, and small numbers of older people that characterized early agricultural and pastoral societies. In truth, the ideal of family responsibility for the aged should include a corollary that refers specifically to the women of the family, for they have long borne the burden. To grow old in a traditional society that "takes care of its own" is to rely almost exclusively on a stable network of family relationships and a deep reservoir of unpaid female caregiving.

The aged have their own traditional obligations as well. Growing old is difficult, and the aged have long been expected to bear its acknowledged hardships with as little complaint as possible. Those who come to depend on their families are expected to minimize the burden they place on those who love and care for them. There is a deep-seated belief that to complain is to make oneself into a burden, and to become a burden is a terrible thing. This stoic impulse remains largely in force and is one of the reasons the abuse and neglect of older people has been so hard to eradicate.

In traditional societies, each family is responsible for its elders, but in reality many families lack the knowledge, skills, and maturity needed to cope effectively with the last years of an elder's life. Many more older people have suffered from abuse and neglect at the hands of their blood relatives than will ever be mistreated in nursing homes. The important thing is not to romanticize traditional family caregiving by suggesting that it is naturally superior to care given by those outside the family. Being knowledgeable about the basic strategies for dealing with the sometimes difficult and unpleasant changes that are part of old age is important and can be life saving. Still, no matter what shortcomings a family might have, most older Americans do express a clear preference for spending their last years at home, surrounded by the people they love.

Folktales, myths, and religious writings usually take care to emphasize the duty the young have to the old. Relying only on such sources, it would be easy to believe that there is a singular authority that can be derived from old age itself. This is not true. In fact, all the respect and prestige reserved for the aged is given in the form of a voluntary (and revocable) grant made by the young to the old. In a stable society, it makes sense for the young to surrender a portion of their power to the old. Doing so provides the surest guarantee of safety and comfort for their own dotage, should they be blessed with so long a life. A folktale, first collected by the brothers Grimm but found in many forms, drives this point home:

> A woodcutter lived with his wife, his son, and his father in a cottage deep in the woods. As the years passed, the grandfather grew feeble and developed a tremor. One evening at dinner he dropped and broke his soup bowl. His enraged son and daughter-in-law agreed that the old man should no longer be fed at the table or from the family dishes. The woodcutter hastily fashioned a wooden trough from which the old man was to eat his meals.

> So it was, until the day the woodcutter came home from his work in the forest and found his son playing on the floor with several blocks of wood.

> "What are you making, dear son?"

> "I am making a trough like grandfather's so that you may eat from it when you get old," the boy responded.

That very evening the grandfather was back at the family dinner table taking his meal from the same dishes as the rest of the family.

It pleases us to think that respect for the aged springs solely from an intrinsic value that somehow arises in old age. The woodsman cuts that idea to the quick. Returning his father to the family table did something more than simply honor a divine commandment. The woodcutter struck a bargain in a continuing effort to balance risk and benefit. Honoring one's parents has long been both a divine commandment and the best way to ensure that your children will honor you when you grow old. Such a reward is worth far more than the cost of a few broken dishes. The woodsman, seeing the lesson his son was learning, welcomed his father back to the family table as insurance for his own old age.

The conditions that created and sustained traditional practices and customs relating to old age are vanishing and will likely never return. The value modern society places on high technology, individualism, physical and social mobility, and education and employment opportunities for women all conspire against traditional aging. In less than a century, the extended family has become a nuclear family, which is itself increasingly atomized. Birth rates in many nations are in decline, while the number of people surviving into the late decades of life is increasing. Life in a mobile wage economy, while desirable and liberating in many respects, also cuts deeply into the availability of unpaid family caregivers. Americans spend more than one hundred billion dollars a year on paid caregivers for older people, and

Table 4

The Elements of the Traditional Approach to Age and Aging

Traditional Aging
Old age is both a blessing and a burden.
The aged should be respected.
The aged should be stoic.
Care for the aged is a family responsibility.

that number is sure to rise as the traditional structure of family support for the aged collapses around us.

Consider your own family situation. The odds are that there is, within the past generation or two, the legacy of a family home place. This was the locale, whether it was a neighborhood in Brooklyn or a farm in rural Michigan, around which the extended family was centered. The households of several generations were close by and family members gathered together regularly. This proximity gave rise to a powerful, if unspoken, expectation of mutual aid.

It is likely that the home place is gone. The family has scattered and only the memories remain. Millions of grandchildren are now growing to maturity without regular daily contact with their grandparents. Cousins who once would have shared at least one meal a week together now communicate by e-mail, if at all.

No one forced this dissolution. It was chosen freely and it was actively pursued in the name of independence and opportunity. The truth is that we like this fluid, mobile society better than the fixed localism demanded by tradition. But at the same time, in diners and malls, at church picnics and in airplanes, we yearn for a return to a half-remembered and highly romanticized golden age of old age. The more difficult the issues around aging become, the more fervently we desire to escape the present and find peace in the warm glow of blurred memory.

Industrial-Strength Aging

The Fog of Nostalgia

Proclaiming the loss of a golden old age and condemning contemporary society's thoughtless treatment of the aged is nothing new. Arguments about how society should or could treat old people were well known to the Greeks of Athens and Sparta. There is, after all, the story of the Athenian who, arriving late for the theater, could not find a place to sit. When none of his fellow citizens would offer his own seat to the old man, a Spartan (Sparta espoused a deep respect for the aged) rose and bade him to take his place. Making note of this gallantry, the audience applauded politely. A wag later noted, "The Athenians had no trouble knowing what was right but were loathe themselves to do what was right."

Little has changed. We still prefer nostalgia to any efforts to restore old age to "the way it used to be."

The power of nostalgia to distort and mislead can be seen in the unlikely history of Sir Walter Scott's novel *Ivanhoe*. In the early 1830s Scott decided to try his hand at the old form of the chivalrous novel and produced a tale of bravery, honor, and revenge set in the Saxon England of old. For many readers of the time, the real hero of the book was not the knight Ivanhoe, but rather the Saxon nobleman Athelstane. In Scott's hands, brave Athelstane came to embody the virtues of a lost age of Saxon nobility.

The story took a strange turn after it was delivered to the type-setter. Two-thirds of the way through the novel, the man came upon Scott's description of the death of Athelstane. The loss of this great man was more than the typesetter could bear. He went to Scott's home and, wracked with grief, begged the author to spare the Saxon's life. Moved by this plea (and against his better literary judgment) Scott rewrote the final chapters of the book. He added a bizarre scene in which Athelstane, whose family had gathered for his funeral, is found to have escaped death: ". . . the door flew open and Athelstane, arrayed in the garments of the grave, stood before them, pale, hag-gard, and like something risen from the dead!"

Understandably, critics reacted negatively to this crazy plot twist, and although the book was popular with readers of the time, *Ivanhoe* is not one of Scott's better novels.

We are much more like Ivanhoe's teary typesetter than we imag-ine. The longed-for golden age of Saxon nobility had disappeared seven centuries before, but the need to cling to romantic notions about that time remained strong. The typesetter was in love with the idea of Saxon nobility, not the reality. In truth, Scott's countrymen would never have tolerated and did nothing in practice to promote a return to the society of that era. It was the power of nostalgia that converted the idea of a lost era into a balm that could soothe the painful dislocations of life in an emerging industrial economy.

In similar fashion we plead with our leaders to set things right with respect to old age. We cling to and are often deceived by a flawed collective memory of old age. Life in Saxon society had little in common with Scott's blatantly romanticized depiction. His read-ers found comfort in the dream, not the reality. We are no different; the old age we think ought to be restored is mostly a nostalgic inven-tion—it bears only a passing resemblance to the old age that truly was.

Scott had the luxury, however ill-advised, of rewriting the story. We do not. The old way of being old is dying and will soon be dead, nostalgia being a sure sign that what we long for has already slipped away. If we are ever going to define the future of our longevity, we must turn our attention to old age as it is now.

Social Insecurity

The old age we know today first came into being on a mass scale in the late nineteenth and early twentieth centuries. In the United States, European immigrants flooded large eastern cities, crowding into tenements and seeking work in sweatshops and factories. Wage labor offered poor pay for hard work done with dangerous machinery. Left behind in the old country were long-established patterns of family-scale, low-technology enterprises and agriculture. The new employment pattern and the disruptive trauma of immigration destroyed the ability of many extended families to function as effective economic units.

In spite of the massive dislocations it spawned, the modern industrial economy and its attendant machines and technologies did reduce the physical vigor needed for day-to-day survival. While much has been made of the contributions water and sewage systems made to reducing the transmission of infectious diseases and improving public health in general, little has been said about the longevity-promoting effects of gasoline engines, electric lights, electric motors, central heat, and air conditioning. These technologies foster longevity by harnessing and deploying energy in forms that reduce the demands our environment places on us. The relationship between technology and longevity becomes clear every summer when heat waves overwhelm the air conditioners used by older people. The rash of deaths that follow, sometimes numbering in the thousands, is the result of the environment overwhelming first air conditioners and then the diminished reserve capacity of elders. When the technology that protects elders from the heat fails, hyperthermia and dehydration soon follow. Too often, the results are fatal. Life expectancy would plunge if we were suddenly returned to a preindustrial level of technology and our daily survival once again depended on our capacity to chop wood and carry water.

Life in highly urbanized, technically sophisticated societies yielded a parallel reinvention of longevity. The standardization and mechanization of work, along with the modern economy's unrelenting demand for productivity, led employers to insist that workers be able to keep pace with machinery that never tired. Young adults were valued for their ability to tolerate twelve-hour shifts six days a week; older people rarely possessed the required strength and stamina and were deemed unfit for full employment. This distinction was alien to the traditional pattern of family-centered, nonindustrial farming and production enterprises. For millennia, human families and communities created roles for older people that matched their changing energy and endurance levels. The factory, however, lacked this flexibility, and had little use for the aged.

Wage labor and the disintegration of the extended family as a cohesive unit opened a gap between life span and economic productivity. In industrial societies, older people became ineligible for paid employment long before they reached the ends of their lives. This gap gradually developed into the novel idea of retirement. The family, which had been the traditional refuge of the aged, was transformed as well. Poverty and the migration of women into the paid workforce compounded the difficulties of growing old in the New World. Particularly within urban ethnic immigrant communities, the need to rethink old age became urgent.

Part of the response formed by these communities came in the form of private charitable institutions dedicated to the care of the infirm and elderly. Members of immigrant communities came together to create what had been a rarity in American society: homes devoted especially to the aged. Supported by private donations, the homes were intended to serve the members of particular ethnic or religious groups. Many of these institutions remain in operation today and are among the oldest long-term care organizations in the nation.

Urbanization, the industrialization of work, and the disassociation of the extended family as a cohesive economic unit all contributed to the rise of retirement and reinforced the declinist view of old age. It is ironic that even as waves of technological progress increased longevity, there was a simultaneous reinterpretation of aging as a process of physical and mental decline. The wrenching social dislocations that swept through urban immigrant communities at the turn of the twentieth century foreshadowed the changes that would remake American society in the decades that followed. Communities and families that had always been able to make do with traditional forms of family-based caregiving for older people were no match for the demands made by a new kind of society. In the 1930s, the Great Depression strained and broke the ability of families and local charitable institutions to meet the needs of the aged. It is worth remembering that the Social Security program was originally conceived of and referred to as "old age unemployment insurance." It was developed in explicit recognition of the fact that, in a modern industrial society, the aged could no longer be sheltered purely and only by family, church, and community.

After World War II, the nuclear family became the operative economic unit. Automobiles and freeways vastly increased mobility and decreased the attachment to place that had long defined settled rural communities. Millions of people left the countryside in search of a better life, moving to the city and then the suburbs. At the same time, women were given increasing access to educational opportunities and employment outside the home. The number of women enrolled in colleges and universities started growing dramatically. (By 2001, female students outnumbered male students in higher education 56 to 44 percent). Added to this picture were the simultaneous improvement in general health and nutrition and the development of antibiotics, which enhanced longevity in industrial societies. Extended life spans expanded the need for caregiving even as the family's capacity for caregiving was shrinking.

The twentieth century gave us a mobile, fully industrialized society and the increased longevity of millions of people. It also enabled and often compelled women to work outside the home. This created a growing mismatch between the demand for family support of older relatives (created by better medical care and greater longevity) and the shrinking supply of female family members able and willing to stay home with older relatives. Traditional approaches to aging proved unable to close this gap. A new approach was needed, and with typical zeal, modern industrial society set out to create an old age in its own image.

Mitigated Aging

The contemporary view of old age borrows, as it should, from traditional beliefs. Despite the unbridgeable gap between the ideal and reality, an idealized view of traditional aging retains a powerful hold over us. In daily life, however, old age has ceased to be understood as a blessing (a reward from God for a life of piety) and a burden (the undeniable reality of pain and the loss of strength and vigor) and has become something very different. By lionizing youth and using the benchmarks of a healthy adulthood as the gold standard of well-being, contemporary society has created a simple but radical reinterpretation of age and aging. Old age has been recast as a merciless descent from the apex of youth—a hurtling fall and a peculiar form of brokenness that must be resisted with every available means.

Within the context of modern industrial societies, the equation of age and decline is accepted without question. Unlike the traditional view of old age, which tempered the admitted difficulties of late life with the comforts of family, faith, and hearth, industrial society has chosen to *emphasize* the physical and mental decline associated with aging. This prejudice is so ingrained that it sometimes seems that no other perspective is possible.

Deeply held beliefs can, however, give way with surprising speed. The history of childbirth provides a case in point. For centuries people believed that the pain of childbirth was a consequence of Eve's original sin and that birthing itself was in some way shameful. These traditional ideas were swept away by a philosophy that emphasized the careful management of pain and the joyful participation of the family in the birth experience. Childbirth remains unchanged; the revolution concerns our reinterpretation of what it means to give birth.

Society has not only been closed to the notion of aging as a virtue, it has stressed the negative. The declinist perspective is dominant today because this pessimism serves powerful interests. Equating aging with decline fosters the development of a social science and public policy empire that is dedicated to shielding us all from the dreadful realities of aging. This tidy package blends beautifully with the prevailing ageism of our time. Long established ideas about aging and the aged have given way to a public health philosophy that sees the "graying" of industrial societies as a looming disaster that must be met with ever more creative programs and policies. Missing from these experts' equations is the idea that this bloom of longevity might actually represent a vast reservoir of meaning and worth.

In the clinic and laboratory, medical technology is used to mitigate the mental and physical defects associated with aging. It is every doctor's dream to make the blind see, the deaf hear, and the lame walk. In my practice as a physician, with the help of modern technology, I have been able to make each of these dreams come true, not once but many times. Intraocular lens implant surgery removes the clouded lens of the eye and replaces it with a crystal-clear plastic substitute. Laser surgery performed on retinas gives new sight to long-term diabetic patients. Presbycusis (loss of hearing due to aging-related changes in the ear) can be mitigated with sophisticated digital hearing aids. The skillful use of rehabilitation medicine and physical therapy has helped millions of older people learn to walk again. Each of these miracles is a normal everyday element of the geriatrician's practice.

Success on this scale has upset the traditional acceptance of the difficulties imposed by old age. In its place, we can now find a robust faith in the power of science to reduce the difficulties associated with old age. The pharmaceutical industry, in particular, is relentless in its search for magic bullets that can mitigate aging. Whole new classes of medications are being dedicated to the needs of older people (table 5). The aged are, from a corporate point of view, an ideal market segment. They tend to have stable chronic illnesses and need their medications consistently for years, often decades.

The unshakable equation of aging with decline plays to the strengths of a highly technological, industrial society. Health care technology has contributed vastly to the well-being of older people and shows every sign of being able to continue doing so. The problem is that the technologies that drive this progress are complex and expensive; many of the most important advances cost much more than the ordinary family can afford to pay. For example, the average

Table 5

Old-Age Pharmacology

Classes of Drugs Commonly Used in Old Age	Indication
Anti-inflammatory	Degenerative joint disease
Antihypertensive	Cardiovascular disease
Hypoglycemic	Diabetes mellitus
Psychoactive	Mood disorders, especially depression
Dementia-related	Alzheimer's and other dementias
Sexual performance enhancement	Erectile dysfunction

cost of one year of skilled nursing care for an aged relative is 125 percent of the median family income. Cost was much less of an issue when the best we had to offer was a gentle touch, a cup of hot tea, and a seat by the fire. Now, an older person crippled by degeneration of the hip joints can be pain free and walking after receiving titanium artificial hip joints. But who will pay?

Industrialization has changed the nature and function of the family and radically transformed the meaning and experience of work. It has given us powerful tools with which we may mitigate many of the most difficult aspects of aging. The fact that these technologies are both effective and expensive has led us to extend the reach of mitigated aging beyond the research laboratory and doctor's office. Mitigated aging has become the de facto standard for making public policy and has remade the patterns of obligation that bind young and old.

Every major industrial nation now makes explicit guarantees of material support to its aged citizens. When the Social Security program was launched in the 1930s, its founders understood perfectly well that it would take income from current workers and put it into the hands of current retirees. The program was accepted for the same reason that the woodcutter invited his father back to the family table. The transfer of wealth between the generations was fully justified by faith in the idea that tomorrow's workers would support tomorrow's retirees.

Social Security did much more than simply monetize the wood-cutter's social security. It changed the nature of obligation between young and old. Modern social welfare programs for the aged, while massively generous by historical standards, have defined our society's obligation to its elders in strictly material terms. The purely economic nature of this social compact is made plain in the Social Security eligibility standards and payment mechanisms. Rules and regulations extend into the tens of thousands of pages and are concerned exclusively with the objective facts and processes that guide eligibility and terms of payment.

Social Security is the most popular government program ever created. It became the legendary "third rail" of American politics that no elected official dared touch. Its logic was extended with the passage of the Medicare Act of 1964. Together, these two programs have indeed done immeasurable good for older people and their families. Far less obvious is the way that publicly provided resources and services have gradually replaced the idea that the bonds that unite young and old must also include important non-economic dimensions. We have created, and continue to maintain, a massive bureaucracy that serves the financial needs of the elderly. The fact that it does so completely without affection or tenderness is seen as beside the point. The end result is a bizarre reverse alchemy wherein long-held ideas about honor and obligation are reduced to purely economic considerations. In practice, "honoring thy father and thy mother" might as well be a line item in our government's budget—its ultimate dollar value subject to fierce political and fiscal debate.

It is a credit to our society that older people have access to the public purse. Public resources are necessary if older people are ever to afford the best methods of mitigating aging. Still, that access cannot be taken for granted. An ongoing program of grassroots organizing and professional lobbying exists to maintain and extend old-age entitlements. Lobbyists for the aged routinely scuffle with advocates for other causes—children, defense, lower taxes, and so on. Nothing is guaranteed. In the constant struggle for resources, the aged (as one special interest group among many) are entitled only to what their political influence can command.

Mitigated aging has clumsily divided responsibility for the aged between the public and private spheres. Governments and families are now uneasy partners in the effort to cope with what is, by any measure, a substantial effort. The boundary line between public entitlement and private obligation is hazy. As a result, there is a nearly constant struggle to shift responsibility for the aged from one sphere to the other. The outcome is a peculiar public-private dance in which each side attempts to minimize its burden without appearing to abandon its obligation.

This struggle can be seen clearly when we ask who will pay the bill for expensive nursing home services. Adult children, eager to have the government pay for long-term care services for their parents, devise complex legal strategies that both shelter their future inheritance and qualify Mom and Dad for government assistance originally intended for the poor. Hundreds of thousands of affluent Americans have used this loophole, happy to benefit from the legal but false impression that their parents are impoverished and thus eligible for public support.

For its part, the government specifically and in many cases intentionally underfunds the long-term care system. The result is low pay for workers, chronic understaffing, and a widespread loathing of skilled nursing facilities. The government can rightly claim to be fulfilling its pledge to provide "access to care," but many families will do anything to keep from having to put their loved one in a nursing home. A 2001 survey of the American public found that 43 percent of respondents found the idea of being placed in a nursing home "totally unacceptable." Those who make public policy fear that if they ever did create a publicly funded system of long-term care that had people's full faith and confidence, families would "come out of the woodwork" in a mad rush to gain such services for their own family members. Adult children and their aged parents, formerly terrified of nursing homes, would bankrupt such a system in short order.

Mitigated aging has been woven into the fabric of our culture. Social programs provide substantial support to the frail and infirm, even though families contribute much more. Science and industry pursue technologies that can lighten the physical and mental burdens of aging but retain a devoutly pessimistic perspective on old age itself. Old age is taken down from its traditional pedestal above petty adult politics and becomes just one of many competing special interest groups. Once solely the responsibility of their families, older people now face the dangerous prospect of relying on both family and government, and potentially neither.

Modern society makes real and ongoing efforts to honor ancient commitments to the aged. Governments approve massive expenditures to ensure that older people are not subject to the misery of poverty that for so long accompanied old age in industrial societies. But this assistance casts a long shadow. These programs give much but also take away. Older people rarely go hungry, but they have little assurance that they will find the love and affection that gives life meaning. Their health and life span can be extended, but those extra years may be burdened by boredom and loneliness. We may assure "access to care" but insist that that care be received inside loathsome government-financed institutions.

There are two useful lessons that come from all this. First, despite all our modern pretensions, we continue to struggle as did the

Table 6
The Reinvention of Aging

Traditional Aging	Mitigated Aging
Old age is both a blessing and a burden.	Aging is defined by mental and physical decline.
The aged should be respected.	The aged are entitled to high-quality medical and surgical treatments.
The aged should be stoic.	The aged must lobby for access to resources.
Care for the aged is a family responsibility.	The obligation to care for the aged is shared by the family and the government.

ancients with the tension between the short-term gains that can be had from neglecting or even eliminating the aged and the long-term cost that would inevitably accompany the destruction of old age. Second, old age and the place of the aged in society are both much more complex than we realize. There is no single story that can explain them to us. Shadowing the kind and gentle treatment accorded to millions of elders—haunting the enlightened, even divine endorsements of old age as a social good—is a long and terrible legacy of abuse, neglect, and gericide.

These ambiguities are the source of aging's greatest strength. Aging endures *because* it is so full of complexity and contradictions. In fact, our experience with longevity is entering into a new phase that will test and overturn some of our most cherished assumptions, new and old. Like a great conquering army resting quietly outside a sleeping city, old age is preparing for its greatest triumph.

Victory

The New Old World

Grasshoppers don't write books, but if they did, the mid-nineteenth century would deserve a volume all its own. During those years their golden age unfolded on the great plains of North America. Food was plentiful and the climate ideal; their numbers swelled into the hundreds of millions. Later locusts (a variety of grasshopper) would have recalled those days with relish. At night, they might have gathered the little ones around them and treated them to tales of wheat fields stretching hundreds of miles. The birds, who had been their enemies, were gone, denied nesting places and food by the tireless working of John Deere's sod-busting plow. Those were the good old days.

Not surprisingly, the human history of that time and place tells a different story. The people who were there shuddered as they recalled the plague of locusts. The locusts came in such vast numbers that they turned the sky black at noon and consumed everything in their path. Of course they ate the crops, but then they ate the weeds. They ate clothes hung out to dry. Then they ate the clothesline. They claimed millions of acres of grain for themselves and drove farmers and their families to the brink of starvation. This plague of locusts changed human history. It brought misery, poverty, and suffering to the people unfortunate enough to be in its path.

We are the natural allies of the farmers and find it easy to mourn their ruined crops. Few can muster sympathy for the millions of gnawing insects who took what was not theirs. This feeling is actually part of a broader cultural bias that favors beings who are productive, be they human or insect. Those who take without giving are always seen in a negative light.

This bit of history is especially relevant today because it previews the dynamics that will define the course of the global age boom. All over the world, societies are "graying." Declining birth rates combined with increased longevity are creating something new: old age on a massive scale. The old are descending on us by the hundreds of millions. No longer considered to be productive members of society, they will, nonetheless, continue to make demands on the people who must support them.

The "plague of locusts" rhetoric can become heated at times. Will the aged empty our treasury and strip our cupboards bare? Many fear that the age boom will ruin us all. But there is an alternative to this dark pessimism. When we set aside our customary preference for youth, we can see that old age is growing and developing in new and different ways. It is succeeding on an immense, history-making scale. We are, in fact, the beneficiaries of staggering good fortune. What name, other than success, could be applied to the modern ability to bring forth a generation imbued with the health, wealth, and wisdom not only to survive into old age, but to thrive there? Far from a plague of locusts, the coming age boom represents one of the greatest windfalls of all time.

Healthy, Wealthy, and Wise

I live in a small rural county in upstate New York that is characterized by little industry, few tourist attractions, and no college campus. Taken together, these factors have limited the area's economic growth, and the county lost population in the 1990s. Not surprisingly, the local chamber of commerce is always searching for ideas that could boost the county's economy. While I was writing this book, the chamber's director called me up to talk about economic development. I listened as she described her efforts to lure manufacturers to the community and her frustration with the difficulty of this work. What, she asked me, would I suggest the county do to spur growth?

I told her that old age is the answer.

Many people believe, usually without giving it much thought, that older people represent a net drain on community resources, the idea being that the fewer older people in any given community, the more healthy and prosperous that area is likely to be. This bias grows from our society's careless ageism. In truth, older people represent a net social and economic gain for communities fortunate enough to recruit them. Rather than trying to lure a defense contractor to our county, the chamber of commerce should be making the area attractive to older people.

This is the healthiest generation of elders ever to walk the Earth, and the elders to come are likely to be healthier still. Advances in pharmacology, surgery, and medical technology will continue and even accelerate as the population ages. The provision of high-quality medical and surgical services to an increasingly affluent and discriminating older population will be a growth industry for decades to come. Older people want a greater health span to go along with their growing life span, and communities that can help them achieve that goal will be amply rewarded.

Even though income disparity persists or grows in late life, older people emerged from the twentieth century as the wealthiest segment of our population. Households headed by people over sixty-five years of age hold claim to hundreds of billions of dollars of wealth. Even when their household income is at or below the median, older people tend to have as much or more disposable income than younger people with the same income.

Examining the material wealth of older people tells only part of the story. Older people are richly endowed with what author and professor of public policy Robert Putnam calls "social capital." Older people are more likely than younger people to read newspapers, vote, follow civic events closely, and contribute time and energy as volunteers serving community organizations. The people who will grow old in this century will be better educated, more widely traveled, better read, and thus more aware than any generation of elders in history. As an added bonus, older people are also much less likely than younger people to commit crimes.

More than any other age group, older people are engaged in civic life. Putnam has argued that these attributes define a specific generation (those seared by the Great Depression and World War II) and are not attributes of old age in general. Such an argument has much to recommend it, but we should also recall that members of the coming age boom have their own history of (fitful) social awareness and action. Given their health, wealth, and long-held beliefs, there is reason to hope that these new elders will contribute a unique form of social capital to twenty-first-century society.

Imagine for a moment an economic development strategy that recognized and aimed to make use of the value in old age. Why should we not seek out and develop a partnership with a demographic group with so much to offer?

Being Elder Rich

For the most part, a steady rise in the number of older people would seem an indication of a healthy society. The age boom is a flesh-and-blood testament to our success in creating a healthier society in which vast numbers of people are able to experience the fullness of human longevity. In fact, we are witness to the history-making triumph of old age. Far from being ravenous locusts determined to consume an ever-increasing share of scarce resources, our elders represent an unprecedented windfall.

The aged will live longer in greater health and security than their forebears a century ago. In terms of political power, they form one of the most powerful political advocacy forces in our society. The amount of life experience they can bring to bear on the important problems that face our society is huge and will only grow as the decades pass. We are living in an era of enormous wealth and possibility and should be welcoming the age boom with cries of joy from every rooftop. It is ironic that this victory should be confused with disaster. Even more worrisome is our collective failure to recognize and respond to the danger that comes with not acknowledging this victory. The windfall of old age is in danger of being snatched away, taken from us before it can bestow the blessing that only elderhood can provide.

NAVIGATING
LIFE

*No written law has ever been more binding
than unwritten custom supported by popular opinion.*

Carrie Chapman Catt

Living on the Edge of the World

The Packer Family

Four times each year, I teach part of a medical school course in geriatrics. The students are in their final year and are close to graduation when they come to me. Many dread the prospect of spending a month in a nursing home. They have already chosen their specialty and it can be hard for future obstetricians, pediatricians, and surgeons to muster much enthusiasm for the problems associated with longevity. Part of their reluctance comes from my chosen field's admitted lack of drama. Working with older people just doesn't make the pulse pound the way the operating room or emergency ward can. In the brief time I am with these students, I do my best to open their eyes to the subtlety and depth that make geriatrics, in my opinion, the best of all medical specialties.

I usually allow my students a week or so to become accustomed to the rhythm of the nursing home before I round them up for a field trip to a nearby cemetery. There is nothing like a cold, wet autumn day and a long, lingering walk in the local graveyard to awaken the slumbering knowledge of one's own mortality. As we wander among the stones, the excited chatter of successful young adults fades into a pensive silence. When they are quiet, I call them to the Packer family monument.

Dr. Perez Packer, 1790–1832, was buried beneath the epitaph "Being first in his profession, his work was well done." It doesn't take long for someone to do the math—Dr. Packer was just forty-two when he died. His wife, Nancy, says the monument, died sixteen years after her husband, when she was forty-seven. Walking around the stone, and taking time to understand the story it tells, opens the door to a tale of love and loss that played out in the first half of the nineteenth century.

1819–1831

It is likely that Dr. Packer was a veteran of the War of 1812. The headstone, however, gives no hint of his rank or branch of service. Whatever his past, he and his young wife (she was probably only seventeen or eighteen when they wed) chose the life of what was then a frontier settlement. In the decade that followed his arrival, he established a thriving medical practice and his family grew apace. Their first child, William, was born in 1819. Maria arrived the following year. Then, in 1826, another daughter, Caroline, was born. By the time their last child, a boy they named Theodore, was born, Dr. Packer was a respected physician and a pillar of church and community. It is easy to imagine peering through a frosted windowpane as Dr. Packer and his young family celebrate a merry Christmas Eve in 1829.

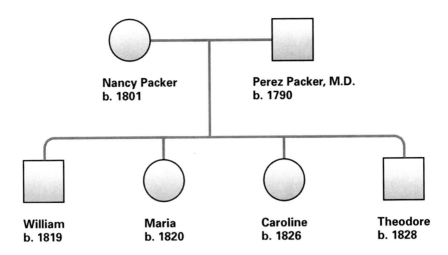

The Packer family circa 1829

1832–1847

Disaster struck on July 10, 1832. The stone bears no clues as to the illness or injury that cut the good doctor down. Perez Packer, M.D., was dead, and the result must have been pure calamity for the Packer family. (A frontier family, even one headed by a physician, would have had little defense against poverty after the loss of its breadwinner.) The students and I stand at the gravesite and, using the dates carved into the stones, create a picture of Dr. Packer's burial ceremony. There was his wife, standing where we stand now. Formerly so full of life and optimism, her face is now ashen gray. She holds Theodore's hand. He is three or four years old and does not understand that his father will never return. Two girls, the dead man's daughters, pour out their grief. Maria is twelve and Caroline is six. Then there is William; he stands slightly apart from his siblings. At thirteen, he is old enough to know that he will not be returning to school in the fall. He will go to work and do what he can to become the man of the house. There is no other choice. Whatever he imagined for his own future, those dreams were laid to rest alongside his father's casket.

We imagine that Nancy raised the children and did everything she could to give them a start in life, but the ache in her heart must have grown more painful as time went on. As expected, she gradually sold her most cherished possessions, including her husband's medical equipment and books, to buy food and clothing for the children. This painful parting occurred again and again until everything of value was gone. She lost Caroline in May of 1845, just before the girl's twentieth birthday.

1848–1850

Nancy, who had once been the young bride of a dashing older man, and the wife of a war veteran and physician, lived only forty-seven years. Surely those who mourned her when she died in 1848 remarked that she had aged greatly in the years since the deaths of her husband and daughter. Maria, the older daughter, followed her mother to the grave a year later, in 1849. She never saw her thirtieth birthday. Neither of the sisters had ever married.

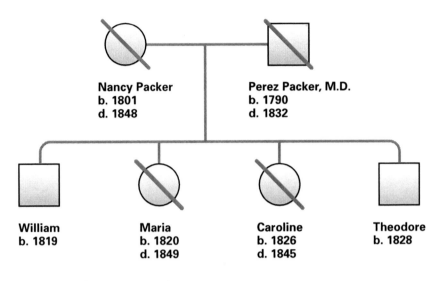

The Packer family circa 1849

At the start of the 1850s there was some reason for hope in the Packer family. Despite the loss of their parents and sisters, both boys had reached adulthood. In 1848, the older brother, William, was twenty-nine years old. Like his father, William married relatively late and chose a younger woman as his bride. Mary Packer was in her early twenties when she gave her husband a son, William W. Packer Jr. The baby was born in the winter of 1850.

1851–1855
Then came 1851. William the elder fell ill in March and died on the first day of spring. An epidemic of some kind was probably responsible, because William Jr. died just four days after his father. Mary, grief stricken and perhaps not well herself, died that summer.

That left Theodore, the youngest of Perez and Nancy's children. By the time he turned twenty-two he had attended the funerals of five immediate family members. He was an orphan with no surviving siblings and no wife or children of his own. His grief must have been profound. It is doubtful that those who knew him were surprised when he died in 1855. He was just twenty-six years old and was survived by no one.

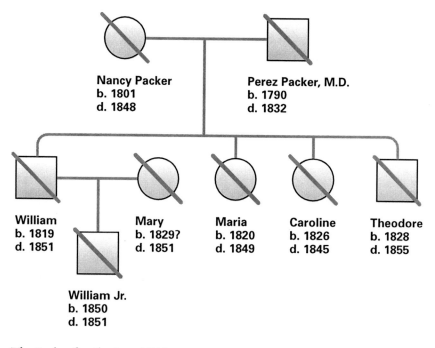

The Packer family circa 1856

Knowing the Living from the Dead

The saga of the Packer family interests my students partly because of Dr. Packer and his unusual epitaph but also because so many of the story's principals died at ages so close to their own. Given these connections, they are quick to speculate on the details of these people's lives. They wonder if Caroline had tuberculosis or if influenza killed William and his infant son. They want to know more. Where did the Packers come from? What was it like to live in that time and place?

They ask questions I cannot answer; all we have available to us are our imaginations and the dates inscribed on the stone. The lives these people led are lost. Their loves and losses, their victories and sorrows, their joy, passion, despair—all these things are reduced to a solitary mark, a hyphen carved in stone. A human life condensed into such a tiny space becomes a kind of dark matter. Hidden and mysterious, it exists beyond our reach. We can be confident that a life was led only because of the dates that surround that solitary mark.

Most medical students are ill at ease when they come to the nursing home. During their first week in the nursing home (before our visit to the cemetery), they are tentative in their words and actions. This is hardly surprising; it is rare to find anyone who feels immediately comfortable in this environment. Unlike fearful friends and relatives, however, the students can turn their attention to the stream of lab values and radiology reports that pour in every day. The visit to the graveyard brings something new to their outlook. They bubble with curiosity and questions. The problem is that even this fresh burst of enthusiasm is driven by the desire to avoid the unsettling truth of life as it is lived in the nursing home.

They have plenty of company in this regard. Professionals of all types have a tendency to think of the residents of nursing homes, especially the most frail and disabled, as being partly dead, or at least not fully alive. I go to the burial ground with my students because being among people who are dead and buried sharpens the contrast with the living. The people laid to rest under those stones are dead—the Packers are all dead, with the last of them laid in his grave in the decade before the Civil War. Nursing home residents, in contrast, are alive. My students have in fact spent the past week in a building that is bursting with older people who are truly, fully, and completely alive. We can ask for and listen to their stories. The difference between the living and the dead is the difference that matters most of all.

Medicine can heal afflictions and mend injuries in ways undreamed of in the early nineteenth century. It is probable that modern medicine could have extended the life span of every member of Dr. Packer's family. For all its power, though, medicine remains strangely silent on the question of what use we are to make of our extended life spans.

Despite the calamities visited upon them, the Packers knew how to live the lives they had been given. The terrain of their society was as familiar to them as the hills that stand around the family plot. Nancy Packer understood the role of the young widow even when her husband was alive and well. How many nights did she sit up worrying for the safety and health of her husband when he was out visiting patients? The day Perez died, she ended one part of her life and began another. Widowhood may have been grueling, but her place in the world was never in question.

Consider this: In the nineteenth century, living to an old age was rare—but one's place within family and community was secure. In the twenty-first century, living to an old age is commonplace—but one's place in family and society is profoundly uncertain. This is a tragedy deeper and more enduring than the deaths recorded on the Packer headstone.

A brooding walk through a cemetery illuminates the humanity of the nursing home residents for my medical students. Exposing the social calamity that gave rise to the nursing home itself is much more difficult. The nursing home is, for the aged and the infirm, a peculiar form of exile, simultaneously strange and familiar, local and very far away. Like all émigrés, nursing home residents long for a home and a way of life that no longer exist.

In ways that would have been incomprehensible to the Packer family, we live in a world prone to repeated society-wide upheavals. The very cultural and technological forces that protect us from early death are also redrawing the social maps we need to find our way through life. Long-settled ideas about how life is to be lived are remade in less than a lifetime. We now know people born in the first half of the last century who are confronted with an old age they could not have imagined when they were young. The Packers, in particular, were well acquainted with the ordinary forms of grief and shared their losses freely with others. We are coming to know something very different: a public tragedy that masquerades as a purely private grief. This is what comes from having the lives we were meant to live snatched from us by circumstances that are beyond our control. Medicine has no salve for an injury such as this.

OLD MAPS

Knowing Where You Are

Living seems such an ordinary thing that there should be little reason to create a map that describes its passages. Think about your daily routine. You do not need a map to go to the store or pick up the kids at school. Local landmarks are so familiar that they escape notice. A road map can prove its worth only when we enter unfamiliar territory. So it is with the human life cycle. Our need for a map of life is most acute when our place in the world is least certain. Members of a settled society can and do live out their lives with little concern about what lies ahead. They don't need to navigate because everything is and remains familiar. Contemporary society offers no such comfort. How are we to live? What comes next?

As I write this I am sitting at the corner table in a diner in my hometown. My geographic position is 42 degrees 41 minutes north latitude, and 75 degrees 30 minutes west longitude. This information is accurate, precise, and potentially useful to the reader (you can find me on a map). I offer it as a parallel to the following accurate, precise, and potentially useful information about society:

- Since 1900, the percentage of Americans over the age of 65 has more than tripled (4.1 percent in 1900 to 12.7 percent in 1999), and the number has increased by a factor of eleven (from 3.1 million to 34.5 million).

- Persons reaching age 65 in 1998 could expect to live on the average another 17.8 years (19.2 for females and 16.0 years for males).
- Almost 2.0 million people celebrated their 65th birthday in 1999 (5,422 per day). In the same year, about 1.8 million persons 65 or older died, resulting in a net increase in the over-65 group of approximately 200,000 people (558 per day).

Numbers such as these are meaningful only when they help us understand where we are in the context of history, culture, and society. Latitude and longitude are useful because we have maps on which they can be plotted. Demographic data are and will remain so much statistical gibberish until they can be transposed onto an accurate map of the human world. The better the map, the more useful the data become.

An individual life can be fully understood only within the context of the society in which it is being lived. Even our shared past, which would seem to be fixed and unalterable ("in 1492 Columbus sailed the ocean blue") is constantly being remade by the present. The future, which we like to imagine as an infinite sphere of possibility, is actually bounded by the way things are today. Even the tiniest, least memorable moments of our lives require the adhesive properties of memory and culture before they can be assembled into a meaningful story. Finding one's way through life, from beginning to end, has never been easy. Human beings have been making maps of the difficult terrain of the human life. When we turn our attention to these maps, we can see how urgent and enduring has been the question, "How are we to live our lives?"

Genesis

There is a childhood riddle that turns on the belief that Adam and Eve lacked belly buttons. Our navels are a remnant of birth, so only those who are born can have them. Since Adam and Eve were made, not born, they must have had unblemished abdomens. Human history would be completely different if belly buttons were the only things the first couple lacked. Being formed into an adult human from earthen dust or the fragment of a rib creates difficulties that those of us born into a human society have a hard time imagining. What could the first two created people on Earth know about how life is to be lived?

An adult without a childhood is like a house without a foundation. An adult living life without the benefit of elders is like a house without a roof. Those who lack both would have to face life's inevitable difficulties with no shelter at all. Adam and Eve lived their lives without the benefit of received wisdom and lived experiences. There was no community to draw on and no knowledge to acquire. Although the weather was perfect, food was plentiful, and the Creator was nearby, the Garden of Eden was a flawed paradise. Adam and Eve suffered terribly from the absence of human tradition. For them, all the problems of living were unprecedented. Because they had never been parented themselves, it would have been impossible for them to know how to be parents. When Cain and Abel whined, "Mom and Dad just don't understand," they were right. Given how poorly the first family was prepared for the challenges of being human, the subsequent eviction and murder are hardly surprising.

The story of Adam, Eve, Cain, and Abel reminds us of the perils of attempting life without a map to guide us. While we are accustomed to the idea of a moral compass, we are much less familiar with the need for a map of life to which such a compass might be applied. People, unlike the plants and animals that surround us, lack an inborn understanding of how to live. Somewhere in our distant past this instinctive knowledge passed out of our genes and into the wisdom that human societies hold in common. Human cultures exist, in large part, to instruct us in the manners and customs that define the boundaries of a life well lived.

The book of Genesis gives us a map of life that is bounded by the place we hold in the family. In this context, no life can be understood apart from the evolving web of family relationships that defines it. No person can or should stand alone, nor can any single family. This ethic comes through clearly in the verses that describe the repopulation of the Earth by Shem, Ham, and Japheth, the three sons of Noah:

Sons were also born to Shem, whose older brother was Japheth; Shem was the ancestor of all the sons of Eber.

The sons of Shem: Elam, Asshur, Arphaxad, Lud, and Aram.

The sons of Aram: Uz, Hul, Gether, and Meshech.

Arphaxad was the father of Shelah and Shelah the father of Eber.

Despite its obvious lack of interest in the daughters of Shem, the quotation provides us with a way of knowing how life was to be lived. Shem was the son of Noah, brother of Japheth, father of Arphaxad, and great-grandfather of Eber. His life was defined by relationships that no power, human or divine, could alter. For thousands of years, people navigated life using a map made from the permanent latitudes and longitudes of blood relations. Indeed, it was the very permanence of these relations (no father will ever be his own son's son) that formed the highest recommendation for their use as a guide for how to live.

Life can easily be understood and lived on such terms. When one is a child, the things of childhood are taken up. The child prepares to become the adult. The adult puts away the things of childhood and enters into the responsibilities that belong to spouse and to parent. Old age, if and when it comes, is to be received as a blessing. Living into old age was thought to be a God-given reward for piety. But that was not all. Old age was also a gift given by one's children as they fulfilled a sacred duty to provide for and honor their mothers and fathers.

Solon

Solon loved numbers. Installed as the lawgiver after a period of turmoil in ancient Athens, Solon remade Athenian society in dramatic numerical fashion. Starting in 594 BC, he reformulated the system of weights and measures, revalued the city's coinage, and created the Athenian Council as four groups of one hundred men each. My interest in Solon is based on his strikingly modern picture of the map of life in Athenian society. His poem "The Ages of Man" is possibly the first map of life drawn from the perspective of the individual rather than the family or bloodline:

A child in his infancy grows his first set of teeth and loses them
Within seven years. For so long he counts only as a child.
When God has brought to accomplishment the next seven year period,
One shows upon his body the signs of maturing youth.
In the third period he is still getting his growth, while on his chin
The beard comes, to show he is turning from youth to a man.
The fourth seven years are the time when every man reaches his highest
Point of physical strength where men look for prowess achieved.
In the fifth period the time is ripe for a young man
To think of marriage and children, a family to be raised.
The mind of a man comes to full maturity in the sixth period,
But he cannot now do as much, nor does he wish that he could.
In the seventh period of seven years and in the eighth also,
For fourteen years in all, his speech is best in his life.
He can still do much in his ninth period, but there is a weakening
Seen in his ability both to think and to speak.
But if he completes ten ages of seven years each, full measure,
Death, when it comes, can no longer be said to come too soon.

The poem is a lightning bolt of modernism. Solon replaces the traditional idea of age as a function of one's relationships with the radical idea of an individual life. The map he creates revels in mathematical precision. Indeed it is so orderly and predictable that it is doubtful that any person ever experienced such a life. But that is not the point. His poem is offered as an ideal, an archetype against which each of us can evaluate the life we *are* living. Solon uses the very arbitrariness of his scheme as a lever with which to pry life loose from its traditional attachments. This poem marks the beginning of age as a meaningful numerical concept in Western civilization. "How old are you?" is a question that has importance only in a society in which law and politics are given dominion over family and tribe. The next time you gather around a birthday cake with its flickering candles, one for each year, thank Solon for teaching us that in the life of an individual, the question "How old are you?" matters.

Shakespeare

In one of the best-known pieces of English literature, William Shakespeare offers his own map of the human experience. These lines from *As You Like It* show the way:

> All the world's a stage,
> And all the men and women merely players:
> They have their exits and their entrances;
> And one man in his time plays many parts,
> His acts being seven ages. At first the infant,
> Mewling and puking in the nurse's arms.
> And then the whining schoolboy, with his satchel,
> And shining morning face, creeping like snail
> Unwillingly to school. And then the lover,
> Sighing like furnace, with a woful ballad
> Made to his mistress' eyebrow. Then a soldier,
> Full of strange oaths, and bearded like the pard,
> Jealous in honor, sudden and quick in quarrel,
> Seeking the bubble reputation
> Even in the cannon's mouth. And then the justice,
> In fair round belly with good capon lin'd,
> With eyes severe, and beard of formal cut,
> Full of wise saws and modern instances;
> And so he plays his part. The sixth age shifts
> Into the lean and slipper'd pantaloon,
> With spectacles on nose and pouch on side,
> His youthful hose well sav'd a world too wide
> For his shrunk shank; and his big manly voice,
> Turning again toward childish treble, pipes
> And whistles in his sound. Last scene of all,
> That ends this strange eventful history,
> Is second childishness and mere oblivion
> Sans teeth, sans eyes, sans taste, sans everything.

Shakespeare's life cycle goes well beyond Solon's rigid formula. It imagines not only an individual but also one man who in his time "plays many parts." The scenes are well worn, but how they will be played can never be known in advance. A part is nothing until a flesh-and-blood human inhabits it. We may be mere players upon the stage, but we are players. The ages of man are ours to explore. This speech represents a second giant leap in the creation of the individual. Solon cut the cords that bound individuals to their birth-family circumstances, but it was Shakespeare who set us free to live out the scenes of our lives—to play our parts as well or as poorly as we are able.

In the late 1990s, I wrote a novel called *Learning from Hannah*. In an effort to bring its message to a wider audience, I also made the story it told into a play. I performed this one-man show in dozens of cities during the summer of 1999. Before the tour began, I was worried that playing the same scenes and saying the same lines night after night would bore me. What I found instead was that I had much to discover, even in my own words. By the end of the tour, it was painfully clear to me that I was only just beginning to understand the role I was playing. This is Shakespeare's insight—the player on the stage may be confined by the role he plays, but within that role there is a universe of meaning. Life is the ultimate human performance, our greatest opportunity for imagination, creation, and meaning.

Erickson

Psychoanalyzed by Anna Freud herself, Erik Erickson accepted and then extended the Freudian theory of psychosexual development. Erickson's most important innovation was the addition of another three stages of development to Freud's original five (table 7). Each of these stages was thought to unfold as a consequence of what Erickson termed "the epigenetic principle"—that progress through each stage is determined in part by one's success or lack of success in the previous stage. Events that interfere with this orderly pattern of development are likely to lead to difficulty or even pathology in later life.

Erickson gives us the life cycle as an individual journey that is at once perilous and satisfying. The constraints of kinship, the numerical rigidity of Solon, even the plodding normality of Shakespeare are swept aside by the pristine image of an individual mind and its struggle to develop. This approach was, partly, the product of the mid-twentieth-century world that Erickson inhabited. He shared the impulse to organize, categorize, and rationalize all elements of human experience. The inclination to mechanize living processes strongly influenced Erickson's understanding of how life should be lived.

To his credit, Erickson saw the remarkable degree to which one generation depends on another. He labeled as "mutuality" the tendency of members of different generations to interact. Freud made

Table 7

Erickson's Human Life Cycle

Age	Crisis	Modalities	Virtues
Infant (0–1)	Trust vs. Mistrust	To get, to give in return	Hope, faith
Toddler (2–3)	Autonomy vs. Shame	To hold on, to let go	Will, determination
Preschooler (3–6)	Initiative vs. Guilt	To go after, to play	Purpose, courage
School age (7–12)	Industry vs. Inferiority	To complete, to make things together	Competence
Adolescence (12–18)	Ego identity vs. Role confusion	To be oneself, to share oneself	Fidelity, loyalty
Young adult (19–29)	Intimacy vs. Isolation	To lose and find oneself in another	Love
Middle adult (30–55)	Generativity vs. Self-absorption	To make, to take care of	Care
Late adult (55 and up)	Integrity vs. Despair	To be, through having been made; to face not being	Wisdom

the influence of the parent over the child the focus of his work. Mutuality broadened this view, recognizing the additional age-old truth that children actively shape the development of their parents. We can easily add the observation that grandparents can also be powerful influences in the lives of their grandchildren, and vice versa.

Finding Our Way

To a degree far greater than we recognize, our lives are molded by the cultural evolution (and revolutions) in which we are immersed. These forces are not easily located and even when we can pinpoint them they are often hard to interpret. Engaging in a daily struggle for individual success and well-being is a most difficult and solitary undertaking. Such an expedition is made easier whenever we can rely on a map to guide us.

The usefulness of any such map is determined by how well it describes the terrain. A map of a mountain range, once completed with confidence, will remain accurate for millions of years. Political maps include national boundaries that can and do become dated, sometimes in less than a generation. Maps that describe the terrain of our society, that can show us how we are supposed to live, are the most difficult to make. Unlike mountains that remain rooted in the earth itself, our culture is changing day and night, changing without our permission, changing in ways we cannot comprehend. Expectations about how we are to live our lives are colliding with the reality that defines life within a modern industrial economy.

The social terrain within which we live our lives has less and less in common with what we believe our lives ought to be like. We need a new, updated map that describes the way we live now.

The Way We Live Now

Creating a New Map

A new map is called for because the old ones are increasingly out of date. Familiar landmarks have been relocated; our culture's rivers and valleys flow in new and disconcerting directions. While these changes are unnerving, few of us would be willing to dust off the old maps and press them into service once again. Living a life tightly bound by a rigid pattern of kinship holds little appeal for those accustomed to modern freedoms. I cannot recall ever receiving a business card that read, "John, son of Jason, brother of Albert, husband of Patricia, and father of Abigail," and I doubt I ever will. Though the choice can be agonizing at times, we choose freely to live and be known as individuals.

Reared as members of an industrial society, we can readily see the folly of dividing life into arbitrary seven-year periods. Solon's once-daring metaphor seems antiquated—worth remembering for its intent rather than its utility. Even Shakespeare, author of immortal insights into human nature, trots out a dull and dated picture of life that is bound to a single place, time, and gender. His "lean and slip-per'd pantaloon" is unlikely to make a comeback. Finally, Erickson puts forth a life cycle so detailed and so focused on the self that it is difficult to appreciate it fully except in a college lecture hall.

I was trained in the practice of medicine. When I am faced with difficult questions, I am inclined to seek practical answers. As a result,

I choose to spend as much time as possible observing people as close-ly as I can. I watch how children play, I listen to their speech, I note how they dress—and it makes me wonder why, year by year, child-hood is changing. Why does childhood increasingly look and feel like a dress rehearsal for adulthood? I see and feel the suffocating busyness that infests the lives of most adults. I hear people complain about the Alice in Wonderland futility that comes from running faster and faster just to stay in place. Why are we so busy? Everywhere I turn, I see the crazy paradox that lauds the older people we know and love even as old age itself is savagely attacked. I want, as much as anyone else, a map of life that can give me useful information about where we are and where we are going.

Without a research team or even a proper preparation for aca-demic inquiry, I must make do with what I have. Simple observation has led me to see life as a dynamic and unfolding interplay between the states of doing and being. The human experience is a peculiar form of living alchemy that combines and recombines doing and being in ways that create the moment-to-moment essence of a human life. The manner and circumstances in which these elements are compounded can be used to create a map of life as it is lived in modern industrial society. Before we can put such a map to its high-est and best use, though, we must develop a better understanding of what it means to do and to be.

Doing

It is entirely possible to live one's life without ever giving a single thought to what it means to *do*. Looked at as a question, "What is *doing?*" is on a par with "Why is the sky blue?" The sky is always with us, hanging over our heads every day, and yet we rarely think about its blueness until a curious three-year-old pesters us. The answer to "What is *doing?*" should be much more obvious to us than why the sky is blue, especially since it does not require any knowledge of physics or chemistry. We all ought to know what *doing* is because, as adults, our lives are devoted to doing. We do our work. We do our best. We do what we can. We do what needs to be done. We do what we are told. When I drive to town, I am doing. When I prepare a meal, I am doing. When I draw a bath for my child, I am doing. Breathing is a form of doing, as is the digestion of the food we eat and even the circulation of our blood. It is impossible to live and not do. Even the laziest person in the world has to do something. Death itself can be defined in its terms: dying requires a complete and final cessation of doing.

Doing is what happens when we come into relationship with and manipulate the visible, material world that surrounds us. Human work is usually thought of in terms of doing. This emphasis ensures that work will result in discrete, measurable (sometimes profitable) changes in the environment. Even management is a form of doing because its end product is the same as if the managers had done the work themselves.

All living things depend on doing for their survival. The bird gathers twigs in order to build its nest. The fox digs its den in the side of a hill. The lion stalks its prey. *Homo sapiens,* and many other species, have learned how to make other creatures work for them. Animal energy has been diverted to human goals for at least ten thousand years. With their herding dogs, draft horses, and honeybees, human communities continue to depend on what animals can do.

The purest expression of doing, however, is found in the tools and technologies created by humans themselves. Above all else, machines do. They engage and manipulate matter and energy with visible, measurable results. Best of all, from a human point of view, machines are insensible. Repeating the same task ten thousand times wears the parts but does not change the machine. As a society, we live in awe of the power of machines to detect, respond to, process, and transform our world. Faith defined the Middle Ages, and reason drove the Enlightenment, but now it is the machine that drives our society and we are said to live in the Age of the Machine. Any person who is capable of rising above the limitations that bedevil ordinary people is said to perform with machinelike efficiency and is given high praise. Executives pine for the day when their organizations will finally begin to function like the well-oiled machines they are meant to resemble.

Being

Living, as we do, in the Age of the Machine, it seems slightly suspect even to ask, "What is *being?*" The very question suggests a woolly-minded lack of seriousness. Whereas doing is visible and quantifiable and generates useful, real-world results, *being* concerns itself with things that cannot be seen. To *be* is to create and sustain relationships with the invisible and the intangible. For example, being married involves the mutual exploration of an invisible bond between two people. Being yourself requires a continual refashioning of the relationship between who you were, who you are, and who you will become. Being spiritually faithful requires us to strengthen and deepen a relationship with a deity or a force that can be felt but not seen or touched. It is being that guides us to the deepest, richest veins of human experience. We find meaning in being. This meaning can easily become more important than life itself.

I can tell another person to do something and easily determine whether the work has been done. It is impossible to command another person to be something. One cannot require another person to be in love. Love is a product of the intangible being and as such cannot, itself, be physically sensed (seen, touched, smelled, heard, tasted) or measured. Love is a feeling, and feelings possess a sovereignty that kings and queens can only dream of.

Those with great power have often failed to appreciate this. There is a long and sorry history of attempted coercion within the realm of being. During the Inquisition, the Catholic Church forced the "conversion" of thousands of Jews. Using the threat of torture and persecution, the Church was able to force Jews to do the things that Catholics do (eat pork, for example) and to profess the things that Catholics profess (the holiness of the Trinity, for example), but the Church was never able to know for certain if the converted truly believed what they had been commanded to believe. In fact, there is a Spanish word, *marrano,* that is used to describe a Jew who had been forced to convert. The term exposes the residue of suspicion among Catholics that the true beliefs of the *marranos* could never be known with certainty, despite their actions.

Centuries later, in the Age of the Machine, we have convinced ourselves that being matters much less than doing. Being, and the active pursuit of beliefs (political, social, spiritual, and so on)—along with the ambiguity that attends to them—have receded from the forefront of daily experience for hundreds of millions of people. Still, there are those for whom being remains an essential feature of daily life. Sages from all of the world's religions continue to seek the path that can lead them to purer forms of being. The ascetics among them condemn eating and sleeping as distractions and pursue the truth in the furthest reaches of human experience. In doing so, however, they overlook the instances of pure being that can be found within every human life.

In the early years of my medical practice, I attended births. The work was rewarding and I always savored the time I spent examining the newborn. Alert or asleep, each child seemed to me to be a nearly perfect expression of being. Human infants are notable for how little they can do (eat, sleep, and fill a diaper about sums it up), but they possess a nearly unlimited potential for creating human relationships. Somehow, they understand that these invisible attachments are essential to their continued growth and survival. To look deep into the eyes of a newborn is to glimpse a human, being.

A similar and equally powerful depth of being can be found among those who are very near to death. It has been said, and with good reason, that dying people never wish they had spent more time in the office. Doing matters little to the dying. As death draws near, it is relationships—with family, with friends, with God—that hold the greatest appeal. The carefully controlled breathing of the skilled meditator is, in a way, a rough approximation of the last breath we draw. When that breath is released into the atmosphere, we return at last to the pure essence of being that we last knew as a babe in our mother's arms.

DOING-Being and BEING-Doing

Presenting distinct definitions of doing and being creates the false impression that one can be separated from the other. Doing and being are best thought of as two sides of one coin. The human experience is the product of a fusion of doing and being that joins the two into one. When we flip a coin, it is just as likely to come up heads as tails. The human experience with being and doing is different; similar circumstances may, in fact, call forth very different responses.

You can see this in something as simple as driving a car. When you find yourself stuck in a frustrating traffic jam, you can focus on the thing you are kept from doing: getting from one place to another. On another day, in another situation, the same snail's pace might call forth the fullness of being. Creeping along, you reflect on your life and relationships—your faith, your loves, your past or future—invisible things that give richness to your life. Same car, same traffic, but a very different experience.

Religious observances, supposedly centered on faith and God, contain plenty of doing. Prayers are said in unison, songs are sung, ritual gestures are made. This is doing, but not a doing that could be confused with the mindless repetition of the machine; this is doing informed and enriched by being.

One of the most important freedoms offered by modern society is that we are entitled to adjust and readjust the proportions of doing and being that suit us best. Imagine that the fabric of human experience is a ribbon. One edge of the ribbon holds experiences that are defined mostly by doing rather than being (DOING-being). The other edge of the ribbon holds experiences that are defined primarily by being rather than doing (BEING-doing). The middle of the ribbon holds experiences in which the two are in balance. Moment by moment, our experience finds a place somewhere on this continuum. At one instant we are inclined to give precedence to doing but remain capable of being. In another situation we give precedence to being, though we can never let go of doing.

BEING-doing

DOING-being

The thread of human experience

Five Ages

Childhood

Newborn humans are helpless and highly dependent on their mothers, even by primate standards. The demands imposed by a human infant are so great, so insistent, so enduring that a powerful guarantee of reliability on the part of the caregiver is essential to every newborn's survival. This guarantee is delivered in the form of a human-to-human relationship. The mother-child bond is almost always a human's first and most enduring creation. The connection between a mother and her newborn may be invisible and intangible, but its existence cannot be questioned. As noted earlier, human newborns can do almost nothing, but they are masters of being.

This preference for being over doing persists as the child grows, and it can be seen in the chief preoccupation of every healthy child. Child's play and playgrounds offer ideal venues for studying human behavior that gives precedence to being over doing. The ascendance of being is subtle and may not be apparent on first inspection. Most of what we see and hear involves running, tumbling, laughing, and shrieking. Kids climb, chase, wrestle, and argue. Beneath all this activity, and much more important than any of it, is the practice of make-believe. When children play, they sail ships that cannot be seen, touch clouds that cannot be felt. What children do when they are playing is secondary to what they can be while they are playing.

Most parents can testify to their children's relative lack of interest in doing things that need to be done. The parent identifies an urgent need for the child's room to be cleaned, top to bottom. The child rarely shares this interest. The parent declares that the garbage will be taken to the curb every Thursday morning. The garbage frequently misses its appointment. Frustration builds. Stern lectures are delivered regarding the need to take responsibility for one's assigned duties. The child listens attentively and very soon afterward drifts back into the comforting womb of BEING-doing. It is hard for a child to understand what all the fuss is about. Doing matters little to the child; being matters very much.

At the deepest level, adults appreciate this basic truth of childhood. Part of the outrage that shadows the use of child labor is related to the feeling that it is a particularly ugly kind of theft. The child's right to play—the right to soak in the richness of being, without the press of adult responsibility—is taken away with little or nothing given in return. The loss is especially damaging because a healthy childhood is the best available preparation for the harrowing ride through adolescence into adulthood.

Adolescence

Like a shutter that flaps back and forth in the wind, adolescence is a time of indecision and loud, unpredictable banging. Adolescents are attracted by the sweet lures of adulthood—the freedom, the possessions, and the opportunity to "make it under their own steam." At the same time, the joyfulness of play is still a reliable part of daily life. The result is a persistent ambivalence wherein the benefits of acting like an adult can be sampled and rejected like cold peas on a dinner plate. What shall I choose: the comfort of childhood BEING-doing or the excitement of adult DOING-being? Both? Neither? The adolescent doesn't really know, and the answer varies according to the day of the week and sometimes the hour of the day.

A prolonged transition from childhood to adulthood is a luxury that only the prosperous can afford. Adolescence is a product of affluence. Instead of following the biblical injunction to put away the things of childhood so that we can enter into adulthood, we are indulged with a period of indecision. Over time, and each at his or her own pace, adolescents begin to play less and perform more. The chaotic imaginative play of the schoolyard gives way to the discipline demanded by the soccer coach. Learning for its own sake is set aside in favor of textbooks, advanced-placement coursework, and college boards. Childhood art is replaced slowly and fitfully by the graded art-class projects now signed and hung in the hallways of the school. Gradually, embarrassment envelops childish things—the beloved stuffed animal is set discreetly aside.

Parents, who function as active co-conspirators in this process, watch with heavy hearts. They know that the child must become the adult, and yet they are very sorry to lose the child who loved them more than anything else.

When does adolescence begin? When does it end? Age markers have little value in delineating adolescence. This is a developmental process, and while it usually unfolds against the backdrop of puberty, the years devoted to adolescence vary from person to person. It begins when the child expresses an independent interest in the discipline required for real achievement. This is the first stirring of an adult's preoccupation with DOING-being. Adolescence continues in its characteristic fitful and unpredictable way until the playfulness of childhood becomes a memory rather than a reality of daily life.

Adulthood

The adult is chained, willingly, to the rock of doing. Adults are obsessed with doing—it fills their lives, and for the most part they enjoy it. Confirmation that adulthood is solidly in place happens when a person displays a clear preference (in his or her actions if never in words) for DOING-being.

When two adults meet, it is rare for more than a minute to pass before one of them pops the question, "What do you do?" Adults use to-do lists, ticking the items off in order as their work gets done. Adults inhabit a world of tasks and schedules, payments, obligations, and jobs that need to be done. They may maintain a nostalgia for childhood, but they play very little or not at all. Indeed, to "play" at something implies a disappointing lack of intensity and purpose. Becoming an adult entails the completion of a complex and irreversible transformation. Over time, an adult loses the desire to once again be the child he or she was.

The closest adults come to a sustained experience of BEING-doing comes with the annual vacation. If the desire and the means exist to arrange a holiday that is not itself a hectic race to an imaginary finish line, the vacationers will tell a story something like this: "It took me about a week to unwind and let go, and then I had the greatest time of my life." They will describe the sheer luxury of sleeping when they were tired, eating when they were hungry, and playing with the people and things that surrounded them. In other words, they tasted, however briefly, a way of being that they had all but forgotten. The reprieve is temporary—even before the holiday is over, the calloused hand of adulthood grabs hold and pulls them back into the orbit of routine and responsibility. DOING-being reasserts its power. The sustained focus on what has to be done and the comparative disregard of just being return in full force. There is no slavery more powerful than a servitude that is self-imposed.

The adult's devotion to DOING-being also influences how adults see, think about, and speak of their older friends and relatives. Anywhere adults are gathered together, you can hear the "Adulthood Forever!" anthem being played if you listen for it. It starts slowly, modestly: "My mother is eighty-seven, but she's still as sharp as a tack; she lives by herself in Phoenix." Such an unassuming claim is sure to be followed up with something more substantial: "Well, my grandmother—she's ninety, but you would never know it; she manages her own stock portfolio online and is finishing her master's dissertation in French literature." Then comes the coup de grâce. A man, silent until now, speaks up: "My great-uncle is ninety-six years old and he just got back from climbing K2. He spends his winters in Florida because he likes to barefoot water-ski, in the nude." Game. Set. Match. Adults think that everyone should be an adult no matter how long he or she lives; nothing else quite measures up.

Senescence

One of the reasons I wrote this book was to try to rescue the idea of senescence from the clutches of declinist thinkers. I think the word is worth saving because it can reflect a complex ripening, a richness that is unavailable to those who remain in the fevered vigor of adulthood. Just as adolescence ("growing into adulthood") is a complex and turbulent time, senescence ("growing into old age") is not to be undertaken lightly.

The first sign that a person is preparing to grow out of adulthood is the dawning awareness of how heavy a toll is taken by the things he or she "has to do." Sheltered for decades by the energy and vitality of youth, adults are utterly convinced of the rightness and goodness of their family and their chosen work. The shadow of doubt appears only tentatively and intermittently at first. Gradually there emerges an understanding that one's family, while beloved in every way, is very much like millions of other families. Slowly the adult begins to understand that his or her work, while undoubtedly important, is very much like the work being done by millions of other people. These uncomfortable insights are slowly and painfully transformed into a desire to set aside the world of "have to do" in order to begin exploring the mysteries that cloak the world of "want to do."

The consequences of this shift can be seen in the distinct differences in how adults and senescents bake cookies. The adult tends to approach cookie baking as one more item on a long list of things to do. The children are either banished from the proceedings or—if the adult is feeling particularly guilty about a perceived deficit in the "quality time with the children" account—the children will be included, with some apprehension. The cookies are baked with dispatch, and dire warnings about eating raw cookie dough (possible salmonella) are issued along with lessons about the virtue of cleaning up as you go.

The senescent is much more likely to *want* to bake cookies than to *have* to bake cookies. As a result, children are usually more than welcome. Eating raw cookie dough? "Never mind what your mother says; go right ahead." Flour, sugar, and eggs are used with abandon.

Bizarre and experimental cookie shapes are welcomed. The crucial difference between the adult and the senescent is that the former is fixated on the doing while the latter seeks the being. The adult cares about the cookies and is happy to log some quality time if possible. The senescent cares about the relationship and is content with the cookies no matter how they turn out.

Senescence, like adolescence, is a time of transition. It is a letting go of something comfortable and familiar (in this case the practices of adulthood) and a reaching out for something new and different. There is no biological trigger for this transition; it is a function of culture and shared expectations. It is the beginning of ripening, just as adolescence is the beginning of maturation. When I first made notes for this book, I knew that it would include a description of this phase of life; however, I did not have a name for the phase. Again and again the word *senescence* suggested itself to me. Finally, I realized that it was time for someone to stand up for this beautiful word. The declinists, who have tainted it with their bleak dread of aging, do not deserve to keep it. The purpose of senescence is to prepare a person for the final stage of human development, elderhood. What could be more beautiful than that?

Elderhood

Far from its crude caricature as a second childhood sans hair, sans teeth, sans everything, elderhood offers a richness that can only be known near the end of a long life. Elderhood has a revolutionary, liberating potential that is often misinterpreted and misunderstood. The source of its richness lies in the transition to a life defined by the experience of BEING-doing. This is a gift of great value.

The fact that children and elders share a preference for being over doing accounts for the considerable mutual attraction that exists between the two groups. Watching older and younger people together, one gets the sense of a secret (or at least submerged) collusion that excludes adults. I remember visiting a nursing home that had a child day-care center within its walls. A group of elders and children were engaged in painting flowerpots when the adult overseers declared that

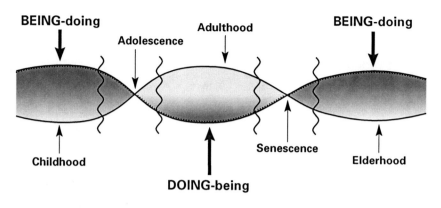

A contemporary human life cycle

it was time to move on to the next activity. All but one of the children trooped obediently out of the room. Andrew, who was curled up in an elder's lap, wouldn't move. As he was being prodded to leave, I heard him say, "I want to be with Frank." The time they were spending together soothed them both. The adults could not be expected to understand. They pried the boy gently from the elder's lap and sent him scurrying on to the next scheduled event.

Elders develop a new relationship with time. As the years pass, the pressures created by living one's life in the thrall of the future abate. The past, long exiled from the bustle of daily life, gains new prominence. New experiences and relationships are evaluated from the perspective of how well or poorly they elicit pleasing emotions and memories. Elders recount scenes from their lives, intent upon distilling, from the pale liquid of memory, the meaning of the life they have lived. Busy adults are apt to receive the telling and retelling of stories with an eye-rolling tolerance. Memories, and the lessons that can be drawn from them, are discounted among those who inhabit the busy world of the doer.

Death is close. The body, a faithful companion for so long, is now near its end. As a geriatrician, I have had the duty and pleasure of talking with hundreds of older people about the end of their lives. Because the days of "doctor knows best" are past, I need to know what my patients want me to do when their time comes. With only rare exceptions, I have found elders to be quite interested in having this conversation and very willing to make their views known. I ask, "What should I do if you stop breathing and your heart stops beating?" By far, the most common answer I receive is, "I've lived my life. Just let me go." I follow this affirmation with an assurance that we have much to offer in terms of comfort measures and pain control. Then, I promise my patients that they will not be made to endure the piercing, the electrical shocks, and the drugging that is medical technology's distorted response to death in old age. A half smile comes, and fades just as quickly—a subtle sign that I have been allowed, inadvertently, to glimpse a deep secret, one that I am far too young to understand. The subject is changed. I move on to complete my duties. The elder waits and remembers, ready to depart for a destination unknown.

TRAGEDY

All great truths begin as blasphemies.

George Bernard Shaw, *Annajanska*

The Cult of Adulthood

Three Sets of Questions

Before his untimely death in the early 1960s, social theorist C. Wright Mills published a series of provocative and enduring studies of American society. *White Collar* and *The Power Elite* dissected the structure and uses of power in mid-twentieth-century America. *The Sociological Imagination* addressed the study of society itself. Mills was wary of the trend toward purely quantitative methods of investigation that were then sweeping the field of sociology. He feared that an exclusive reliance on numerical certainties like those that fueled research in physics and chemistry would obscure the distinctively human interrelationships that actually compose life as it is lived in a community. In developing the ideas that make up this book, I accepted Mills's premise that "no social study that does not come back to the problems of biography, of history, and of their intersections within a society has completed its intellectual journey."

The best preparation for understanding age and aging in contemporary society comes from a careful look at the past. We do, after all, live in a world that was shaped by ten thousand generations of elders. Their contribution, however, is often overlooked and for the same reason that stars aren't seen in the daytime sky. In fact, there is a canopy of stars over our heads all day long, but the tremendous glare of the sun hides them from our eyes and makes it easy to forget that they are there.

Likewise, we are blinded by the overpowering, action-oriented role that *adults* play in society and history. Mills urges us not to let the obvious obscure the important. Our only hope for understanding the lives we live, the society we inhabit, and our place in history rests on an accurate understanding of how this society, distinct from all others, came to be. Mills puts forth three sets of questions that can lead us to a deeper understanding of our world:

1. What is the structure of this particular society as a whole? What are its essential components, and how are they related to one another? How does it differ from other varieties of social order? Within it, what is the meaning of any particular feature for its continuance and for its change?

2. Where does this society stand in human history? What are the mechanics by which it is changing? What is its place within and its meaning for the development of humanity as a whole? . . . How does it differ from other periods [of history]? What are its characteristic ways of history-making?

3. What varieties of men and women now prevail in this society and in this period? And what varieties are coming to prevail? In what ways are they selected and formed, liberated and repressed, made sensitive and blunted? What kinds of "human nature" are revealed in the conduct we observe in this society in this period? . . .

It is the third set of questions that supplies the pry bar that we need for understanding longevity in contemporary society. When we name the "varieties of men and women [who] now prevail," we find that we live in a world that is dominated, as no society ever before, by adults. Those of us who wish to understand the role of old age in contemporary society are well advised to pay close attention to adults and the ways that adulthood is shaping the society in which we live. In a way that Mills would surely recognize, we are so thoroughly drenched in the doctrine of youth's perfection that we no longer recognize its scent. Every important social institution has been bent to the task of forming or reforming adults. Contemporary society has placed adult influence and prestige at its apex. Its power is so great that all else is scattered before it.

Adult Power

Modern society has given us many perspectives on power. Feminists have developed a powerful critique of male control, and they show how that power is used to limit the opportunities afforded to women. Economists draw attention to the growing gulf between rich and poor and document the consequences of this inequality. Other writers emphasize the value of information and point to the rise of a new educated class, a pedigreed elite with its hands on the keyboards of power. Each of these points of view offers something useful, but none grasps the attribute that is common to them all—it is adults who govern. Man or woman, rich or poor, educated or illiterate, each of us participates in or is subject to the power of adults. Adults rule.

Their power is so complete, their control over our lives so encompassing that we have to ask the question, "Does adulthood function as a cult?" Common sense suggests that the answer is no. After all, adulthood is the most ordinary of things. When we are young, we crave its promised freedoms. When we grow old, we cling to the social status it can confer. Wherever we look, we find ordinary men and women living out their lives in the most conventional circumstances. Being an adult is as mundane as buying groceries, driving to work, and balancing a checkbook.

But what *is* a cult? The definition depends heavily on who is asking the question, because the word *cult* lacks a universally agreed-upon meaning. Religious leaders, alert to the dangers posed by schismatic cults, look for important variances from standard theological truths. Sociologists probe organizations that self-consciously divorce themselves from and actively oppose mainstream values and lifestyles. Mental health professionals measure the damage done by leaders who manipulate others to enforce conformity with their own desires. Journalists tend to use the term *cult* loosely, applying it to any group or movement that diverges importantly from the orthodoxies of the day.

Identifying a cult is easiest when it is headed by a madman. A powerful conviction that the Maker of the Universe is riding into town on the tail of a comet is a real tip-off that something is terribly wrong. A much more challenging case is presented when a cult's beliefs mesh agreeably with society's most conventional wisdom. This is the cult hidden in plain sight.

Mayhem ensues whenever a society surrenders to the ideology of a cult. The twentieth century was studded with cultic catastrophes that were recognized only in retrospect. Still, it is hard to imagine something as soothing and comfortable as adulthood as being kin to communism or fascism. Familiarity does have its virtues, but we should never forget that it can also conceal more than it reveals.

Despite great variation in size, history, and ideology, cults do have a common underlying framework. They must recruit new members while maintaining control over existing devotees. They make themselves remarkably easy to join and devilishly difficult to leave. At the same time, heretics and unbelievers must be identified and expelled before their influence can damage the integrity of the group's ideology. All cult members are required to participate fully in the group's beliefs and practices. Priorities are ordered on the basis of what will allow the cult to extend and consolidate its power. Neither the common good nor an individual's well-being are considered.

Cults use outlandish promises as currency. It is the wondrous nature of these promises and the glowing confidence with which they are made that people find so enticing. Ordinary cults content themselves with promises of love, fame, fortune, or spiritual enlightenment. Adulthood pledges something that not even mighty Zeus could deliver—an active life combined with eternal youth. In what amounts to a self-fulfilling prophecy, adulthood erases the distinction between acting young and being young. The appearance of youth becomes youth itself.

That adulthood's central premise is demonstrably false does nothing to reduce its allure. In contemporary society, to act young is to be young. No limits are set on the means that may be employed in the pursuit of that illusion. Older people who are able to cling, however tenuously, to a credible claim of active adulthood possess the modern equivalent of Ponce de Leon's fountain of youth. Meanwhile, the young are made subject to adulthood's fanatical devotion to doing. Long-settled ideas about youth and childhood are being set aside in favor of patterns of living and learning that give primacy to the dictates of DOING-being. The aggressor is a cult of adulthood that can see no limit to its power and believes unquestioningly in the righteousness of its cause.

It Is All Around You

Mills was always keen to overcome the blindness that accompanies familiarity. When he asks us to explore "what kinds of 'human nature' are revealed in the conduct we observe in [a] society," he is inviting us to do the hard work of seeing the ordinary. Nothing is more familiar to us than the totems and practices of adulthood.

We are adults living in the Age of the Machine, and the mechanization of society has created an immutable bias toward speed and uniformity. Without our being conscious of it, we are compelled to eat fast, walk fast, and talk fast. The irony is that it is easy to imagine just the opposite: hundreds of millions of people living within a cocoon of efficient, productivity-enhancing machines would seem to have little need for urgency. All our machines could be devoted to the task of enabling leisurely afternoon walks by the riverside or freeing us to pursue a long-submerged interest in reading and writing poetry. Instead, the human being has become entangled in the machine's feedback loop of productivity, speed, and consistency. The greater the power of our machines, the more urgent the need for human speed becomes.

Pointing out the problems associated with the mechanization of society has often been taken, wrongly, as an attack on mechanization itself. Contemporary society is so sensitive to criticism on this point that I must take a moment to clarify my position. I am not denying the importance and utility of machines. As a physician, I depend on and my patients benefit from a wide variety of lifesaving technologies. I would not give up the progress that has been made since I first became a doctor. At the same time, I feel an increased intensity and demand for speed and productivity within my practice. I'm not alone. Many people feel that the pace at which they are living is accelerating in tandem with their ever more efficient mechanical partners.

I suspect that you feel these changes in your own life. Cause and effect are hard to disentangle, but the outcome is a human society that is increasingly fused with the world of the machine.

When we step back far enough to place the stages of the human life cycle into this context, it quickly becomes clear that adulthood is the phase of life in greatest harmony with the machine, and the phase that has the most to gain from such a union. It is the grand alliance between the adult and the machine that is warping the human perception of time, information, and relationships. Adults, who have always had difficulty seeing beyond doing, are often unable to recognize these distortions for what they are.

Stanford researcher Laura Carstensen has developed a theory of human experience that illuminates the distinctive ways young and old perceive time. She argues that our perception of time shapes our priorities. This perspective on human motivation blends nicely with the distinction between DOING-being and BEING-doing (table 8).

Carstensen asserts that those who believe, rightly or wrongly, that they have a virtually unlimited amount of time to live tend to act based on knowledge-related motives. They routinely and unthinkingly value doing over being. In contrast, those who believe, rightly or wrongly, that the time left to them is limited tend to act based on emotion-related motives. As we age, the normal course of human development should take us from one set of motivations to the other.

The quackery that makes up so much of the antiaging fad perverts the human developmental process by altering our perception of time. Our youth-obsessed society trumpets the value of dietary sup-

Table 8
DOING-Being and BEING-Doing: Two World Views

Knowledge Related	Emotion Related
Gaining information	Meaningfulness
Social comparison	Intrinsic satisfaction
Identity strivings	Deeper intimacy
Achievement orientation	Emotional gratification

plements and ancient healing herbs that promise to protect our youth. Whether any of these pills and therapies can actually "slow and even reverse the effects of aging" is actually beside the point. What really matters is that the promises allow people to believe, no matter how old they are, that they still have *an unlimited amount of time left to live.* The illusion of unlimited longevity strengthens and maintains the characteristic adult devotion to doing, having, and getting.

The ideology of antiaging infects a substantial part of the contemporary adult population and obstructs the ancient progression from adulthood to elderhood. The result is an underdeveloped, increasingly dysfunctional population of developmentally delayed adults who are prone to catastrophic errors of judgment. The highly mechanical, outcome-oriented adultish worldview is wreaking havoc on the lives of people of all ages and even on the well-being of the planet itself. At the root of it all is the adult fantasy of unlimited time, unlimited wealth, unlimited resources, and unlimited information.

Since hardly a day goes by that we are not reminded that we have entered into a history-making information age, this idea of unlimited information deserves further attention. In the fashion of the telegraph, the wireless, and the telephone, the Internet is touted as a panacea. Cyberspace is supposed to give us lower prices, better service, more rapid progress in science and technology, and a faster route up our chosen ladders. What is left unsaid is that the Internet has an almost exclusive preference for adult-oriented, knowledge-related types of information. There are being-related resources available in its domain (mostly confined to online support groups and virtual communities), but these offerings are tiny bits of flotsam carried along by a tsunami of *useful* data and images. Taken together, emotion-related resources are far less popular than those that provide the up-to-the-minute information we crave.

Here's a test you can perform the next time you log on to the World Wide Web. Look at the sites included on your list of favorites. How many of them are on your list primarily because of the achievement-oriented, identity-striving, goal-directed, DOING-being information they contain? Visit some of them with a fresh perspective.

How many of these sites are designed specifically to bring meaning and intrinsic satisfaction into your life? How do they deepen and enrich the intimate relationships that you have formed with the people you care most about?

Adults value information in proportion to what they can do with it. The information revolution (like most heavily hyped revolutions) is really just a coup d'état. It marches under the banner of unlimited information when in fact it is a front for the power of adulthood, for the adult's obsession with doing and the strategies required for success in adulthood.

Adults are increasingly structuring their personal relationships around actual and hoped-for economic benefits. This bias first rears its head in adolescence, when ambitious high school students begin selecting extracurricular activities with an eye to the impression these affiliations will create in the minds of college admission officers. The tendency accelerates when people begin their careers. Adults network furiously at business meetings, though they have little interest in knowing or understanding the distinctive personhood of the people they meet. They are modern hunter-gatherers in determined pursuit of the contacts that can advance them toward their goals. Nor is this phenomenon limited to the ambitious Ivy Leaguer. Soap, plastic dishware, and cosmetics companies are just a few of the thousands of businesses that have persuaded millions of adults to convert family relationships and friendships into selling opportunities. Multilevel marketing schemes are founded on the ease with which ordinary people will inject commerce into their otherwise personal relationships.

The adult mind is also adept at transforming the fantasy of unlimited time into the parallel illusion of unlimited resources. The preeminence of doing is the foundation of our voracious appetite for getting and having. In modern industrial economies, social rank is defined in large part by wealth, and few adults willingly exchange the chance to acquire wealth for an opportunity to deepen the intimacy of and satisfaction in their relationships with the people they hold most dear. Whenever government officials and business executives announce that they are stepping down so that they can spend more time with their family, we know the truth. They were fired.

The mania for having and getting diminishes the value of stewardship in our culture. The preservation of resources for the benefit of those yet to be born, or even for the common good of those living now, is airily dismissed as simple-minded idealism. With this in mind, it is interesting to watch the interplay between environmentalists and those who speak for corporate polluters. There is an unmistakable hint of paternalism in the way corporations address those who would preserve natural resources for the use of others. They cast environmentalists as little children who still believe in Santa Claus, and deride their foolish faith in the unseen and the indefinite. The corporation, in contrast, presents itself as the embodiment of the responsible adult, unwilling to yield, even for a moment, to anything other than the merciless pressure to do, to get, to have.

The Buddha's insights into human suffering *(dukka)* are practically a catalogue of adult obsessions and concerns. Karen Armstrong, in her excellent biography of the Buddha, examined these ideas carefully and summarized them and the "adult mind" in this way: "The ego is voracious and continually wants to gobble up other things and people. We almost never see things as they are in themselves, but our vision is colored by whether we want them or not, how we can get them, or how they can bring us profit. Our view of the world is, therefore, distorted by our greed, and thus often leads to ill-will and enmity, when our desires clash with the cravings of others." The Buddha knew the adult mind well, and we can see how little the centuries have changed that mind.

The Assault on Childhood

Trampled Boundaries

Sometimes we find that the most important clues to the workings of a society are uncovered when we ask ourselves what should be there but is missing. For example, human societies have long drawn a bright line between childhood and adulthood. Colin Turnbull, author of anthropological works such as *The Forest People* and *The Mountain People*, spent his life looking for this line and the initiation ceremonies that have long defined the transition from child to adult. In his book *The Human Cycle*, he pays special attention to the ways in which societies organize people of different ages into specific social roles and how these roles allow people of every age to contribute to the well-being of communities as a whole.

> In cultures such as those of the Ituri villages and the Mbuti, the period of transformation from childhood to sexual and social maturity is often highly formalized in rites of passage, generally accompanied by ritual initiation. These rites are frequently among the most important in the life of the society; the focus is as much on the social good as upon the good to the individual participants, for with this transformation from childhood to young adulthood there is a corresponding and vital transformation of an individual into a social being.

While many religious groups in our society continue to practice such rites (the bar mitzvah participant's proclamation that "today I am a man" comes to mind), these ceremonies now lack secular force or meaning. The line between childhood and adulthood is indistinct, perhaps purposefully so. The right to drive comes at sixteen years of age, the right to vote at eighteen, and the right to drink alcohol at twenty-one. The absence of modern initiation rituals is actually an alarming sign of the tremendous power of adulthood in contemporary society.

Initiation rites emphasize the distinction between children and adults. The rites mark a social boundary line that must be respected by all parties. The ceremonies are used to mark an irreversible transformation that launches the young into adulthood. Modern industrial society emphasizes transition rather than transformation. Much has been made of children who supposedly "refuse to grow up," while little or no attention has been paid to the ways in which this hazy line allows adulthood and its devotion to DOING-being to impose itself on the young. The creation and maintenance of a boundary between these two phases of the life cycle serves mostly to protect children, who are and always will be the weaker party.

All nations, strong and weak, are expected to respect political boundaries, but those boundaries serve, mostly, to protect the weak. They offer little advantage to the strong. Modern industrial society has dispensed with the boundary between childhood and adulthood largely because such a line is not perceived to serve adult interests. We are witnesses to the relentless adultification of childhood. We see it. We feel it. We mourn its consequences in our own lives. The forces of adulthood are trampling the childhood most of us recall, and there is nothing that children can do about it. Absent a formal barrier capable of restraining its power, adulthood is free to continue dismantling childhood, piece by piece.

Shakespeare's whining schoolboy, with his satchel and shining morning face, would struggle to keep pace with the industrial model of childhood. Far from an idyll of play and learning, contemporary childhood throbs with adult attitudes and behaviors. The adult community, which equates maturity with productivity, imposes its standards on the young whenever and wherever it can. As occupiers are wont to do, adulthood shines the light of benevolence upon its conquest. The transformation of childhood is justified with the argument that children need an early and thorough education in the habits that bring success as an adult. These trends also create alarming images of ever younger children adopting adult language, behavior, and beliefs. These children inadvertently illustrate the conflict between what we believe childhood should be (innocent and unblemished) and the way it is being lived today. Angered by such behavior, many adults resort to blaming children themselves for their increasingly adultish ways.

Children, for their part, are well aware of which way the cultural wind is blowing. Most voluntarily adopt the behavior, language, and desires of their conquerors. The ingrained preference for BEING-doing that has long been the hallmark of a healthy childhood is being replaced by an accelerated program of academic work, organized sports, media consumption, and extracurricular activities. Childhood is ensnared by a ruthless social ethic that defines success, even for the very young, through the objective, doing-oriented metrics of adulthood. Even toys, once the embodiment of the pleasure children take in BEING-doing, are increasingly conceived of as tools for fostering improved performance. Spend some time in a toy retail outlet and make a note of how many packages proclaim (in bold colors), "Makes Learning Fun!"

Industrial Education

Learning, supposedly a principal element of childhood, has been remanded to a massive adult-run education industry. I say industry because the school system is a first cousin of the corporate model of manufacturing. Schools sort and track students by age and ability, like so many raw materials, and pass them through a highly structured, technically sophisticated curriculum. The resemblance to an assembly line is obvious and intentional: the taxpayers who fund public education are ever eager to know whether they are getting their money's worth.

Public policy in the field of education is increasingly centered on the idea that standardized tests provide the best measures of learning.

Those who advocate childish ideas about playful learning—the whetting and sating of curiosity and learning as an intrinsic good—are dismissed for failing to understand the urgent need for "tough new standards" and measurable outcomes. Like the managers of manufacturing plants, the leaders of our educational institutions are increasingly disciplined by their production numbers. Some schools have found that the fastest way to achieve the largest increase in test scores is simply to reject, eject, or refuse to serve those who are most likely to be difficult to educate.

The difference between these practices and the ideals of public education as they were described by Horace Mann and John Dewey shows us how far adulthood has gone in eradicating an education that is conscious of both the common good (rather than purely individual achievement) and the pursuit of well-being (rather than vocational success). Listen to how antiquated the words of Mann and Dewey have come to sound:

> [The purpose of public education is] to fashion a common national culture out of a far-flung and often immigrant population, and to prepare young people to be reflective and critical citizens of a democratic society.

> [The goal should be to develop] self-governance through self-respect; a sense of cultural ownership through participation; and, ultimately, freedom from tyranny through rational deliberation.

The industrialization of education is an accelerating but long-established phenomenon. More distressing is the degree to which parents themselves are injecting the overscheduled mayhem of modern adult life directly into their children's lives. Summer vacations are increasingly given over to camps and organized activities. Casual sandlot ball games have been transferred to manicured sports fields. Children at play increasingly find themselves under the management of credentialed adult coaches who are eager to see their charges succeed. The idiosyncratic, self-imposed rules that define casual play are being consumed by written rules created and enforced by adults. This trend has so saturated the daily rituals of modern family life that exceptions are regarded as newsworthy. Bradford McKee penned just such a backlash article for the September 25, 2003, issue of the *New York Times:* "A generation ago, the latchkey child was the most forlorn image in the parental universe. Now it is the overscheduled child, who, whether driven by parental ambition or the necessity for afternoon supervision, never stops moving. Jumping from Spanish to karate, tap dancing to tennis—with hours of homework waiting at home—the overscheduled child is as busy as a new law firm associate."

Parents who are concerned about this phenomenon, writes McKee, participate in programs such as "Take Back Your Family Time Week" and "Family Night: Ready, Set, Relax." Many more succumb to the fear that "scaling back" could result in their child "forfeiting the chance for a competitive edge with a team or a crucial bonding moment with a scout trip."

In the cult of adulthood, not even the little children are suffered to be free from adulthood's endless loop of doing, getting, and having.

The Littlest Consumers

The corporate obsession with effectiveness and time management is increasingly coming to characterize the outlook of ambitious children. Several companies have identified these young people as a large, growing, and potentially profitable market segment. The *Wall Street Journal* made note of this in a profile of time-management and productivity products and services for young people. The offerings ranged from day planners laden with inspirational, productivity-enhancing bromides to software specially designed to enhance the time-management skills of the busy adolescent. There is a whole branch of the productivity industry that is targeted toward people too young to buy a legal drink. Consider the Taste-Berry line of adolescent advice books. The last edition garnered this review on Amazon.com:

> [This is] an exciting new volume filled with stories, commentary and advice by teens (ages twelve through twenty) who tell of their experiences and share their ideas about setting and achieving goals! As most taste-berry teens know, goals spell the difference between wish-

ful thinking and making things happen. Setting goals and reaching them are the keys to making teens' lives purposeful, worthwhile and filled with happiness.

For all teenagers—from master goal-setters to beginners with no idea where to start—this step-by-step guide shows how to:

- Discover what their personality, aptitudes and hobbies reveal about them
- Determine if they are dreaming "big enough"
- Identify goals in nine areas of life
- Set long- and short-range goals for today, tomorrow and the future
- Develop a plan of action to achieve goals
- Break goals into manageable monthly, weekly and daily "to-dos"
- Remove obstacles that stand in the way of achieving goals
- Learn ways to encourage, coach and inspire themselves to reach their goals

Divided into five units, each opens with A Message from the Authors, followed by a story by a teen. A specific concept or skill is then presented along with a "Virtual Practice" section where teens are given the chance to apply what they've learned—actually identifying, setting and charting out how to achieve their goals. You're sure to gobble up this latest volume of taste-berry advice!

Corporations, the purest expressions of adult power, are also eager to cross the line that once separated adulthood from childhood. Advertising directly to children, long considered to be an unwarranted intrusion on the sanctity of the family, took off in the 1980s. Style preferences, fashion trends, and brand loyalty among children are now tracked with a near religious intensity by specialized research firms. A fast-food company, eager to attract children and their accompanying parents, has built the largest collection of private playgrounds in the world. Engaging children as consumers tramples the historic separation of adulthood (and its world of commerce) from childhood, which was, until recently, a socially protected zone.

Once I became aware of this tendency, examples too numerous to count presented themselves to me. A small sampling of those I have collected includes the following:

- Spas and spa-related services are marketed to teens and even preteens.
- Athletes as young as five years of age are used as performers, promoters, and product endorsers.
- Schools are recruited as marketing vehicles for large corporations that are targeting children. Soft drink and athletic apparel companies are the worst but not the only offenders. Some students have been disciplined for wearing the logos of companies that compete with the school's "sponsor."
- Sales of thong underwear to girls aged seven to twelve quadrupled in one four-year period.
- A "super baby" formula has been developed and is being promoted to parents who want to give their child "the mind of a scientist."

With just a little practice you too will be able to recognize the stories that document the dismantling of childhood.

Invading the Womb

Perhaps the most telling, and bizarre, evidence of adulthood's implacable effort to enforce its standards of behavior is the idea that a child can be successfully educated while in the womb. No longer a science fiction fantasy, in utero learning has become the subject of serious academic research. According to a study published in *The Lancet,* there is evidence that the fetus can remember things it has learned in utero. Scientists stimulated late-term fetuses by applying a vibration to the mothers' abdomens. When the vibration was repeated twenty-four hours later, the fetuses showed evidence of remembering it. Scientific research of this type is inspired by a desire to see pregnancy as a crucial developmental period in which active parental intervention can improve the likelihood of success after birth.

One parent who was clearly concerned about improving the performance of her newborn wrote to an online advice columnist asserting that a pregnant mother should "constantly recite the alphabet and count to 100. If she really wants her child to compete in the world, she should recite multiplication tables." While it is unlikely that maternal recitation of the alphabet makes any difference in the educational success of the offspring, the urgent belief that it does shows us just how far adults are willing to take their view of the world. The adultification of childhood is an active and continuing process that is being pushed ever closer to the moment of conception.

But will it stop there? Already there are debates over the development and use of designer genes for children. If some parents are able to endow their children with preternatural strength and intelligence, will their children race into adulthood (and success) with an unfair advantage? Who could resist providing the same or even better genetic enhancements to their own offspring? This is where the distortions of contemporary adulthood come into plainest view. The cult of adulthood does not and cannot value childhood except as a staging ground for the real purpose of human life. Under attack is the idea of childhood as a time of exploration and play, enriched with vast quantities of time from which no outcome is expected. Given the forces arrayed against it, childhood can hardly be expected to withstand the assault.

ADULT FOREVER

There Be Dragons Here

I once asked an older friend of mine if she imagined that she would be an adult for the rest of her life. Her response was nearly instant: "Of course," she said. Most people would agree with her. Society offers little prospect for meaning and fulfillment beyond the margins of adulthood. We all understand this and cling instinctively to the role of adult. The sad irony is that we live in a time that, like no other before it, has put the treasures of *elderhood* within the grasp of millions of people. Modern society has created a situation not unlike that of a host who lays out a feast for the guests and then insists that the food is spoiled and the wine has gone rancid. They sit before a banquet, their hands folded in their laps, not daring to eat or drink.

Adulthood keeps people away from the richness of old age in much the same way that medieval cartographers warned travelers away from the edge of the world. Convinced that the world was flat, and that those who strayed too far from familiar terrain were bound to perish, they marked the far limits of their maps with these words: "There be dragons here." We now know that the world is round and that dragons are figments of superstitious imaginations. Old age, however, remains shrouded in mystery. As adults, we cling to a fearful declinist interpretation of the realities that define old age. We tremble before the loss of function that defines the edge of our social world. There is a calamity, nearly as fearsome as death itself, which is ready to claim those who wander off the path of adulthood. Old age threatens us with social death, a banishment from our accustomed place in society. Like all cults, adulthood monitors its adherents closely and warns them against wondering about what might lie beyond the pale.

Strangely enough, it is retirement that forms adulthood's first line of defense against old age. Retirement acknowledges the impact of aging on productivity but blocks the traditional transition into elderhood by creating the special class of *adult emeritus.* Retirees are released from the burdens and expectations imposed on productive adults but must continue to make DOING-being the central theme of their lives. This obligation is what lies behind the avalanche of books and articles devoted to showing previously employed adults how to keep busy. The highest prestige is reserved for those who master the practice of "active retirement."

This fierce dedication to activity is evident when older people talk about life after employment. The mantras of active retirement never grow stale. "Gosh, I've been so busy since I retired that I don't know how I ever had time to work!" These words are said with feeling, and they are meant to reassure both listener and speaker. Retirees, it must be remembered, are still adults, still faithful to the ideology of DOING-being.

Antiaging Gurus

Cults work to inspire a slavish devotion to their doctrines and are intolerant of any who stray from those beliefs. Antiaging proponent João Pedro de Magalhães provides a classic expression of this intolerance in his essay "A Vision of Senescence." Feeling that the bulk of work in the field of gerontology is dedicated to "healthy" and "successful" approaches to aging (a feeling that is not supported by the evidence), he rails against this supposed emphasis: "I find these concepts [healthy and successful aging] pathetic. Why ameliorate aging's consequences when you can focus on its causes? Have in mind that the goal is to diminish, not extend, age-related debilitation. The idea is not just to make people live longer; the idea is to end all forms of age-related involution."

He wears his idealism as a shining medal of honor attesting to his deep and unquestioned devotion to the doctrine of youth's perfection. It is the fall from that perfection, I believe, that he fears most of all. As with any shameful fear, its source is made most plain when its expression is emotional and overwrought. The essence of his argument—that aging is an unnatural and immoral imposition on us all—depends on an abiding faith in an imagined human potential for eternal youthful vigor. He sees in the advancing technology of our time the seeds of potential immortality. He is not alone.

Most of the spokespeople for the antiaging philosophy veil their prejudice against aging more carefully. Michael F. Roizen, M.D., has developed an "age reduction program" that, he claims, can make the people who use it "live and feel up to twenty-six years younger." After acknowledging the intrinsic nature of human aging, Roizen turns to his true purpose. He tells us, "First, [we must] stop thinking about health as the prevention of disease and start thinking about it as the prevention of aging." Throughout his book *RealAge*, he gives well-founded advice on how to reduce the risk of developing many of the diseases commonly associated with old age. His advocacy of stopping smoking, losing weight, being physically active, lowering stress levels, and eating a healthy diet relies on solid scientific proof. What is interesting about Roizen's work is not the content of his recommendations, which are in the mainstream of preventive medicine, but the reason he gives for *why* they should be adopted: "The better condition you are in—that is, the younger you stay—the better prepared you will be to fight the factors that age you. When you take care of your body, time slows down."

The term *antiaging* is a euphemism for youth perpetuation. Those who embrace this philosophy hold a very limited, highly distorted view of human longevity. For them, old age is really just a cardboard villain. They have little passion for simply avoiding the ravages of aging; their aim is much higher than that. They seek the divine gifts of perpetual strength, energy, and health so that they may remain in full possession of the pleasures and prerogatives of adulthood. A cover blurb from a satisfied reader of *RealAge* makes it clear that this message is coming through loud and clear. Kim C___ of

Greenville, Ohio, informs us, "I was so inspired by Oprah's show, which featured your book, that I have decided to further improve my RealAge. Thanks to you and your book, I'm working every day to become younger . . . I never want to grow old!"

Who can blame her? The prospects for those unwilling or unable to use the latest antiaging nostrums are dimmed by an intractable ageism. One plastic surgeon counsels prospective patients to factor "the economic costs of looking 'tired and worn out' into the decision to have cosmetic surgery." It is not just the old who are penalized; even those who simply look old are placed at a decisive disadvantage in contemporary society.

Rabidly intolerant social systems always have a ready supply of epithets that can be used against the "other." Once-vibrant adults who can no longer conceal the effects of aging are relabeled as "the frail elderly." Former masters of the universe are scorned for being "infirm." No longer able to command a share of social resources, the aged come to rely on the noblesse oblige of adults who cannot imagine growing old themselves. The government organizes services, programs, and support for the poor and the disabled—and the aged. All of these unfortunates are maligned in everyday language.

The aged, in particular, comprise an alien presence in this adult-driven society. It is possible to be disabled and still worship youthfulness. It is possible to be poor and still ascribe to the primacy of doing, getting, and having. But to be old *and frail* is to move beyond hope and become an object worthy only of fear and pity. We love our older relatives even as we declare our wish to "never grow old" ourselves. Elected representatives, many of whom are older than those they refer to as "the elderly," routinely make decisions about "them" and the role government should play in providing "them" with services. Modern industrial society, with its adultish preoccupations and churlish attitude toward old age, does spend heavily (if somewhat grudgingly) on services for the elderly. But money can't buy respect.

There is a great but so far unrequited faith in the ability of science and technology to render old age obsolete. Faith in antiaging products supports an essential coping strategy for those trapped between the demands made by the cult of adulthood and the reality presented by their own aging bodies. This faith provides an avenue of escape for those who cannot face the contradictions created by adulthood's equation of youth with the appearance of youth.

This conflict provides an opening for a range of antiaging gurus, many of whom stray very far from Dr. Roizen's reasoned recommendations. Following are summaries, provided by Amazon.com readers, of just two popular antiaging books:

> *The Baby Boomers' Guide to Living Forever* by Terry Grossman
>
> **Reader Comment:** This book supports the method of using biostasis (cryonics) at the time of death as a means of reaching the future era of advanced nanomedicine, much anticipated by many scientists who work in this nascent field. About fifteen pages are devoted to cryonics, a very good introduction to this subject, an idea and practice that is slowly becoming "mainstream." In fact, Terry Grossman, himself an M.D., is signed up for cryonics.

> *Look and Feel Fabulous Forever: The World's Best Supplements, Anti-Aging Techniques, and High-Tech* by Oz Garcia
>
> **Reader Comment:** Clearly written and well organized, it actually covers everything you need to know about health and fitness, from nutrition and fat burning to state-of-the-art life extension and enhancement techniques.

The jacket photos (and they're always there, somewhere) make it obvious that the aging movement is promoted by some very attractive spokespeople. The movement generates a seemingly inexhaustible supply of new products and services, and its "no-wrinkle, live forever and die young" ideology is guaranteed to continue setting advertisers' hearts aflutter. Denying the truths of human aging is a very profitable business.

Antiaging advocates would like to be ordained as the definitive source of information about age and aging. There is, however, a problem—a single irredeemable flaw that dooms antiaging to a peripheral role in our society's future. No matter how clever, how attractive, how entrepreneurial the proponents of antiaging may be, every one of them will, in time, grow old. If they are blessed with a long life (and not all of them will be), they will become frail. While vitamins, vegetables, and exercise may help keep them spry, such regimens can-

Table 9

The Denial of Aging

Traditional Aging	Mitigated Aging	Antiaging
Old age is both a blessing and a burden.	Old age brings mental and physical decline.	Old age is unnecessary.
The aged should be respected.	The aged are entitled to high-quality medical and surgical treatments.	The young should resist old age with all means possible.
The aged should be stoic.	The aged should lobby for access to resources.	Technology has or will have the means to conquer old age.
Care for the aged is a family responsibility.	The obligation to care for the aged is shared by the family and the government.	Perpetual youth will eliminate the problem of caring for the aged.

not keep them young. Time and the inexorable workings of human mortality will, eventually, overtake them all. Remains of prehistoric peoples tell us that old age often came to them in their 30s. Perhaps someday old age will be deferred until we are in our 130s, but it will come. Any person who makes a reputation as an antiaging guru sets a terrible retribution into motion. In time, the guru will get old, the guru will get gray, the guru will begin to forget and will shuffle when he walks. Justice delayed may be justice denied, but aging delayed will not be denied.

The antiaging doctrine will fail us all because of its willful denial of our humanity; aging is the most human thing we do. Antiaging will remain a fringe movement, always able to attract and profit from the same kinds of people who are willing to believe that you can "lose forty pounds, never be hungry, and never exercise!" We cannot base a revised understanding of old age on the shifting ground of the latest gurus' ideas and their hectic pursuit of the ever-elusive fountain of youth.

Challenges to Adult Supremacy

Recently, many writers have developed useful critiques of ageism in modern society. More than a few have gone on to present alternative visions of what old age should be. These affirmative, developmentally oriented visions of late life have garnered far too little attention and acceptance. Popular resistance to these views can be seen in the response these authors have met with in the bookstores. The "aging" and "health" shelves in bookstores often lack any titles dedicated to an affirmative developmental approach to age and aging. Mainstream media tend to trivialize this line of thinking, preferring the more comforting illusion of the old person as young person or, for comic effect, as doddering fool. Hidden from the mass media and publishing conglomerates are a very small but growing number of people who are willing to challenge the doctrine of youth's perfection directly and on their own terms.

These efforts are united by a search for meaning in old age, and they rely on the assumption that there is life beyond adulthood. These writers all identify the need for a changed emphasis in late life, whether the approach be conscious aging, sage-ing, healthy aging, or gourmet aging. They recognize the potential contained within BEING-doing and the opportunities available to those willing to make the leap from adulthood. They all contend with the suspicion, and even revulsion, heaped on those who dare to leave the familiar behind. The cult of adulthood reserves its ultimate scorn for those who question its assumptions.

The conflict between those who adore adulthood as the pinnacle of human existence and those who seek to go beyond adulthood became clear to me when I was attending a meeting of innovative businesspeople in San Diego. During a break in the proceedings, I struck up a conversation with one of the conference organizers. She asked me about my work and we wound up talking about women and old age. I told her about how some menopausal women were beginning to gather for ceremonies where they bestowed upon each other the title of "crone." I might as well have described a visit to a Roman vomitarium. With her face pinched in disgust, she responded, "You have got to be kidding me. Crones? Ugh."

I was not surprised by her reaction and pressed on with an explanation of why "croning" was growing in popularity. The burden of contemporary ageism, after all, falls heaviest on women. Wrinkled, silver-maned old men can, at times, be imagined to be senatorial. Old women have no such refuge. I told her how the growth of croning echoed a strategy that was popular with police officers in the 1960s. Tired of being called "pigs," they grasped the epithet and made it their own. Many of them took to wearing boar-skin jackets when they were off duty. The heavy burden that ageism places on older women creates a paradoxical benefit for women willing to take possession of the word *crone*. By embracing the term and its long history as a term of abuse, these women create a measure of control over their own place in society. I had thought that the innovative, successful entrepreneur and feminist with whom I was speaking would have been sympathetic toward women brave enough to challenge the bigotry of ageism. Instead, she was repelled. She made it plain that she was an adult first and a woman second and abruptly ended the conversation. Such is the power of adulthood.

Another small but growing element in the challenge to adult supremacy is the sage-ing movement. In 1995 Rabbi Zalman Schachter-Shalomi and Ronald S. Miller published *From Age-ing to Sage-ing,* in which they laid out a blueprint for harvesting one's life experience. It presumes that growth is not only possible but necessary for those in the last decades of life. The group has founded dozens of Spiritual Eldering Institutes around the country and has developed a remarkably devoted following. The members are faced, though, with the difficulty that bedevils all those who desire to challenge society's most fixed ideas about age and aging. Given the ethic of adulthood forever, most adults are unwilling or unable to acknowledge the role of the sage. Alternative self-identification can and does soothe the pain felt by individuals but cannot, by itself, influence society as a whole. There is no ritual induction into the mysteries of elderhood because, practically speaking, there is no elderhood into which we can be admitted. This absence cannot be described as a careless oversight. We live in a society that denies the legitimacy of old age and has little tolerance for those who dare to suppose that crones and sages could inspire us as models of healthy human development.

The Best Death

A woman I helped take care of for many years often told me the story of her husband's death. They had a long and happy marriage, raised a family, and retired to Florida. One fine warm winter day they shared a round of golf and then went to the pool. The woman's husband plunged into the water and swam his daily quota of laps. When he was done, he pulled himself out, dried himself off, and lay down on the chaise next to hers. The sky was blue; the sun was warm. He reached over and patted her arm—then died. Her face gleamed with pride whenever she told me this story, the events of which were some years distant. Her husband had lived the dream. He had remained a fully accredited, card-carrying adult right up until the end. This is a dream that millions share. The woman's life, however, took a very different turn. She was in her nineties when she moved to the nursing home and had been living there for five years by the time I met her. Small and pale, she lay curled on her side as she talked to me. She rehearsed her late husband's great victory nearly every day. Every day she grieved her failure to follow his lead. She had missed her chance to live and then die as an adult.

The Old-Age Archipelago

Exile on Two West

Advanced old age is a contemporary heresy because it violates the central premise of adulthood. The frail elder furnishes irrefutable proof that youth is, in fact, fleeting. Despite drugs, vitamins, creams, surgical procedures, and the best intentions, both youth and the appearance of youth will slip from our grasp eventually. The cult of adulthood must remain on guard against those who, despite Herculean effort, are no longer able to maintain the pretense of adulthood. Adulthood, like all cults, must expel its heretics. The steady growth in the number of frail older people makes this type of cleansing an especially important and difficult necessity. Our society has built and continues to maintain more than sixteen thousand nursing homes as part of adulthood's urgent effort to protect us from those who can no longer live independently.

At the turn of the twenty-first century, the United States had more than three times as many nursing homes as it had hospitals, and three thousand more nursing homes than McDonald's restaurants. Many of these skilled nursing facilities were founded by and continue to be led by some of our society's most generous and benevolent people and organizations. Many more are the instruments of huge corporations whose motivation encompasses only operating profit, return on investment, and share price. In truth, the motivations of nursing home operators are of secondary concern. Debate over the

relative merits and weaknesses of for-profit and not-for-profit operators actually obscures a far more important truth: nursing homes
form the backbone of a contemporary old-age archipelago.

During the twentieth century, American society witnessed two
great waves of deinstitutionalization. Children and adults with developmental disabilities were freed from massive state-run institutions.
And people living with mental illness were returned to the community (with highly variable support and consequences) as state mental
hospitals were decommissioned by the hundreds. Now that we have
entered the twenty-first century, only two categories of people still
face routine and even permanent institutionalization. Society sentences its convicted felons to specific terms of incarceration (there are
about 1.9 million prisoners). Using different means but just as deliberately, society confines older people to long-term care institutions,
often for life, when they can no longer live alone or with family members. In the last half of the twentieth century, prisons and nursing
homes both experienced a steady rise in the number of inmates.

Throughout this unprecedented expansion, prisons and nursing
homes shared an urgent need to cloak their growing importance in
American society by emphasizing the benevolent dimension of their
respective missions. Prison wardens deliver cursory endorsements of
the need to rehabilitate prisoners and then proclaim their facilities'
essential contribution to the safety of free men and women. Nursing
home operators loudly announce their devotion to safety and quality
of care for the residents but say nothing of the crucial hidden service
the nursing home performs for the cult of adulthood.

To understand nursing homes as they truly are, you have to see
them as instruments of terror designed, funded, and operated by
adults. Instruments of terror? Isn't that a little over the top? You
wouldn't think so if you opened my mail. I have received many communications like this one from a former nursing home resident:

> I recently returned from "rehabilitation care" in a nursing home. I
> have pretty severe cerebral palsy and had breast cancer surgery, so
> was unable to care for myself at home for a while. However, the
> nursing home environment was a nightmare, and it did more to slow

the healing process than help. I got a terrifying glimpse into a future I doubt I could live through—suicide seems a better option than life in such facilities. Right now I'm only sixty-one, but because of my disability, I am scared that I might end up in another nursing home. I would rather die than have to exist in such a place where residents are neglected, ignored, patronized, infantilized, demeaned; where the environment is chaotic, noisy, cold, clinical, even psychotic. The nursing home is run for the convenience of the staff and administration, not for the patients and residents. Serious medical mistakes are made often, and the patients have to keep constant vigil over their own care . . . if they are able; fortunately I was able to, but may not be in future.

People are placed in nursing homes, often against their will, because they no longer display the behaviors expected of independent adults. The decision to surrender a loved one to a nursing home is emotionally traumatic and is usually made only after all other options have been exhausted. That alternatives are few (relative to the demand) and underfunded (relative to what is spent on institutionalization) is rarely acknowledged. Benevolent adults unwittingly transform a real and often urgent need for assistance on the part of older people into a license for removing elders from their homes and communities. We all know where a road paved with these kinds of good intentions leads.

The true nature of the nursing home is especially obvious to those schooled in the ways of institutions. I recently received a letter from a prisoner. He wrote to me after seeing me on a television program in which I discussed my thinking on the impact nursing homes have on our society:

> I too am very concerned about the way people are treated in nursing homes. As you can see I am currently incarcerated in a correctional institution. I have been in for the last eight years. Unfortunately, this is not my first time in prison.

> I remember when I was free and I visited my two grandmothers in nursing homes. I was very upset at the conditions (and these were supposed to be the better homes where upper middle class people went).

> It reminded me so much of prison it was unreal!

The prisoner is isolated from the community so that he can "pay his debt to society." Stalin sent millions to his gulag archipelago for the smallest deviations (real or imagined) from communist orthodoxy. The elder is confined to the nursing home for the heresy of growing old.

One might think that this exile into a skilled nursing unit would yield, at the least, freedom from the power of adults and the expectations of adulthood. In fact, the opposite is true. Our long-term care system is founded on the principles of mitigated aging. The idea that nursing home residents are best understood as failed adults is reinforced at every opportunity. The staff are highly motivated to create the most complete and accurate inventory of residents' failures. This catalogue is deemed essential for professional and financial reasons. The residents' defects must be known in detail if the institution is ever to mitigate them fully. The nursing home, like the totalitarian re-education camp, seeks to restore the heretics to the status of true believers and, failing that, to keep them apart from the general population. Success, in the nursing home, is determined by how well its residents emulate the adults they used to be.

Those who doubt such an assertion should spend some time reading the medical records of people confined to nursing homes. Page after exhaustive page documents the tireless efforts of adult staff members to return the residents in their charge to the glory of DOING-being. The procedures and incentives that govern life in nursing homes encourage a frenzy of treatment, medical evaluations, and active therapy. It is hardly surprising that nursing home residents are the most overmedicated people on the planet. Even when not receiving treatment, nursing home residents are victims of the facility's mindless emphasis on doing. The professionals who are responsible for the diversions that are intended to lessen the burden of boredom refer to their efforts as "activities." In the world of the nursing home, functional independence and social engagement are the key parameters that separate the well from the ill. The notion of an elderhood with its own purposes and intents is absent and so far removed from the reality of daily life that it is not even missed. Being matters little, or not at all.

The Culture of Negativism

Operators of nursing homes have long held that problems of safety and quality are inevitable because the staff are caring for patients in the final terrible stages of decline. Not everyone agrees. Since 1970, a series of books and research articles have amply documented the painful and repeated failure of many nursing homes to meet even minimum standards of care. In 1986, the Institute of Medicine weighed in on the problems in nursing homes and recommended substantially strengthening federal regulations. That report, coupled with the efforts of many consumer advocate and professional organizations, resulted in the passage of the Omnibus Budget Reconciliation Act, or OBRA '87, as it is better known. This legislation created a new level of accountability for the vast amounts of public money that flow from the public treasury into the coffers of the nursing home industry. It mandated annual inspections and a substantial tightening of quality standards. More regulations have been added every year since then. We can now count nuclear power, mining, and long-term care as the nation's three most regulated industries.

The good news is that early in the drive to regulate nursing homes, small changes in the rules often yielded big improvements in care. Because it emerged from a cottage industry of stand-alone boarding homes, the nursing home industry was born without a coherent set of standards and practices. Regulation and inspection served as a visible and quite effective prod to improve safety and quality. Inspired by these early successes, and well aware of continued problems in the industry, legislators and regulators came to rely on new regulations as the preferred response to continuing negative publicity about nursing homes.

Inevitably, the reliance on regulation to improve quality began to function like a narcotic: it took bigger and bigger doses of rules, regulations, penalties, and fines to achieve smaller and smaller improvements in outcomes. In the early years of the twenty-first century, 90 percent of all nursing homes were understaffed, many dangerously so. More than a third of all homes were guilty of "serious violations" of state and federal rules. These defects (uncovered, it should be noted, by the system of reporting and monitoring) remained despite 120,000 pages of rules and the full-time efforts of five thousand inspectors. Doubling the number of rules or tripling the number of inspectors or quadrupling the number of fines would have little, if any, sustained effect on quality. Seemingly aware of this, the government has opened the final frontier of nursing home enforcement action. Noncompliance with regulations is now being used as one basis for criminal complaints against nursing home managers and operators.

Despite the intense regulation and substantial expense, adequate quality of care and quality of life are not consistently provided to nursing home residents. The long-term care industry remains hobbled by poor public perception and poor performance. In 1995, the top ten most frequently cited deficiencies were as shown in table 10.

While it is easy to point the finger at nursing homes, and most people do, physicians have also been implicated in the abuse and neglect of nursing home residents. Several years ago I was asked to review

Table 10

Most Frequently Cited Deficiencies in Nursing Homes

Nursing Home Deficiencies	Percent of Citations
Failure to conduct comprehensive resident assessments	27
Failure to ensure that food is sanitary	26
Failure to prepare comprehensive resident care plans	24
Failure to provide care that protects the dignity of residents	20
Failure to remove accident hazards	19
Failure to prevent the inappropriate use of physical restraints	19
Failure to prevent pressure sores	17
Failure to provide adequate housekeeping	17
Failure to accommodate the needs of each resident	14
Failure to ensure infection control	13

the medical file of a man who had been admitted to a nursing home for care after the untimely death of his wife. The man became depressed and stopped eating. The physician was made aware of this change of condition but offered no assistance, explaining that the patient's decline was "only to be expected." His condition worsened and the 160-pound man lost half his body weight. In less than a year, he came to resemble a concentration camp inmate. His body, like the biblical Job's, was a mass of oozing sores, four of which extended to the bone. In the end, this man died alone and in pain. His suffering had been enormous, and, worst of all, it had taken place under the supervision of a licensed physician.

Before dismissing this dismal event as a rarity, consider that nursing home abuse and neglect has led to billions of dollars of liability judgments. In 2000, Florida juries handed down $267 million in judgments against nursing homes. That same year, the state's entire budget for nursing home care was roughly $400 million. Not surprisingly, insurers have started pulling out of the market for nursing home liability insurance.

This terrifying chain of failure arose from the mitigated-aging philosophy on which we have founded our system of long-term care for the elderly. Nursing homes are and will always be limited in what they can achieve because they have an essentially negative mission. They are dedicated to mitigating the worst aspects of old age and they devote themselves to providing the least negative experience possible for the residents in their charge. They cannot, however, turn back the workings of time and age. Try as they may, nursing homes have and will continue to attract considerable negative attention.

Understanding the negative foundation of long-term care allows us to unravel its many paradoxes:

- We believe, mistakenly, that old age is an entirely bad thing, and so we establish institutions dedicated to mitigating the "badness" of old age.
- These facilities fail in their mission to create the least negative experience possible. Therefore, a new system must be created that can mitigate the consequences of that failure.

- Vast, onerous, and expensive, the regulatory system itself has yet to mitigate fully the failure of the nursing home to mitigate the failures that are thought to define old age.
- This failure of the regulatory system to mitigate the failure of nursing homes to mitigate the failures of old age has attracted the attention of the trial lawyers. Ostensibly devoted to punishing the failure to protect nursing home residents from pain and suffering, a subset of trial lawyers have become the alpha predators of the long-term care ecosystem.

It is hard to imagine how this downward spiral could serve any part of our society. But, in fact, it enlarges the power of adulthood.

Along with many others, I have devoted years of my life to "fixing" nursing homes, and I continue to believe that this work is important. I have come to understand, however, that "the problem with nursing homes" lies not in their failures (which have been many and are well documented) but in their success. Nursing homes function as instruments of adulthood and they serve a purpose very similar to that of Stalin's gulag archipelago. The damage done to those caught in the web of long-term care is trivial when compared to the emotional and psychological impact nursing homes have on those of us who are still fit enough to be included in the general adult population. Under Stalin, the Soviet Union used the fear of the gulag archipelago to enforce communist orthodoxy. In our society, the terror that surrounds placement in a nursing home strengthens a society created by and for adults. The next time you drive by a nursing home (and you will drive by, because people do not visit nursing homes unless they have to) look closely and you will see, in brick and mortar, a testament to Ohioan Kim C___'s words, "I never want to grow old!"

The Sunny Side of the Street

A few years ago, I stopped in to visit Dr. Chip Roadman at his office in Washington, D.C. Trained as an obstetrician and retired as the surgeon general of the United States Air Force, Dr. Roadman accepted the job of leading the nation's largest nursing home trade association. We settled in for a chat about the state of long-term care and I launched into a critique of the industry quite similar to the one given above. He heard me out. When I was finished, he paused for a moment and said, "Well, you're quite a ray of sunshine, aren't you?" At the time, I took this as a polite way of disagreeing with my argument that nursing homes too often serve interests other than those of the elders. Only later did I realize that Dr. Roadman was politely informing me that the critique I had developed was incomplete—that I was leaving out any comment on positive outcomes of nursing homes.

Despite its flaws and the uses to which it has been put, the long-term care system does have important contributions to which it can point with pride. In the past four decades, significant achievements have been made:

1. We have developed a vastly improved understanding of the anatomy and physiology of old age. We have made dramatic strides in our understanding of diseases and injuries that are common in old age, and we continue to enlarge our capacity to treat them effectively.

2. We have developed a society-wide appreciation for the value of extrafamilial support for the aged. This change has lessened (though not eliminated) the traditional obligation of female family members to serve as caregivers.

3. One of the major, if unintended, effects of the regulatory crusade has been to drive away many people who prefer the comfort of low expectations to the challenge of striving for better performance. People who lack a calling to work with elders have found little reason to remain in the field. It is as if long-term care has been purified by a peculiar form of regulatory fire. Though many people have left the field, many more remain, and among them are some of the kindest, gentlest people this or any other society has ever produced.

4. Long-term care organizations of all kinds, and especially nursing homes, have made a surprisingly durable and effec-

tive commitment to quality improvement techniques. Not surprisingly, these efforts have been centered on clinical processes and outcomes. Mitigated aging requires that long-term care organizations pledge allegiance to the flag of quality care, and elders have benefited from that commitment.

Millions of good people work in nursing homes every day, doing their best to make the elephant dance. They make this commitment because of the elders and in spite of the system they have inherited. These devoted workers would prefer that long-term care were a profession rather than an industry, and they are working every day to earn that title. The remarkable thing is that despite its negative foundation, despite its many and well-documented failures, long-term care has given us sophisticated and eminently useful insights into the clinical needs of older people. For this we should all be grateful. It is easy to scorn the people and the organizations that make up the old-age archipelago, but the temptation should be resisted. There is great value in what we have been able to learn in the forty-year history of long-term care.

PRIVATE GRIEF, PUBLIC TRAGEDY

The Obits

When one arrives at a certain age, obituaries begin to make interesting reading. They are our society's most public record of private grief, opening windows into otherwise hidden lives. Because space on the page is limited, only the most important information about a person can be included in the notice. Tradition demands that newspaper items be organized according to the journalist's rule of descending importance. As a result, obituaries can tell us about much more than the lives of the dearly departed. Obits trumpet society's most treasured virtues and values even as they mourn the dead.

Here are the headlines and leads related to the lives thought worthy of an obituary writer's attention one weekday in the *New York Times:*

> **Riley Housewright, Microbiologist, Dies at 89** Riley D. Housewright, a microbiologist who helped direct United States research into biological warfare from World War II until 1970, died on Saturday at an assisted living center in Frederick, MD. He was 89.
>
> **David C. Morton II, Architect, 61, Dies** David Cummins Morton II, an architect who did the first residential loft conversion in the Fulton Ferry area in Brooklyn, died on Tuesday at his home in San Francisco.
>
> **Paul Monash, 85, Television Screenwriter** Paul Monash, a producer and screenwriter, whose credits include the films

Butch Cassidy and the Sundance Kid, Carrie, and
Slaughterhouse-Five, died at his home in Los Angeles on
Tuesday. He was 85.

One might suppose that the tendency to put professional
achievements at the top of the order is a journalistic practice reserved
for the famous and accomplished. Further inspection reveals the same
pattern, though in much smaller type, in privately placed death
notices as well. The celebration of achievement in this section is, if
anything, even more fulsome. What else are we to think of "a giant
of a man who lived a life of scholarship, heroism, philanthropy, and
family"? Another begins, "Renowned authority on international and
tax law, educator, writer, lecturer and philanthropist." The tri-
umphalist tone in many of these notices suggests a hope that one
final recitation of the virtues of the deceased might somehow stay the
hand of oblivion.

Dedicated readers of the obituary page will be quick to point out
that there is a second, distinctly different form of obituary. It is much
more emotional and it celebrates the personhood of the beloved man
or woman who has passed. These notices are so personal, so intimate
(even though they stare at me from a newspaper page) that it seems
indecent to reprint them verbatim. They begin, "Cherished husband," "Beloved Mother," "Matriarch and Beloved Wife of,"
"Beloved father of [daughter] and [son], proud grandfather of
[granddaughter], beloved brother of [sister], father by affection of
[step-daughter], adoring and loving friend of [lifelong friend]."
Notices that begin this way tend to be shorter and less prominently
placed than the others. They are perhaps the most deserving of our
close attention because, when we read them with care, they never fail
to remind us that being and feeling can be the defining characteristics of a life.

Surviving relatives are expected to honor the dead by posting
these public notices. While certain causes of death may bring shame
to surviving family members, there is nothing dishonorable about
death itself. After all, aging and death are preordained biological
necessities. But because we adhere to the doctrine of youth's perfection and because an adult-dominated society sees the encroachment

of old age as a personal failing, we find age-related changes shameful in ways that death is not.

Hidden Losses

I remember one of the speakers at my medical school commencement ceremony. He was a distinguished neurologist with an international reputation. There were whispers that he had been considered for a Nobel Prize. When it was time for him to speak, he approached the lectern carrying a battered, dusty case. In the sober tone of the successful, he began to lecture his audience of new graduates on the importance of taking time for things outside of medicine. At the midpoint of his speech, he opened the case and produced a clarinet. Holding it up for all to see, he described how much he had loved music when he was young. He told of playing for hours alone in his room, just for the pure pleasure of the music he made. In preparation for this speech, he had gone searching for his beloved instrument. He found it in the distant reaches of a hallway closet. It hadn't moved from that spot in more than twenty years. He rued the fact that his (fabulously successful) medical career had shoved aside his love of music.

This demonstration seemed at the time to be offered as a piece of hard-won wisdom. These young graduates ought not to do as he had done. They must understand that some things should not be sacrificed on the altar of one's career. As I reflected on it years later, however, I came to see a deeper and much more powerful message in his performance. The professor was, in fact, speaking as a proud adult standing on the pinnacle of professional achievement. He had given himself completely to doing and getting (both money and fame). When he held the clarinet high over his head, it was hard not to see it as a vanquished foe. Young graduates, if you seek my kind of success, you must do as I have done. You, too, must set aside the joy of being.

The man died a couple of years after he gave this speech and I have no doubt that when his possessions were cleared away, a dusty clarinet case was found in the far back corner of a hallway closet.

It is easy to stand up in public and brag about how complete your devotion to the cult of adulthood has been. Far braver are those willing to proclaim their failure to achieve and maintain the cherished independence of the adult. Such failures are deemed shameful because our society defines them as purely personal lapses. Gossip reinforces the idea that if the sufferer had been better, faster, or smarter, such a loss need never have occurred. We define criminal delinquency in terms of lawbreaking, and whenever possible we name the lawbreakers publicly. Social deviancy is defined as a violation of adult standards of behavior. These losses are hidden whenever possible. People who die are honored with an obituary; people who commit crimes are identified in the police blotter; those who lose their grip on the vigor and virtues of energetic adulthood hide themselves and their shame from public view. The truth of this assertion is made plain when we imagine a newspaper page dedicated to publicizing our private griefs:

> **Myrtle Smith Has Crow's Feet.** Myrtle looked in the mirror yesterday morning and could not help noticing how prominent her facial wrinkles were becoming. Formerly noted for her beautiful complexion, she is now quite concerned about her changing appearance. "The creams I have been using just aren't doing the job anymore," she said. Questioned about future plans, Myrtle reported that injections have been scheduled for later this month and surgery is a possibility.

> **Megan Panock Hates Her Job.** Having taken her parents' advice that "there's always room for another good accountant," Megan majored in finance in college. Now employed by a Big Four accounting firm, Megan finds that she hates her work. "I want to quit but I can't. I still have student loans and credit cards to pay, and Mom and Dad would kill me." Informed of their daughter's unhappiness, Mr. and Mrs. Panock professed unconcern. "I know my daughter," Fred Panock observed, "and she's no quitter."

> **Former Mayor Placed in Nursing Home.** Robert Ginsberg was placed in a nursing home by his son and daughter last week. According to daughter Emily, "Dad just wasn't safe at the house anymore. We couldn't keep home-care aides there—he kept yelling at them." Robert Jr., who currently

lives in California, disputed his father's contention that "I don't want to go to that damn place." According to the younger Ginsberg, "I've spent hours on the phone with this thing. Dad doesn't really know what he wants. His mind just isn't there like it used to be." County officials note that, due to actions taken by the family attorney, Mayor Ginsberg is now qualified for Medicaid. His children have taken possession of the now empty house. A sale is planned for the spring. "Dad would have wanted it this way," Robert Jr. said.

Earl Cordell Confined to a Locked Alzheimer's Unit. The staff at Merry Dale nursing home report that Mr. Cordell will no longer be allowed to live among the general nursing home population. The director of nurses, Gina Centrello, says, "We did everything we could for him but it got so that he just wasn't cooperating." His offenses ranged from drooling and letting food run out of his mouth at mealtime to screaming during showers and becoming violent toward staff members. "He kept swinging at nurse aides when they were trying to change his diaper. We won't tolerate that kind of behavior." Other nursing home residents were said to be relieved by news of the transfer. "I'm glad they got rid of him," one resident commented. "He was a wacko."

The reason we won't be seeing notices like these anytime soon is that these are private losses, to be hidden from society whenever and however possible. We hide them because they shame us, and while that shame is experienced as a purely personal phenomenon, it has its roots in the public domains of society and history.

The Tragic Flaw

The cult of adulthood demands that people don the mantle of adulthood as soon as possible and keep it for as long as possible. This dictate conflicts directly with a hundred thousand years of human experience. We have succeeded as a species precisely because we have been able to turn the biological necessity of aging to our collective advantage. We stand experience on its head when we proclaim that old age is neither virtuous nor necessary. The brazen effort to certify adulthood as the only truly worthy part of the life cycle delegitimizes both youth and old age and creates unavoidable and painful conflicts in our personal lives. We cannot and will never be adults forever. To attempt such a thing is to invite repeated and progressive failure into our lives. Worst of all, the cult of adulthood slathers these failures with shame and demands that, whenever possible, they be hidden from others.

The private grief that accompanies the visible signs of an aging body is a singular, personal expression of a vast public tragedy that is created and maintained by the declinist view of old age. The grief, shame, and anger experienced by a child who is compelled to institutionalize a parent is but one facet of the public tragedy that comes from exiling elders after thousands of generations of faithful service.

The power of adulthood to distort our understanding of how life ought to be lived is also seen in the increasing use of medications to control the behavior of children. Elementary school students who cannot sit still or focus for long periods on the assigned task, and who fail to produce acceptable measured educational results, are diagnosed and started on treatment with the aim of improving their compliance in the classroom. Their parents grieve in private, but that grief is nonetheless a part of a historic assault on the meaning and experience of childhood.

When old age does become a matter of public debate, the issues are most often framed as a generational conflict that pits the young and old against each other. These battles damage the ancient alliance between the very young and the very old. Both parties are forced to independently confront adults in the public arena and demand access to resources and advantaged treatment.

This drama is wrongly framed as a generational conflict. It is better understood as a tragic and unnecessary collision between the doing and getting of adulthood and the being and feeling of childhood and elderhood. The losses we find so shameful and hide so carefully are actually shared in full by millions of our fellow citizens. They are like the tiny points of color that make up a printed photograph. When we view it up close, we can see only the dots. When we back up and enlarge our field of vision, the dots resolve into a picture that is crisp and informative.

We speak in grave tones of the "graying of America" and worry about whether the demands made by an aging population will lead to our ruin, but these concerns are trivial compared with the real danger confronting our families, our society, our government, and the global environment. The social trend that jeopardizes our collective well-being is not age and aging. In fact, old age has never been stronger or better positioned to do good in the world than it is now. The real villain is the ideology of adulthood. Whenever and wherever adulthood breaches ancient barriers and tramples ways of living that were previously outside its control, it weakens the delicate fabric of human community.

DOING-being and its associated totems, rituals, and machines are fast becoming the only legitimate basis for a successful life. We are hurtling into a future that is eager to exchange for beads, baubles, and adult power the indescribably rich cultural inheritance that is the product of our long experience with longevity. What will become of elderhood and childhood is a matter of urgent concern; the threat posed by adulthood is both real and imminent. Teetering atop its

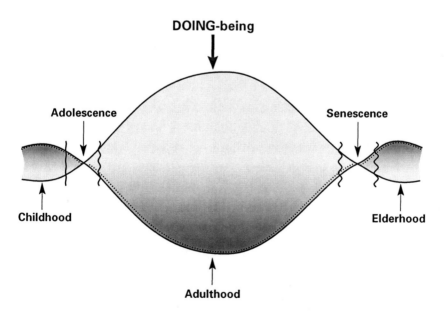

The malignant enlargement of adulthood

own overweening pride, adulthood threatens to collapse the very foundation on which human community is built.

In his three sets of questions (page 132), Mills reminds us to ask, "What is the structure of this particular society as a whole?" The central social and cultural challenges of our time revolve around the malignant enlargement of adulthood and the adult obsession with DOING-being. Elderhood and childhood are reeling, ill equipped to answer the challenges posed by adult power.

While it could be argued that, in fact, adults have always formed the most powerful group in human communities, and that the young and old have always been subordinate to adults' power, it is the magnitude of that power that has changed. Youth and old age have long inhabited social spheres that were given special protection from the power of adults. Adulthood, intoxicated by its own might, is intent on remaking youth and old age in its image. It has already defined the best child as the most precocious child. The wunderkind mimics adult behaviors and styles of work and learning. Likewise, adulthood demands that those who would remain worthy defy their age and continue to think, walk, talk, look, and work like adults.

Hearing this, Mills might ask, "What is the meaning of adulthood? How is it strengthened and how is it changed?" We must remember that adulthood itself is a right and fine thing. I am an adult. I love adulthood. I find daily pleasure in living as an adult and have no interest in returning to the childhood I have outgrown. Nor am I ready to enter into an elderhood that requires perspective, experience, and judgment that I do not yet possess. Adulthood, rightly understood, provides us with a productive, potentially glorious interlude between youth and old age. The problems begin when we conceive of it as a permanent necessity, an apex of human experience that must be defended and enlarged no matter what the cost.

Though the suggestion might seem absurd at first, I believe that the elders of our time form the only force capable of returning adulthood to healthier bounds. So far, this is more hope than reality because relatively few older people have made the leap into elderhood. Most choose to live instead as increasingly enervated adults, marginalized or even exiled from the mainstream of the adult community. These senior citizens must fight political battles to ensure continued access to promised entitlements. These are necessary battles, but they should not be confused with the immense influence available to those willing to leave adulthood behind. Older adults remain, for now, unaware of the nature of elderhood. This is hardly accidental; society explicitly discourages these ideas.

Still, I am confident that this consciousness will emerge because elderhood has always flourished in affluent societies. It is a hard-bitten tribe that cannot afford to invest in old age. By a wonderful coincidence of history, the enlargement of adulthood (which has improved our access to material things) has also created the conditions needed for the emergence of a new elderhood.

We are stumbling into an era that is blessed with the largest group of (potential) elders the world has ever seen. They are well educated, materially secure, healthy, and socially engaged. The stage has been set for a culture-making (or destroying) confrontation with the cult of adulthood and its remorseless campaign to enshrine DOING-being as the only valid way of living. The battle over the meaning and worth of our longevity will remake our world, and the revolution will begin in the most unlikely place, among the least powerful people we can imagine.

DISTANT THUNDER

Awake, arise, or be forever fallen!

John Milton, *Paradise Lost*

THE EDEN ALTERNATIVE

The Three Plagues

In the early 1990s, I took a job as a physician in a small nursing home in upstate New York. The facility had a proud history of compliance with state and federal regulations and was, in every way, a credit to the community. At one point, it boasted five consecutive "perfect" state inspection surveys. It had everything such a facility could ask for—a modern, well-maintained building; a thoughtful and committed board of directors; and a dedicated staff and management team, many with long tenure. There were just three problems at the nursing home:

- Loneliness
- Helplessness
- Boredom

My eyes were opened to these plagues one day when I was asked to see a woman about a rash that had developed on her arm. Accompanied by a nurse, I strode down the hallway, confident that I could diagnose the cause of the inflammation. I found my patient lying in her bed in the very sparely furnished room that she shared with another resident. I pulled the curtain aside and presented myself in what I supposed was a very friendly, confident way. In a too-loud voice I questioned her about the red splotches on her arm, how long they had been there, whether they itched, and if she had ever had such a rash in the past. When I prepared to leave, she reached up and took hold of my arm and pulled me toward her. I will never forget the whiteness of her hair and the blueness of her eyes. In a soft, sad voice she said, "I'm so lonely."

At first I could not answer. Nothing in my training or experience had prepared me for this. I clumsily excused myself and staggered back to the nurses' station. There I wrote a medical note documenting my visit and prescribing the appropriate cream. I finished my rounds and left the facility—but those eyes, that face, that voice would not leave my mind. Indeed, they are with me still, even to this day.

When I returned to the nursing home I was determined to understand the true causes of suffering among the people I called my patients. I quickly came to see that the three plagues of loneliness, helplessness, and boredom were tormenting these people. The plagues were relentless, remorseless, and too often fatal. Despite this, the organization devoted very few of its resources to alleviating them. Such passivity was hard for me to comprehend, given how committed the facility was to quality care and how seriously these afflictions were harming the people who lived there. My distress was gradually tempered by the understanding that the harm was being done in spite of the best efforts of the people who were working there. The true culprit was the system of long-term care itself. The ideal of mitigated aging was leading staff to "help the residents compensate for their losses." This was a near-perfect description of the medical model of care, and it was blinding everyone to the very urgent needs of the human spirit.

Together with my wife, Judith Meyers-Thomas, I began thinking about creating a different kind of world for people living in nursing homes. The Eden Alternative is the product of that effort. It was created as a response to the withering toll that institutionalization takes on people who must live in nursing homes. Although we had no sense of it at the time, the Eden Alternative, together with a variety of other innovations and philosophies, would later become part of a sustained effort to change the culture of long-term care.

The Eden Alternative (described fully in a book I wrote called *Life Worth Living*) acknowledges that the bulk of the suffering experienced by those confined to long-term care environments is due to the plagues of loneliness, helplessness, and boredom. The Eden Alternative's response to this suffering proceeds from the rather ordinary observation that human beings thrive in gardenlike environments. This is one of the lessons of the original story of Eden. A nursing home, dedicated as it is to combating physical and mental disease and disability, is particularly inept when it comes to confronting the wounds of the human spirit. Careful study of each of the three plagues led us to identify and then develop effective antidotes.

Loneliness vs. Companionship

A lonely person needs companionship the way a thirsty person needs water. Companionship is one of the essential ingredients of well-being, yet we pay it little mind. It is too often confused with friendship or even passive participation in group activities. In fact, companionship is the product of knowing and being with others. We are not the companions of people seated near us on a flight to Los Angeles because we do not (and may not want to) know them. Similarly, our best old friends from high school, while still dear to us, are not our companions because we no longer share the rhythms of daily life with them. The professional staff of a nursing home may well take pride in how well they know "their" residents, but they offer little in the way of companionship because they have so little time to *be with* the elders. The cult of adulthood demands that staff members always remain busy, and so it structures human relationships around the routines required to ensure that work gets done. Long-term care encourages friendliness in the place of true companionship.

The Eden Alternative shows people how to integrate knowing and being into the daily rhythms of life in long-term care settings. Whereas the medical model stresses the idea of "professional distance," Eden helps people develop meaningful relationships with each other by teaching them how to learn and understand each other's stories. The art of giving care depends on companionship to give the care depth and substance. Without companionship, long-term care can offer only the cruel comfort of strangers feeding, bathing, dressing, and entertaining strangers.

A frequent objection in the long-term care industry is that the staff members of any given nursing home are so busy that, no matter how motivated they may be, they cannot provide all the companionship that lonely elders need. I agree and am relieved to report that help is nearby. Humans and animals have been living together for millennia, and those relationships have added immeasurably to the quality of human life. I have often asked people in the audiences I address to raise their hands if they have had experience with companion animals in their lives. Nearly every hand goes up. The beauty of the human-animal bond is that it is capable of providing round-the-clock unconditional love and affection. "Visiting animal" programs are nice but don't solve the need for ongoing companionship. Florence Nightingale made the same observation 150 years ago. Writing about the role of the nurse in facilitating recovery from illness, she observed that companion animals had a natural place in the sick room and could do much to alleviate the loneliness that came with a long convalescence.

Helplessness vs. Opportunities to Give Care

Nursing homes are academies of helplessness. The buildings themselves, ostensibly designed to foster long-term care, actually disable the people who live there. The most ordinary elements of self-care—eating, bathing, and dressing—are taken out of the residents' hands and given over to paid staff members. Being made to feel helpless is an unintended and too often unnoticed consequence of life in an institution.

The logic of long-term care consistently violates the deep-seated human need to balance the giving and receiving of care. People are trapped in a situation in which they receive far more care than they give. This imbalance inevitably leads to helplessness. The Eden Alternative teaches how to provide elders with easy access to opportunities to give care. One of the great virtues of companion animals is that although they require daily care, their needs are far less complex than those of human beings. In the Eden Alternative, we harmonize the need that plants, animals, and children have to receive care with the need that elders have to give care. Elders must be able to wake each morning and know, in truth, that their life matters—that they are in some way contributing to the well-being of another.

The people who work in nursing homes are expected to perform feats that would have fatigued Hercules. They are asked to give care all day, every day—even when the organization fails to care for them. Giving care every day without being cared for every day is a prescription for frustration, cynicism, and ultimately failure. Perhaps the most important part of our work when "Edenizing" a facility lies in teaching members of the management how to rebuild their relationships with the staff. The people who work in long-term care are some of the biggest-hearted, most loving and giving people I have ever known. The tragedy is that they are trapped in a system that defines care in terms of treatment, and caregiving in terms of tasks. The Eden Alternative teaches long-term care organizations that imbalances in the giving and receiving of care are as dangerous to the organization as red ink on the financial statement. Successful Edenizing organizations are constantly exploring the art of cherishing and being cherished.

Boredom vs. Variety and Spontaneity

Boredom is a great crushing weight that can squeeze the life out of any human being. It is the pain we suffer when we seek but cannot find variety and spontaneity in daily life. Because nursing homes are operated as therapeutic institutions, machinelike efficiency is their ideal. The best facilities are thought to be those that deviate to the minimum extent possible from predetermined schedules and routines. Inside the organization, the people who are most adept at maintaining routine and order are promoted into management positions where they are consistently rewarded for suppressing variety and spontaneity.

This approach to daily life has a deadening effect on all who must live and work under its sway. Everyone needs to feel the fresh breeze of the unexpected, even if it does not blow every day. Spontaneous events and happenings are the source of interesting conversation. Conversations grow into stories that can be told and retold. Stories become memories. To live in a typical nursing home is to endure a famine of new memories. By choosing to model daily life in the nursing home on a life-giving garden such as the biblical description of Eden, we can reverse some of the most grievous consequences of life and work within an institution.

Because it is intended to function as a human habitat, the Edenizing long-term care organization embraces the concept of social and biological diversity. Lonely people need companionship, and so we follow Florence Nightingale's advice and bring animals into their lives. Pets can be counted on to do the unexpected, and when they do so (for better and worse), moments of variety and spontaneity come into being. Children inject the elixir of life, love, and laughter wherever they are made to feel welcome—and they are always welcome in an Edenized facility. Plants—green, growing plants—remind us of the quiet exuberance that is always available to those that yet live. The challenge is to create a human habitat where people of all ages come together day after day—eager and able to thrive, not just survive.

Making a New Culture

In order for the Eden Alternative to be effective, management must make an uncompromising commitment to the well-being of the caregivers. Nursing homes have historically engaged in a hidden but very aggressive form of social strip-mining. They have long recruited mature, loving people into their ranks and then used them to soften the edges of a hard-hearted institutional structure. Low pay, regimentation, regulation, and hierarchy mine the goodwill of those who choose to do this work. Given this, it is not surprising that turnover at long-term care facilities is high. Through the Eden Alternative, we teach people to create new ways of thinking, dreaming, speaking, and acting. We teach motivated professionals to align the needs of staff and elders.

We believe that all decisions belong with the elders or as close to the elders as possible. This principle might seem strange when we consider that more than three-fourths of those confined to long-term care institutions are living with significant dementia. In fact, though, it is the safest, most humane, most just assumption we can make.

Beginning with the idea that elders should decide helps us hear their voices. When elders cannot decide, those closest to them—those most aware of their stories, their likes and dislikes—should make the decisions.

One reason the conventional approach to management in long-term care is so dangerous is that it moves decision-making authority too far away from the elders. This disenfranchisement is rarely questioned and, in truth, is just one of the many levels of disempowerment that can be found within the institution. Residents will have little opportunity to become the elders they are meant to be until we remake the relationship between management and staff. Our work in the Eden Alternative has led us to accept, as an ironclad law, the observation that "as managers do unto staff, so shall the staff do unto the elders." An organization that learns to give love, respect, dignity, tenderness, and tolerance to employees creates the potential for these same virtues to be provided, in abundance, to the elders. A commitment to fairness that values this reciprocity is the most elemental form of justice.

While the Eden Alternative began as an effort to improve the physical environment in which nursing home residents were living, it quickly became clear that the social environment had an even greater impact on the well-being of staff and residents. What we think about one another and how we treat one another are ways of being that form the bedrock of daily life; they certainly define the quality of life for people who live and work in long-term care facilities. We learned slowly and painfully that the Eden Alternative flourishes only when creative, courageous leadership that is truly dedicated to this difficult work remains committed to the process.

By the late 1990s it had become clear that the Eden Alternative was part of a larger emerging struggle to remake the daily realities of long-term care for staff and residents alike. Other people, such as Barry and Debbie Barkan of the Live Oak Institute, Charlene Boyd at Providence Mount St. Vincent, and Joanne Rader at the University of Oregon, were also pioneering new approaches to the problems faced by those living in and working in nursing homes. It is often said, "When the student is ready, the teacher will appear." The field was ripe for change and more open than ever before to new ideas and practices. What was needed was some kind of proof that the effort to change the culture of long-term care could offer measurable, sustainable improvements in the quality of life and the quality of care.

Outcomes and Ideals

As a follow-up to the research conducted during our first attempt to Edenize a nursing home in the early nineties, the Texas Long-Term Care Institute organized an Eden Alternative multifacility among nursing homes in Texas. A total of seven homes were recruited, and the management teams were taught to implement the physical and organizational changes developed in the initial project. Would these homes be able to replicate the startlingly positive results we had achieved in our first effort? Because we had limited funds, we chose to concentrate on readily available quality measurements that were generally regarded to be markers of both quality of life and quality of care. Even though we were optimistic about what the Eden Alternative could achieve, nothing could have prepared us for the magnitude of the success.

A summary of significant cumulative findings includes these data:

- 60 percent decrease in behavioral incidents
- 57 percent decrease in Stage I–Stage II pressure sores
- 25 percent decrease in number of bedfast residents
- 18 percent decrease in use of restraints
- 48 percent decrease in staff absenteeism
- 11 percent decrease in employee injuries

Because we are eager to continue improving our ideas and practices, we continue to conduct research on and evaluations of Edenizing organizations. A report from the state of Michigan summarizes the benefits for elders and staff alike from embracing the Eden Alternative approach. Some of those results follow.

A high level of staff turnover has long been regarded as one of the costs of doing business in long-term care. The expense, industry-wide, is enormous. Training a single replacement caregiver costs approximately $3,000. In the state of Michigan, studies have found that the annualized turnover rate for nurse's assistants is 72 percent. Thus, nurse's assistant turnover in a typical 120-bed nursing facility costs about $210,000 a year. Significantly, Edenizing homes report reductions in staff turnover rates and improved attendance among employees. This trend not only strengthens the financial performance of the nursing home; it also improves the care provided to the elders. Consistent staff-elder relationships have been shown to increase the satisfaction of both elders and their caregivers. Some examples of this trend at work are the following:

- Lapeer County Medical Care Facility (CMCF) in Lapeer, Michigan, began its Eden journey in 2000 and became a registered Eden home in 2001. It has reported a 75 percent decrease in staff turnover as well as a 60 percent decline in absenteeism.

- Oak Crest Manor of Holland, Michigan, also launched its Eden journey in 2000. Since then it has reported a decrease in staff turnover from 104 percent to 42 percent in just eighteen months. The cost of using outside agency staff plummeted from $60,435 in 2000 to just $247 in the following two years combined.

- Lakeland Specialty Hospital in Berrien Center, Michigan, started to Edenize in 1999 and was named to the Eden Alternative registry in 2001. The facility reports the reduction of staff turnover from 87 percent in 1999 to 33 percent in 2001. The use of outside agency staffing has been eliminated.

- Leelanau Memorial Health Center in Northport, Michigan, started its Eden journey in 1996 and became a registered Eden home in 1998. It experienced a decrease in turnover from 72 percent in 1997 to 17 percent in 2001. Staff absenteeism over the same period improved from 451 call-ins to 276 call-ins in 2001.

- Lenawee CMCF in Adrian, Michigan, began its Eden journey in 1998 and became a registered Eden home in 1999. Staff retention rates have climbed from 58 percent to 78 percent, allowing the organization to keep experienced caregivers, which, in turn, leads to improved care.

The Eden Alternative provides a framework for culture change in long-term care. Its principles and practices nourish a relationship-rich environment in which elders and staff can continue to grow and learn together. Homes that embrace the Eden Alternative and take on the difficult work of culture change enjoy many positive results. Numerous surveys have shown improved elder, family, and staff satisfaction. More fulfilled staff and happier elders lead to improved quality indicators and lower turnover among staff who provide the care.

The Eden Alternative has grown in size, scope, and complexity since its inception in 1992. What began as an effort to improve the quality of life for residents in a single nursing home has developed into a worldwide movement to reform the structures and practices of long-term care as a whole. The Eden Alternative has labored to develop a comprehensive approach to change in long-term care, complete with its own language, stories, and fellowship. The Eden Alternative philosophy has been implemented successfully in every state of the Union and in New Zealand, Australia, Europe, and Asia. There are two factors that help explain its global success. First, in the industrialized world (both East and West), the problems created by a growing reliance on institutional forms of care are largely the same from nation to nation. Institutionalized elders everywhere suffer from the three plagues of loneliness, helplessness, and boredom. Second, no matter what language is spoken within their walls, long-term care facilities the world over all answer to the dictates of the cult of adulthood and its attendant theology of mitigated aging. The Eden Alternative responds to that challenge in a substantial, effective way, and that is why it has grown so much and spread so far. No matter where it is practiced, its work is founded on the ten principles on the facing page.

These ideas are the purest expression of what Eden is. They do not change. The techniques that Eden makes available to those who

Eden Alternative Principles

1. The three plagues of loneliness, helplessness, and boredom account for the bulk of suffering among our elders.
2. An elder-centered community commits to creating a human habitat where life revolves around close and continuing contact with plants, animals, and children. It is these relationships that provide the young and old alike with a pathway to a life worth living.
3. Loving companionship is the antidote to loneliness. Elders deserve easy access to human and animal companionship.
4. An elder-centered community creates opportunity to give as well as to receive care. This is the antidote to helplessness.
5. An elder-centered community imbues daily life with variety and spontaneity by creating an environment in which unexpected and unpredictable interactions and happenings can take place. This is the antidote to boredom.
6. Meaningless activity corrodes the human spirit. The opportunity to do meaningful things is essential to human health.
7. Medical treatment should be the servant of genuine human caring, never its master.
8. An elder-centered community honors its elders by de-emphasizing top-down bureaucratic authority, seeking instead to place the maximum possible decision-making authority in the hands of the elders or in the hands of those closest to them.
9. Creating an elder-centered community is a never-ending process. Human growth must never be separated from human life.
10. Wise leadership is the lifeblood of any struggle against the three plagues. For it, there can be no substitute.

wish to pursue these principles, however, continue to evolve. The methods used by Edenizing organizations today are substantially different from the methods in use in 1996, and what works best in 2006 will, I hope, be substantially different from what is done today. Like them or loathe them, nursing homes will be with us for decades to come. Millions of people will spend, too often against their will, substantial time as nursing home residents. A generation of men and women will devote their careers to trying to improve these homes. The Eden Alternative is the beginning, not the end, of an epic journey. It shows us what is possible and encourages us to continue exploring—to continue asking how we can improve the well-being of our elders and, in doing so, bring a new elderhood into being.

RESISTANCE

The Peril of Great Power

Every person who, on a humid summer night, hears the rumble of distant thunder cannot help but ask, is the storm moving nearer to or farther from me and mine? If the sound recedes, we settle into a peaceful slumber, finding little reason to lie awake worrying about the faraway strangers who live in the storm's path. If the thunder draws near, we cannot sleep. We are up—alert—watching, thinking, planning. The wind rises, rustling the trees in the darkness. If the storm gathers strength, the radio is switched on. We worry and pace, little imagining that miles away others are pulling their covers close, confident that the tempest will pass them by.

The catastrophe of institutionalization seems very far off to most people. It just doesn't seem possible that, someday, it might touch us directly. Although the Eden Alternative offers elders a refuge from loneliness, helplessness, and boredom, we should not let this achievement divert us from searching out deeper, more penetrating insights into the workings of the cult of adulthood. Even a cursory examination of contemporary society will show that the plagues of the nursing home are much more widespread than we might suppose. Loneliness, helplessness, and boredom are seeping into the lives of adults and, even more sadly, those of children. Youth offers no immunity.

We are all in the path of this storm. We should pay close attention to the lives we are making for our elders, for their plight is but a forewarning of the suffering we are preparing for ourselves—not in some distant future but in the near term. The cult of adulthood is always working its way among us, ceaselessly refining the image of the worthy adult. Each year the standard of expected performance is nudged higher. Each year we grow one year older. A collision is inevitable. Even so, it can be difficult to muster much enthusiasm for the problems of the aged. Our collective denial of aging helps us forget the fact that we must follow in our elders' footsteps. Hundreds of millions of people find comfort in this illusion.

We all want to avoid unpleasant situations and we share a preference for what a philosopher might call the unexamined life. The rhythms of faith, work, and home lull us with their familiarity. Unhappiness, when it comes, is most palatable when it is the consequence of personal troubles—the loss of a job, the collapse of a marriage, a spiritual crisis. Difficulties of this kind are part of every life, and the pain they bring can be tempered by the knowledge that "this too shall pass." Social upheaval, however, is much more disturbing because we fear that it will bring, directly into our lives, hard truths that cannot be denied.

In a youth-obsessed culture, denial and aging are bound tightly to one another. Denial is powerful, but it does have limits. Eventually the gathering storm will touch us directly, endangering our comfortable illusions, upsetting or even destroying our hopes and dreams. Issues of social and economic history, which might ordinarily be left to experts, become matters of grim, personal importance. The status quo, which served us so conveniently and for so long, vanishes. Sources of unease, which were previously nameless and mostly hidden, emerge from the shadows.

~

Several years before I started work on this book, I was invited to give a series of lectures in Texas. I spoke in Austin and spent a day there teaching people about our Eden Alternative approach to long-term care. I was scheduled to be in San Antonio the next day, so a small group of us piled into an SUV and headed south on I-35. I was tired, and since the vehicle was full, I volunteered to ride in the luggage compartment. I crawled over the back seat and arranged the bags so that I could sleep.

An hour or so into the trip I began, very gradually, to wake from my nap. The setting sun soaked the hill country in a rich red light. I lay still and watched as the land gave way to something else. Mile after mile of "strip"—seemingly endless formations of burger joints, muffler shops, themed restaurants, and clothing outlets—passed before my eyes. Together they formed the monotonous procession that can be seen anywhere and everywhere. Lulled by the hum of the highway, I drifted into a way of seeing without looking, watching without thinking.

I nodded off, and when I woke again the light of day was nearly gone. We were close to San Antonio, and the parade outside the window continued, now illuminated by electric lights. I felt in the grip of some strange, waking trance. Everything I was seeing—the cars, the streets, the streetlights, the shops, the faceless cinder-block walls, the garish flashing signs—was perfectly ordinary. At the same time, I was shaken by the appearance of something entirely new. All of the steel, neon, and concrete had merged into a whole that was far larger and much more menacing than the sum of its parts. Where I had once seen only the hectic jumble of the usual, I now sensed the presence of something powerful and mysterious.

It took me years to understand this vision. I filled volumes of black-and-white speckled composition books with questions, ideas, and possibilities. This work helped me to realize, slowly and fitfully, that I had glimpsed the cult of adulthood—not as it would wish to be seen but as it truly is. Somehow, I had caught unawares the business, the busyness, the blithe disregard for the genius of place and person, and the antlike devotion to DOING-being that characterize the cult of adulthood. In my early descriptions of this vision, I called the thing I had seen "It" because I could think of no other name. With practice, I was able to see "It" in a thousand different places. "It" was in the mind-numbing standardization of the food we eat. "It" was in the sprawling, stereotyped housing tracts that I could see from the air. "It" was in the mass-produced music, entertainment, ideas, and opinions that clogged the radio and television.

"It" can be found wherever the cult of adulthood has crushed the belief that *being* has been, is, and should always be an honored partner of *doing* in the affairs of daily life. "It" is a world in which meaning is too often reduced to numerical terms.

Slowly, I began to appreciate how this insight connected to my work with elders. My peek behind the curtain was a stroke of good fortune because it let me, a vigorous and able-bodied adult, see what elders see. It let me look at adulthood from the outside. The essential truth of any social system is always most evident to those who live on its periphery. I had been living my life deep inside the cult of adulthood and had imagined that the energy and enthusiasm I was pouring into the work of reforming long-term care was a benign form of rebellion against its power. I was wrong.

In fact, my crusade for change did not directly challenge the cult of adulthood. Working to improve the lives of frail elders—fighting for human habitats that might help them thrive and not just survive—is necessary but not sufficient. The roots of declinism remain undisturbed. The suffering that comes with aging springs from the tragic misinterpretation of the role that elderhood should play in a healthy society.

Our longevity is not simply a matter of chronology or even biology; it is, most of all, the product of a collective imagination. The old age that we know, and so often loathe, is the creation of adulthood. Adults have sculpted and shaped each feature with chisel and file. We recoil from the grim visage they have made for us and too often forget that it sprang from the cult of adulthood and its campaign to remake the whole of human experience in its image.

Adulthood (along with its close ally, technology) gains and holds its power over us by promising us the perpetual union of youth with vitality. Such a combination is, of course, impossible, and if it were only a hopeful daydream it would do little harm. But the denial of both aging and the ancient practices of elderhood distorts and degrades human life from the first breath to the last. The cult of adulthood is creating a mighty reservoir of grief and anger.

A betting person would put money on the continued dominance of adulthood. After all, its control of society, government, and culture has become so complete that it no longer fears to trample traditional boundaries and beliefs. Childhood is increasingly being redirected away from its own pursuits and made into a proving ground for the adults of the future. Elderhood has been marginalized, its rightful place as an epic human achievement minimized or denied outright. Those whose existence defies the slogan of "adulthood forever" are held inside vast adult-run institutions that are dedicated to the isolation and, whenever possible, reformation of its aged inmates. Like any colossus, adulthood would seem to have nothing to fear.

Histories of empires remind us that great concentrations of power frequently sow the seeds of their own destruction. Day by day, the social conditions needed for the reemergence of elderhood as a potent sociocultural force are developing. The unprecedented global age boom has already started supplying the numbers. We can already feel the influence of a remarkable generation of senescents. These men and women are better educated, more affluent, healthier, and more socially engaged than any group of older people the world has ever seen. More than any generation in history, they have demonstrated an eagerness to challenge and even overturn long-established beliefs. There is little to suggest that the role of the quiet, uncomplaining grandparent will appeal to them. What they are missing—what we are all missing—is the vision of an elderhood with its own claim to greatness. Given the immutable fact of aging (yours and mine included), a new appreciation of longevity seems very likely to emerge. When it does, it will lead millions to question, challenge, and, finally, overthrow the doctrine of youth's perfection.

The Liberation of the Elders

Liberation is a distinctly human ambition. Animals instinctively struggle to free themselves *from* cold, hunger, confinement, and pain. None, as far as we know, can yearn for the freedom *to* become something other than what they are. Accordingly, liberation cannot be limited to the struggle for freedom *from* what is wrong, immoral, or evil. Such victories are valuable, but they represent the beginning of a struggle, not its end. Alone, they will never bring the fullness of human freedom into being. The logic of liberation demands that we go beyond the struggle to be free *from* injustice. Those who strive for liberation must shoulder the even more difficult work of gaining the freedom *to* become all that we are capable of being.

Early advocates for the aged understandably concentrated their efforts on eradicating the mistreatment of the old. They were among the first to speak openly against the ageism and overt bigotry practiced toward the aged. Their fight to improve the standing of the older adult in an often hostile, youth-oriented society has been carried bravely forward for decades and has succeeded in important ways. The much broader effort to liberate elders and elderhood, however, has yet to be truly begun. Such a crusade is necessary not because it can right wrongs that are visited on older people (although it can) but because it is the essential precondition for a new culture committed to a better quality of life *for people of all ages.*

Elderhood first took root in human society as one component of a vital intergenerational exchange that joined children, adults, and elders in a healthy web of interdependence. It flourished because it contributed importantly to the well-being of people of all ages. Today, we speak mostly of the assistance that the young provide to the old and pay little heed to what people of all ages receive from the old. This is a tragic oversight because it is the experience of life in a complex, interdependent, multigenerational society that, more than anything else, teaches us *how to be human.* Still, there are those who will see little correlation between the liberation of elderhood and a general improvement in the well-being of all. They should not be so quick to reject such a link. In nineteenth-century America it gradually became clear that the institution of slavery was damaging the fabric of society—that the wrongs inflicted on one group actually harmed all.

The drive to abolish slavery in antebellum America succeeded in large part because the effort was not limited to simply tempering injustice. It was relatively easy to argue that those held in involuntary servitude had a right to be *free from* brutality, forced labor, and inhumane living conditions. The truly radical idea was that these same people should also be *free to* live their lives as full citizens of the

American nation. The abolitionist movement transformed a plea for justice into a cry for liberation that convulsed the American nation. When Lincoln declared, "A house divided against itself cannot stand," he named the danger that slavery posed for the nation as a whole. Lincoln knew well that the question of slavery, the conflict over slavery, and the injustices of slavery were harmful to *all* people, free and slave, from North and South.

This century will be defined by our struggle over questions related to aging and longevity. History will judge us by how well or how poorly we advance the liberation of elders and elderhood. Those who have devoted their lives to the abatement of the worst elements of ageism, those who have struggled to secure basic human rights for the oldest and frailest of the old, have long felt themselves to be laboring in some distant and little-regarded vineyard. In fact, they are the vanguard of a looming worldwide cultural upheaval. The liberation of elders and elderhood is not an aging issue. It is not a generational issue. It is not about government programs or public policy. It is not about aching knees, weakening eyes, or even the wrinkles that line our faces. It is a world-changing struggle that can remake the experience of life from cradle to grave. It is our last, best hope for saving our world from the all-conquering power of adults.

In the twentieth century, capitalism was pitted against communism in a struggle that consumed the sweat and blood of three generations. Citizens of communist nations who set themselves against the will of their totalitarian governments contributed importantly to the communist system's collapse. Their resistance began, indeed could only begin, by nurturing dissent as far from Moscow as possible. Party leaders, secure in their Kremlin offices, had no reason to question the regime's actions. (The powerful have little appetite for dissent.) Instead, anti-communist ideology took shape within the very Siberian concentration camps that Stalin had created to uproot and destroy those who opposed the Party.

Those who would oppose the cult of adulthood cannot afford to ignore this history. Because they live every moment of their lives in its thrall, adults are unlikely by themselves to reverse the dangerous enlargement of contemporary adulthood. Our society needs to see, be inspired by, and learn from the weakest, frailest, most forgetful of us all. Elders are the true dissidents of our time. Their existence offers proof that adulthood does not last forever. Their lives speak to the possibility of life beyond adulthood even when their voices have fallen silent. Millions are being held, like Soviet-era political prisoners, at the farthest remove from power, unseen but not forgotten.

The liberation of elders and elderhood will be launched by an alliance of adults who are awakened to the perils created by an out-of-control adulthood, and elders who are living examples of what elderhood can be. Adult biases make it easy to overlook the potential influence of people living with memory loss, urinary incontinence, paralysis, and multiple chronic illnesses. Then again, revolutions are known to germinate in unexpected places among unlikely people.

The Allies

The oldest of the old cannot overthrow the cult of adulthood by themselves. In fact, they represent the polar opposite of the conventional image of the revolutionary. To say the least, the very old lack the swaggering panache of the insurgent. However, power has never been the currency most appropriate to elderhood. Elders' influence has always been distinct from the direct, mandatory DOING-being power of the adult. They rely, instead, on the subtle, indirect influence of BEING-doing. For those living in a manic world that is drunk on doing—even as it thirsts for meaning—the influence of elderhood can be especially appealing. It entices us with the very virtues and gifts we need most. The discovery of longevity is the greatest of all human achievements; it made us and it made our world. We now await the rediscovery of longevity, the reinvention of elderhood. The emergence of a distinctive twenty-first-century elderhood is crucial to the future of our society, our environment, and the well-being of people of all ages. Old age exists not as a threat but as a promise, ready, as it has always been, to lead us toward a richer, more rewarding way of living in this world.

Because it seems absurd that elders could inspire an overthrow of the cult of adulthood, those who choose to give the idea a second thought usually urge me to turn my attention to the young old instead. Senescents would seem to have all the time, money, and energy that activists require. They have set aside the compulsions of "have to do" in order to embrace the universe of "want to do." And they are joined by millions among us who are already making important contributions to the well-being of people of all ages.

Senescents are the kings and queens of volunteerism, and no community would ever want to be without them, but they are not ideal candidates for leading the struggle against the cult of adulthood. They are aware, they are energized, they are engaged, and they are, in so many ways, still adults—and that is the problem.

In a youth-worshiping society, senescents live perilously close to the precipice of obsolescence. While they are no longer enchanted by doing, having, and getting, they are fearful of losing their status as adults. The strength of this fear is often lost on advocates for social change who are eager to capture and make use of senescents' retained ability to "do." It is true that senescents find value in the shift from "have to do" to "want to do." The young old voluntarily build houses, deliver meals, and organize voter registration drives. Hidden in the can-do ideology of the older volunteer, however, is a much less useful dynamic.

These contributions of time and energy are often used to furnish proof of the senescent's continued success in living and working as an adult. The tip-off here is that the work has its reference point in the past, in the flower of youth. This emphasis is crystallized in the word "still." The volunteer is still active, still contributing, still a valuable member of the community of adults, still faithful to doing, getting, and having. We are so accustomed to this orientation that we rarely notice its influence over us.

This is a very different thing from the person who volunteers in the community in order to prepare for the future, for the ultimate attainment of elderhood. Until we have a social consciousness that values elderhood, the most energetic senescents will remain collaborators of adults and adulthood.

So what are we to do? If the old old are not meant to confront these injustices alone, and the young old are mostly still in the grip of adulthood, how then is the struggle against the cult of adulthood to be sustained?

Our elders will need allies, and these allies will have to come from within adult society. Most adults have no reason to care about elders and the indignities visited on the aged. They ignore elders in an ongoing effort to deny the truth of their own aging. Sometimes, adults with older relatives become enraged when someone they love is exiled from adult society and made to live in the old-age archipelago. These family members can become fierce critics of the nursing home industry. Far fewer, however, are those adults who can peer unblinkingly into the lives of the oldest and frailest among us and see, in magnified form, the growing injustices they are experiencing in their own lives.

These adults understand that the inclination of the nursing home to value the safety of residents over their human rights is but an echo of a public policy that too often allows security concerns to trump the Bill of Rights. They wonder at the growing power of corporations and the tendency to equate consumerism with citizenship. The nursing home is, after all, the bizarre ultimate end point of the consumer lifestyle. The corporations that run nursing homes have the most detailed databases on their "customers" of any companies in the world. The management knows what the residents eat, when they sleep, even when they move their bowels. They are paid to assume total control over the most private and intimate needs of all. The numbing sameness of the food we eat, the opinions we hear, and the buildings we live and work in has already reached its conclusion in the old-age archipelago. Inside the walls of the institution, the only choices are those approved by the professional staff. So it is that ninety-year-old Korean women are served mashed potatoes and gravy for dinner, just like everyone else. The medicalization of late life that debases our longevity by translating advanced old age into a litany of defects, injuries, and illnesses has a parallel in the rising number of children who are being treated for disorders that were not long ago unknown to parents, children, or teachers. The malaise of the institution is gradually becoming our malaise.

People often say to me, "Hey, Dr. Thomas, you'd better get this all fixed before I get old." I laugh and tell them that I will do my best.

People like to imagine that such problems all lie in the future and, if they are lucky, might be sorted out before they enter their own old age. What they do not realize is that the fault lies not in our aging but in the denial of aging. The damage that the cult of adulthood is doing to us all is simply magnified among our elders. The destruction of elderhood creates a danger that people of all ages must share.

Still, the elders have allies. There is a small but growing number of adults who share a progressive orientation toward the true nature of our longevity. They see meaning and worth in aging. They dream of a better way to be with and provide for the most frail among us, but they are also increasingly aware of the defects that mark a society without elders. Fortunately, their influence is larger than their numbers. Many of these men and women have been actively challenging declinism in their work; others are making the brave decision to set their own adulthood aside so that they may move, deliberately, into elderhood. Some have met with startling success. All have stories to tell. They are the true allies of elders and elderhood.

The progressive movement may be small and scattered, but it can take pride in being the vanguard of a long, worldwide struggle to liberate elders and elderhood. Far more than most adults, the people who share the movement's values understand and are willing to confront the damage being done by the doctrine of youth's perfection. Already coalescing into ad hoc groups and factions, the movement is capable of speaking with extraordinary unity about the importance of freeing elders from injustice. As might be expected, there is much less agreement on how the struggle should be conducted.

For me, membership in the resistance against the cult of adulthood has been maddeningly fulfilling, thrilling, and frustrating—and infuriatingly worthwhile. The resistance is and must remain a passionately uncoordinated and lovingly quarrelsome affair. This work matters greatly, for it is within the struggle to free our elders that we will learn how to free ourselves from the grip of the cult of adulthood.

Place and No Place

World Making

When I began my work with elders, I did not understand the importance of place. In those days, I saw nursing homes the way all professionals see them: as convenient, clean, congenial settings that facilitate care for the frail elderly. Somehow, I maintained this pretense despite hearing scores of anguished pleas from elders wanting to return home. I attributed these tearful pleadings to the aged person's supposed distaste for the new. There may well be some of that, but far more powerful is the older person's attachment to place. This should not be confused with nostalgia or simple habit. A sense of place is woven into the being of an elder in ways that adults have a hard time understanding. A sapling can be dug up and transplanted with little difficulty. Uproot a mighty oak and it will die.

Adults cultivate a very open, fluid understanding of place because doing so serves their most important needs. In a highly mobile, modern industrial society, success comes most readily to those who avoid becoming attached to any particular place. While it is easy for affluent adults to feel that the entire planet is within their grasp, this is a difficult conceit for elders to maintain. One of the truths of elderhood is that one's world shrinks with the passing of years. Place is vitally important to elders because the smaller one's world becomes, the more precious the immediate surroundings are.

A few years back, I saw the conflict between adult and elder ideas of place play out in classic tragic fashion. I live in a rural area and one of my neighbors was an elder who had lived in her house for more than eighty years. She had moved there with her family in 1918, when she was just four years old. She never married and by the late 1990s was the sole surviving member of her family. An adult neighbor became concerned about her and began trying to convince her to move to the city, about twenty miles away. The elder said no. The friend persisted. Finally, fate intervened. The elder woman burned her leg on a gas heater. A trip to the emergency room led to a hospital admission.

Well-meaning adults in the hospital saw an old woman who was clearly in need of services. She was transferred against her will from the hospital to a nursing home. A week later, the elder was told that her beloved dog (who had been entrusted to the neighbor) had "died." The woman never went home again. When we visited her, we found not the feisty survivor who had thrived in the country without electricity or indoor plumbing, but a shell-shocked facility resident. Removing the woman from her place may have extended the life of her body, but it destroyed her spirit. She had been torn up by and from her roots.

The gift of place is the gift of meaning. Human beings possess a remarkable ability to unite meaning with the material world. This is how a person, place, or thing becomes sacred. Is a Bible, a Torah, or a Koran made of paper, ink, and glue? Yes. Is it much more than paper, ink, and glue? Yes, again. Holy books are different from telephone books because the former are enriched with meaning while the latter have none.

For the elder, a loss of place carries with it a potentially lethal loss of meaning. Taking meaning away from a person or place is a form of profanity. Pornography is profane because it shears the people it depicts of their essential humanity and displays them as objects. Certain words are profane when they are used without reference to or in defiance of their sacred meaning. When elders leave their own place and enter into a long-term care facility, they are exposed to a ravaging placelessness. Completely without malice, these facilities profane the people who live inside them. Like the factories on which they are patterned, they elevate tasks above people, honor routine over ritual, and value information more than wisdom. Long-term care facilities are workplaces, and the lives of their residents are their product.

A Total Institution

Modern society has invested hundreds of billions of dollars and decades of effort in the creation and operation of placeless environments for the "frail elderly." Any direct challenge to this arrangement must ask and answer the question, why change now? What we have is surely flawed, but change in such a complex system will not always be for the better. Perhaps all that is lacking is a new reform effort, better funding, and improved patterns of regulation. There is a world of difference between those who believe that the current system, with appropriate changes, is worth saving and those who say the nursing home must be abolished. Those who think it can or should be saved would do well to remember where the nursing home comes from and the company it keeps.

More than forty years ago, Erving Goffman set out the characteristics of the "total" institution in his book *Asylums*. He elaborated five specific traits that define such an entity. In the following brief passage he lays out the social and physical terrain of one of those traits, placelessness. In a total institution:

> First, all aspects of life are conducted in the same place and under the same single authority. Second, each phase of the member's daily activity is carried on in the immediate company of a large batch of others, all of whom are treated alike and required to do the same thing together. Third, all phases of the day's activities are tightly scheduled, with one activity leading at a prearranged time into the next, the whole sequence of activities being imposed from above by a system of explicit formal rulings and a body of officials. Finally, the various enforced activities are brought together into a single rational plan purportedly designed to fulfill the official aims of the institution.

The prison system, state psychiatric hospitals, and concentration camps are clearly part of this world. The long-term care system of nursing homes and assisted living facilities, sad to say, fits the mold as well. While the intention of these organizations is clearly different from that of penitentiaries, they share a common, rigid division of people into the guardians and the guarded, the therapists and the sick, the staff and the residents.

Incremental change has done much to improve long-term care in America in the past, but it has its own limits—and we have reached them at last. While I am grateful for the improvements that have made life better for millions of nursing home residents (and have done my best to contribute to those improvements), I know in my heart that the old-age archipelago must go. I am, in this matter, an abolitionist.

The Shiny Roof Tile

Our society faces a challenge that is both noble and dangerous: we must confront the power of adulthood and restore a healthier, more balanced understanding of the human life cycle. The first step in this confrontation will lead us to create a safe place for a new elderhood—a sanctuary that is outside of, distinct from, and independent of the old-age archipelago. There are those who would put off this task until after America's sixteen thousand nursing homes have themselves been reformed. This temptation springs from the illusion that we can "fix" long-term care. A Japanese folktale makes clear the enormous difference between change and transcendence:

> A sage took a young man as his student. The youth was careful and diligent, and he studied the master's every word. Strange as it may seem, this disappointed the teacher and so he resolved to teach the young man the true nature of wisdom.

> The sage cast about until he found a broken roof tile lying on the dusty earth. Taking the shard in hand, he sought his student. When he found the young man, he began polishing the roof tile with a fold of his robe. The student found this behavior quite strange and he immediately asked the master what he was doing.

The sage responded, "I am polishing this roof tile and I am going to keep right on polishing it until it becomes a jewel."

"But master, it doesn't matter how long you polish that tile, it will never become a jewel."

"So true," the sage responded. "It is also true that you will never find the wisdom you seek as long as you insist on changing only what you know. True wisdom comes only to those willing to change what they are."

The liberation of elders and elderhood goes far beyond the "fixing" of long-term care. It will be a decades-long struggle, but it is already under way. In order for it to succeed, it must be nurtured in a safe place, far from the centers of adult power. Elderhood needs a sanctuary. In the past, it could have been said that the family home formed just such a shelter. Most elders throughout human history have lived out the last decades of life within the embrace of an extended family. Changes in society have placed that option out of reach for the majority of older people living in industrialized nations.

Cut off from this traditional refuge, older people are easily snared by the cruel (and utterly false) distinction between dependence and independence. They make it perfectly clear to anyone who will listen that what they want, most of all, is to remain in their own homes. In order to make this possible, they devote themselves to maintaining their independence. To fail in this struggle and lose their grip on adulthood is to descend into the netherworld of dependency.

There is, as yet, no place that specifically and energetically refutes the logic of an old age that is "going, going, gone." We, as yet, have no place that is dedicated purely to the pursuit of the most positive elderhood possible for those whose circumstances require close cooperation with others. We need a safe house that emphatically resists the tyranny of dependence and independence. Old age must have a sanctuary where ideas and practices related to a new elderhood can grow and mature.

Our society needs an engaged and engaging elderhood because such a life stage offers the best possible refutation of the doctrine of youth's perfection. Most of us will need to see, with our own eyes, that a valued and valuable elderhood truly exists before we voluntarily surrender our adulthood. As a society, we, perhaps more than any people who have ever lived, need elders. We need a renewed elderhood that can help older adults become the elders they were meant to be. We need a place where we can learn how best to make this happen. Like the student in the story, we must learn the difference between improvement and transformation. I believe that the foundation for this worldwide transcendent effort can be built on the elemental concepts of warm, smart, and green.

Elderhood's Sanctuary

Living Together Intentionally

Everywhere I go I meet people who are imagining a new kind of old age for themselves. Whether it is on a dirt road in rural Alberta or in a cab in Manhattan, the sequence unfolds again and again. Once my companions learn what I do for a living and my passion for a new longevity, they are eager to share their plans. "You see," they say, "my friends and I, we're not ever going to any nursing home. No, you see, what we are going to do is go in together on a house and we are all going to live together. We are all going to take care of each other." There is a good chance that you have heard someone describe this vision; perhaps it is your dream as well.

There is even a novel that takes this kind of intentional community as its theme. *Where River Turns to Sky*, by Gregg Kleiner, tells the story of octogenarian George Caster. When George's best friend dies lonely and alone at the Silver Gardens Nursing Home, George pledges to help other residents escape that fate. He buys a big old house, paints it fire-engine red, and "liberates" a small group of residents. Together they make a home. One of the characters describes life in the house: "It's a big change here from living in the Gardens. Sometimes I forget how big. In my head too, things are different. Some of the fog has cleared up, the loose wires seem a little tighter. Time's passed. Time. Faster here than in the Gardens. Lots faster. Probably because there is always something going on."

Whatever happens to them, these characters know that they have chosen their own destiny; they live their own lives.

Making the dream come true—that is the thing. More and more of us live alone, without close family members living nearby. The need and the desire to come together with others who are approaching elderhood is growing. The reality is, of course, more complicated than the dream. Kleiner's novel is worth reading for any number of reasons but especially for his honest appreciation of how hard it is for people to live with one another (the only thing harder is being left alone).

We are only beginning to understand how to create and maintain the sanctuaries that elderhood needs if it is ever to develop properly. Those of us who have been working with elders, organizations, staffs, and families to make human habitats bloom in the most unlikely places have learned some things that all those who seek a sanctuary for elderhood are likely to find useful. Living together intentionally requires us to understand the sources and power of human warmth, how it is created, and how it can be destroyed. We must be willing and able to search out the tools and technologies that are best suited to the task of making such sanctuaries healthy and safe. Finally, we must remember that well-being depends importantly on our relationship with the living world that, in the end, sustains us all.

Warm

Human warmth is a peculiar thing that can be felt much more easily than it can be known. Some organizations, like some people, radiate warmth. They are rich in optimism and trust, and they exude the spirit of generosity. Cold organizations, in contrast, demonstrate a distressingly familiar pattern of pessimism, cynicism, and stinginess. The ability to create and maintain human warmth is an essential attribute for any organization that aspires to create a sanctuary for elderhood. Warm organizations are adept at fostering well-being; cold organizations are not. Just as importantly, warm organizations are flexible and adapt readily to new and changing circumstances. Most of us can report bitter personal experiences with the rigid inflexibility that defines cold organizations.

Our efforts to reform long-term care organizations using the Eden Alternative have led us to embrace the practice of "doing good deeds without the expectation of return" as the most effective approach to warming people and organizations. Genuine altruism practiced as an everyday habit rarely fails to touch the human heart. Some organizations, though, have shown themselves to be much better at this than others. Careful review of our experience in this area has shown three attributes that seem to have the greatest influence over the ability of an organization to create and maintain warmth.

Small

Early twenty-first-century nursing homes are the product of a single-minded focus on economies of scale. They collect expertise, labor, equipment, and residents according to the same logic that led Andrew Carnegie to build mammoth soot-belching steel mills. A determined effort to reduce costs and standardize operations has encouraged large size in long-term care facilities. While the financial argument in favor of gigantism is well established, the balance sheet fails to record the human cost of largeness. Being "cared for" along with one hundred, two hundred, or even three hundred other similarly situated people carries a non-economic price that is substantial.

Intentional communities have long recognized the perils of great size. The leaders of fraternities, sororities, churches, synagogues, and monasteries know that the bigger their communities become, the harder it is to maintain the human warmth that grows from knowing and caring about the people around us. Human beings evolved within small social groups and are attuned to their nuances. We have (on the species level) little experience with large, anonymous collections of others. This is not to suggest that small is always warm or even that small is always better than large. Plenty of small towns, small companies, and even small families make life miserable for the people trapped within them. E. F. Schumacher recognized this and described this tension in his book *Small Is Beautiful*:

> What I wish to emphasize is the *duality* of the human requirement when it comes to the question of size: there is no *single* answer. For

his different purposes man needs many different structures, both small ones and large ones, some exclusive and some comprehensive . . . For constructive work, the principal task is always the restoration of some kind of balance. Today, we suffer from an almost universal idolatry of giantism. It is therefore necessary to insist on the virtues of smallness—where this applies.

A sanctuary for elderhood should be built on a human scale, one that answers to the purposes of community rather than the economics of an industrial enterprise. Experts in the field rarely dispute the desirability of small size. They do object that it is not economically feasible. The habit of forecasting financial calamity based on projecting the performance of a typical (large) nursing home artificially shrunken to a more human scale tells us much more about the accountant's unquestioned assumptions than about the potential viability of a small, warm sanctuary for elderhood.

Critics of smallness often overlook the many ways that large size creates diseconomies of scale. Caring for others is an art and, as such, cannot easily be reduced to a repetitive sequence of tasks and procedures. Food, energy, and time are all wasted in a never-ending quest for economy. Industrial long-term care's habit of idolizing machine-like efficiency actually wastes more money than it saves. A visit to the Dumpsters parked beside the loading dock of your local nursing home will give you a good look at the stinking remains of tons of spoiled food. Ordered by the tractor-trailer load; prepared in vast, highly mechanized kitchens; and served according to an institution-defined menu and schedule, as much as 40 percent of the purchased food is thrown away every day. Ever eager to cut its food budget, the old-age archipelago remains stubbornly unaware of its wasteful confusion of the human and the mechanical.

All other things being equal, and with the full understanding that small size does not guarantee warmth, we can say that when it comes to creating a sanctuary in which elders and elderhood can develop, small is better.

Flat

The impulse toward hierarchy and bureaucratic authority grows stronger as human organizations grow larger. In nursing homes, hierarchy exchanges genuine human caring for established-policies-guiding-an-assembled-staff-in-the-efficient-execution-of-tasks-and-procedures-delineated-by-an-interdisciplinary-care-plan-document. Few people work in organizations that are as rigidly compartmentalized and uniformly hierarchical as prisons and long-term care facilities. Even so, millions of elders have learned through firsthand experience that the multiple layers of a bureaucracy can puree care and feed it out with a spoon.

Tragically, long-term care institutions are much more hierarchical than other organizations of comparable size. Although they are often part of multifacility chains, each building usually employs only one hundred to two hundred people. This makes them small businesses by most definitions. Few companies of this size, however, would tolerate, or be willing to pay for, that highly departmentalized and rigidly hierarchical company structure used by nursing homes. Nursing home administrators' intense devotion to the chain of command is usually ascribed to the fact that errors made in long-term care facilities can and do lead to physical pain, emotional suffering, and even death. We expect that organizations dealing with stakes this high will place a heavy emphasis on the internal processes and procedures that can control risk. Society routinely bolsters this behavior with a rigorous pattern of external regulation. Flatness (having a less complex and hierarchical organizational structure) will always come more easily to a hundred-person advertising firm (little risk) than to a hundred-person nuclear power plant staff (huge risk).

Hierarchy promotes safety, predictability, and accountability—but these virtues do come at a price. People who choose to work for the Generals (General Electric, General Motors, General Foods, etc.) understand that their companies are incapable of loyalty. This knowledge helps them guard against arbitrary behavior by the corporation. The people who live and work in long-term care environments, in contrast, are less likely to find refuge in cynicism. They struggle to reconcile the stated goals of the organization (which are noble), their personal sense of calling (which is often profound), and the brutal logic of institutional decision making.

Rigid hierarchy and a near-religious faith in bureaucratic authority may suit an army or a global corporation, but they are incompatible with the tender art of giving and receiving genuine human care. Old age initially developed within the context of family, tribe, and clan, and the organic hierarchy found within these entities has nurtured its development for thousands of years. The formal hierarchy of the corporation is to the nature of elderhood as oil is to water.

Careful observers have noted the vigor with which long-term care institutions enforce systems of control for both staff and residents. People who work in low-status positions nearly always stay at that level. The residents are confined to the role of institutional inmate, and despite the benevolence that inspires resident empowerment programs, they will remain, always, in the inmate role. The slope of the skilled nursing facility's organizational pyramid is steep, and its sides are as slick as ice.

All human organizations have, and need to have, hierarchy. Perfect flatness would create a dangerous anarchy. The struggle in this case is not to eliminate hierarchy but to create an organization in which it is far less steep and far less slippery. Flat human organizations are also notable for their economical use of roles. The family, for example, has survived and thrived while carrying out complex social and economic functions even though it contains only a handful of roles (mother, father, son, daughter, brother, sister, etc.). The hierarchy-making impulse is strong in contemporary society, and flatness, once achieved, will always be a delicate but valuable creation.

Institutions thrive on hierarchy because it simplifies the work of managing highly complex tasks. Unfortunately, it also obstructs the giving and receiving of care. Because bureaucracies confine people to established roles, the knowing, empathic, resourceful relationship that is the hallmark of caring is often placed out of reach. Assigned roles make it easier to delegate tasks and monitor their completion, but they also cloak the people who inhabit those roles. Juanita Jones becomes a housekeeper. Clara Wilson becomes a resident. Within a hierarchical bureaucracy, it is very difficult for Juanita and Clara to know one another outside the roles they have been given. Flat social structures, in contrast, rely on deeply personal relationships as the basis for decision making and mutual responsibility. In order to be a family, mothers, brothers, fathers, and sisters must know each other well. We all know how messy, confusing, and difficult families can be, but we all prefer our families to life in an institution—no matter how efficient the institution might be.

Bureaucratic hierarchy obstructs the work of caring, as it is rightly understood. Human caring is founded on a knowing, empathic, resourceful response to the needs of another. For those seeking to sustain human warmth, a flat organization is better.

Rooted

Social organizations the world over are sustained by rules that are present and active even when they are unwritten or unspoken. Modern industrial society struggles to reconcile the demands of written rules and regulations with implicit but clearly understood norms of behavior. No human community can rely solely on written rules. It is also true that contemporary society would fly apart if it had to rely solely on customs and traditions. We live with a bias toward written rules of conduct because they are so explicit and seem to promise fairness bred from equality and impartiality. This preference also conceals a danger. A strict devotion to doing things by the book devalues unwritten understandings and opens the door to vicious evenhandedness.

Lord of the Flies, by William Golding, offers a literary illustration of the conflict between the moral and the legal. A group of schoolboys, reared within the rigid confines of industrial society, are plunged into chaos after their plane crashes. The boys are stranded on a deserted island, without adult supervision. In the novel's despotic vision, the absence of both formal rules and the authoritarian figures needed to enforce those rules allows the situation to spiral into chaos and death. Civilization proves to be a very thin veneer. The boys' savage behavior is revealed as an unintended consequence of their culture's heavy reliance on formal standards of behavior. The crash exposed the frightening degree to which authority had replaced morality in the conduct of their lives.

Codifying and enforcing rules of conduct that protect the weak, the infirm, and the frail is a cardinal virtue of a just society. In the world of long-term care, government officials and advocates have long shared the sense that these written protections need strengthening. After all, these rules and their enforcement have protected millions of people against abuse and neglect. But that is not all they do. They also uphold the law of unintended consequences. The regulation of the speech and behavior of those who work in the long-term care industry has fostered the mistaken notion that compliance with regulations is equivalent to achieving quality and justice. Regulations are designed to be minimum standards, but official approval is offered in equal measure to those who merely comply with published standards and to those who soar above them. The enforcers equate what is permitted with what is right and what is forbidden with what is wrong. Like a silent and invasive carcinoma, written rules slowly and silently replace unspoken, deeply personal commitments to elders and to the work of meeting their needs.

The regulation of long-term care has improved quality and made life better for millions of nursing home residents. Governments will always have a duty to watch out for people who are being cared for by others. Nursing homes present an especially challenging case in this regard because these large, highly specialized organizations are devilishly difficult to manage. We need to remember that the patterns of regulation that exist today were established in response to an enormous, powerful industry that consisted almost entirely of large, highly bureaucratic institutions. The guardian has been shaped by the threat against which it guards.

For many who work in the industry, officially sanctioned codes of behavior, while onerous at times, can also be said to offer a refuge from the ambiguity that accompanies questions of morality. Legal formality can be attractive, efficient, and objective. Over time, even the most spiritually centered organizations move gradually toward formalized policies and procedures. The road to formalism is well worn. Much less familiar is the path that balances a rooted commitment to elders and the potential of a positive elderhood with the might and desirability of written rules. This is not an either-or proposition. The pendulum has swung too far toward an unthinking compliance with arbitrary rules. We must start it back toward the center before we forget that such a change is both possible and desirable.

When it comes to sustaining human warmth, there is no substitute for having deeply rooted beliefs.

Smart

The technology revolution that is remaking life, work, and leisure in the twenty-first century has done much for people of all ages. The aged, in particular, have benefited from rapid advances in medical technologies that mitigate age-related changes. New drugs, devices, and surgical procedures have done so much to improve quality of life in old age that only a fool would want to grow old without them. Much less obvious are the many ways in which our culture's use and misuse of tools have degraded the meaning and experiences that are unique to elderhood. Our information age continues to promise— and deliver—greater speed, greater bandwidth, and ever-easier access to anything that can be sent over a wire, but it is much less forthcoming with nondigital virtues. To love and be loved, to cherish and be cherished, to hurt and then be healed—none of these gifts will ever be delivered via e-mail. Technology is, and will remain, the friend of longevity (it is largely responsible for sustaining the worldwide age boom), but it has not been an ally of elderhood. We deserve, but have yet to develop completely, the unique new tools we will need to support the liberation of elders and elderhood.

We can begin this work by untangling the confusion between high technology and smart technology. High technology flourishes in the confines of large, sophisticated, industrial laboratories. It is tended by highly credentialed engineers and technicians, and its workings are, from the average person's point of view, shrouded in mystery. Smart technology, in contrast, is and always has been within the province of ordinary people. From the elegant flaked stone tools of the Paleolithic era to the sophisticated bows and arrows of the indigenous Americans, making clever use of available materials is an elegant human art. While I am familiar with advanced medical technologies and deploy many of them in my work as a physician, I also work with the draft horses we keep on our farm. Over the years I have come to appreciate the genius of the harnesses, lines, and hitches. Every strap, buckle, and ring has a purpose, and taken together they are as refined as any airplane wing—and just as useful.

Even more to the point, all of the harnesses being used today are the product of centuries of refinement by skilled harness makers working with simple tools in small shops. I doubt any school of engineering could improve on the convenience, safety, and utility of such a harness no matter how many minds and dollars were set to the task. Smart technology looks and feels comfortable and human. Those who would make a sanctuary for elders and elderhood will need to develop their own tools and techniques for creating and then sustaining the most positive elderhood possible.

Human communities produce tools and are then, to a surprising extent, shaped by their own implements. Technology molds culture, which then influences technology. Our tools and the choices we make about their use have a moral dimension that we ignore at our peril. The smart use of technology demands that we be conscious of the relationship between our tools and our actions, our actions and our most cherished beliefs.

I live with my family on a 250-acre farm and have chosen a path that is distinct from that of most other farmers in our area. Alternative and renewable sources of energy supply the power we need to run the house and farm. We are "off the grid," relying instead on the sun and the wind to generate electricity. In the fields and forest we use draft horsepower to get work done. Instead of specializing in one product as most large farms do, we pursue a version of diversified, low-input, sustainable agriculture. Our philosophy helps us select the tools that are best for our chosen work. We happily employ many different forms of technology, low and high, but we insist that our tools strengthen rather than weaken our commitment to one another.

Much is made of the unwillingness of some Old Order Amish communities to embrace electricity and rubber-wheeled vehicles. Though they are usually pictured as charming if misguided throwbacks to another century, these people are actually among America's most sophisticated technologists. They are engaged in a subtle ongoing effort to balance the usefulness of technology with how they live as a community. They embrace methods and devices that help them sustain their way of life, and reject those that might damage the delicate social fabric of their society. They understand that the smart use of technology will not only help us do what we have to do, it will help us be what we want to become.

Any sanctuary for elders and elderhood must engage in a similar debate. Tools and technologies must be selected and rejected according to how they enhance or degrade the pursuit of the most positive elderhood possible. Technologies (be they simple or complex) that foster a sense of belonging, meaning, and purpose can find a place in such an environment. As a start, properly designed floor coverings and lighting fixtures, accessible cabinetry, and accessible bathrooms and toilets can do much to improve the well-being of elders, but we have so much further to go. We are just beginning to develop a whole new class of technology fitted to the purpose of supporting a true elderhood. I foresee an alliance among elders, those who care for and about elders, and the technicians, materials scientists, and engineers who can create the tools we need. The cult of adulthood always favors tools that help people do more. The liberation of elders and elderhood requires us to develop exceptional tools and techniques that can be placed into the service of being. Those who would make a sanctuary for elders and elderhood must be conscious of the power of tools and technology to support or degrade the experience of BEING-doing.

Smart technology may be high or low, but it must always serve to foster the well-being of elders and those who live and work with elders. Technology (high or low) that restricts, confines, or diminishes elders for the convenience of others or damages the well-being of elders must be abandoned.

Green

A great deal of proof exists that it is better to live in a garden than a machine. Human beings need close and continuing contact with the living world, and it is wrong to deny it to them. In our work with the Eden Alternative, we have had to master the art of bringing the living world into the lives of elders being held within large, inflexible, and sterile institutions. This is difficult work, and success can never be guaranteed. The good news is that years of working to change an intransigent system have strengthened our resolve and sharpened our skills.

Our direct experience with the Eden Alternative is bolstered by research that supports the value of connecting human beings to the living world. The great Roman poet Virgil explored this idea in "The Bucolics," his paean to rural life. Modern thinkers take a somewhat more technical approach, and some of the major themes of their literature are being developed under the headings of "Eco-psychology," the "Biophilia Hypothesis," and "Deep Ecology." Those in pursuit of a new kind of longevity should make use of the insights developed by these investigators. Their work will serve us well when it is joined with the practical aspects of integrating the living world into our lives.

Any sanctuary for elderhood must recognize, from the start, that the need for a connection with the living world increases in the last decades of life. Looking back just a few generations, it is hard to find any example—in any culture—in which older people were not encouraged to partake of the comforts provided by close and continuing contact with plants, animals, and children. Indeed, these are connections that most adults manage without difficulty. Families the world over successfully keep pets, care for children, and tend gardens. Somehow, they do it all without policy committees, executive approvals, and regulatory waivers. Any sanctuary for elderhood must be able to do the same. It will be aided in this work by its small size, flattened structure, and a shared commitment to creating the most positive elderhood possible. The gifts of life, laughter, and companionship should themselves be at home inside elderhood's sanctuary.

It is necessary that a green environment facilitate contact with nature, but that is not all. Although we seem to forget this at times, human beings are part of nature, too. Being green demands a holistic perspective that includes distinctively human virtues. In his study of healing places, ancient and modern, Wilbert Gesler argues that when we think of illness, wellness, and healing we must expand our perspective so that it includes the role played by the symbolic and social environments that surround us. In order to be well, people need to have access to more than the wind, the moon, and the sun. People need to feel safe—to understand their place in the world and be able to participate with others in meaningful rituals. A truly green sanctuary for elderhood must participate in the realm of myth and spirit. It must be part of a new story we can tell ourselves about our longevity and those who live and work with elders.

There is one other meaning of the word *green* that must be considered. Elders have long served as stewards of their community's natural resources. It is in this capacity that they have long spoken for the seventh generation—the people who will not be born until long after the adults of the day are gone. There is a great need for this practice to be renewed in our materialist, use-and-throw-away society. Any sanctuary for elderhood should embody a concern for safe, sustainable use of natural resources. Doing so will strengthen the capacity of the elders to once again speak with authority in their efforts to ensure that the seventh generation will have what it needs to live in safety and security on this planet.

Every sanctuary for elderhood should be a healing environment that makes it easy for elders to partake of the gifts that regular meaningful contact with the living world has to offer. Sanctuaries should be designed and constructed so that they "rest lightly upon the earth" and honor elderhood's ancient commitment to stewardship.

Principles for Elderhood's Sanctuary

Warm: The ability to create and maintain human warmth is an essential attribute of any group that aspires to create a sanctuary for elderhood.

Small: All other things being equal, and with the full understanding that small size does not guarantee warmth, we can say that when it comes to creating a sanctuary in which elders and elderhood can develop, small is better.

Flat: Bureaucratic hierarchy obstructs the work of caring, as it is rightly understood. Human caring is founded on a knowing, empathic, resourceful response to the needs of another. For those seeking to sustain human warmth, a flat organization is better.

Rooted: When it comes to sustaining human warmth, there is no substitute for having deeply rooted beliefs.

Smart: Smart technology may be high or low, but it must always serve to foster the well-being of elders and those who live and work with elders. Technology (high or low) that restricts, confines, or diminishes elders for the convenience of others or damages their well-being must be abandoned.

Green: Every sanctuary for elderhood should be a healing environment that makes it easy for elders to partake of the gifts that regular meaningful contact with the living world has to offer. Sanctuaries should be designed and constructed so that they "rest lightly upon the earth" and honor elderhood's ancient commitment to stewardship.

THE GREEN HOUSE

What If?

There are two great injustices that must be dismantled if a new longevity is ever to take root in our society. First, we must overcome outmoded and dysfunctional ideas about independence and the hallowed role of the private home, which, no matter how lonely, isolating, and boring, is deemed to be the *only* acceptable place to live. Second, we must abolish the old-age archipelago and replace it with something very different. Witness the millions of senescents who are seeing ever more clearly that society has not prepared an attractive way of living into old age. Witness, too, the millions of elders who are trapped in suffocating, tightly managed total institutions. We cannot be free until they are free.

The opportunity here is to transform the *dream* of a warm, loving, nurturing sanctuary into a specific *innovation* that can change how we age. For centuries small groups of people have chosen to live cooperatively in communities of their own making. (Monasteries and convents of all kinds grew from this impulse.) These intentional communities did not rely on blood relations to hold them together. Instead, they depended quite successfully on a shared commitment to specific values and goals. Using this model as a guide, we can exchange the old-age archipelago for a society-wide sanctuary for elders and elderhood. Senescents, in particular, need to learn how to prepare a sanctuary for themselves, their friends, and the people they love. The elderhood that can take root in such places will do more than anything else to heal the wounds that afflict our society.

It is easy for experts in the field of aging to laugh at such assertions. They fully expect the current system, with appropriate modifications and improvements, to endure ad infinitum. I do not. There is a growing awareness that the buildings that make up the nursing home archipelago are themselves growing old. In fact, the buildings are aging much faster than the people who live within their walls. Most were hastily constructed; many were poorly designed. Now roofs are sagging, pipes are clogging, and maintenance expenses are rising. More and more nursing home operators are talking about gaining approval to build replacement facilities. I say no.

There is virtually no chance that the buildings in use today can survive to house the frail elders of the next two decades. Something will have to be done. We could, of course, rebuild them and then be made to suffer another four decades in the cruel embrace of the institution. More hopefully, we could use this moment to launch a revolution. This is our opportunity to put an end to the old-age archipelago. We can use the ideals of elderhood, rightly understood, and the principles of warmth, smartness, and greenness to create a successor to the long-term care system we have known in the past. We can leave Goffman's *Asylums* behind and embrace instead the millennia-old ideals of intentional community. We can take what we have learned from our experience with the institutionalization of our elders and use those insights to transcend that history. We can ask and then answer the question, what comes next?

◇

What comes next must represent a clear break with the past. A massive shift toward the deinstitutionalization of older people is called for, and the foundation for such a shift is being laid right now. A Green House is a sanctuary for a new kind of elderhood; it is an intentional community for people seeking the worth and meaning in late life. Whether they are fit or frail, "sharp as a tack" or living with dementia, the Green House has a place for elders. It generates human warmth through its commitment to small size, the de-emphasis of hierarchy, and the power of its belief in the genius of human longevity. The building and the people who share its spaces are dedicated to fostering a new elderhood.

The culture of the Green House is founded on distinct beliefs about aging and about the people who choose to work with elders. It employs an idiosyncratic vocabulary and cultivates patterns of behavior that reinforce its goals and ideals. Some Green Houses will be home to small groups of friends—people who see a benefit in joining together as they approach elderhood. Those Green Houses will be created by people who are searching, as humans always have, for a better way to live. Other Green Houses will offer themselves as a sustainable alternative to the institutionalization of the aged. Those Green Houses will face the challenge of serving, simultaneously, two conflicting goals. They will need to operate successfully within the regulatory and reimbursement schemes that perpetuate the old-age archipelago at the same time as they are expanding their ability to serve as a sanctuary for elderhood. This conflict will endure for the foreseeable future, and efforts to resolve it will play a vital role in the development of the Green House innovation itself.

Not surprisingly, the physical dimensions of a Green House resemble the typical home far more than any institution. Before the first-ever Green Houses were built in Tupelo, Mississippi, we asked Emi Kiyota to bring her expertise in aging-related architecture and design to bear on a single question: How do the elders of Tupelo make their own homes? Emi visited dozens of homes and took more than twelve hundred photographs. These images helped us think about what a Green House that served the people of Tupelo ought to look like. (The Tupelo story is told in an appendix in this book.) You can be sure that, rich or poor, none of these elders' homes in any way resembled either the stiff, pseudomedical aspirations of the conventional nursing home or the faux nostalgia that poses, at least for visitors, as a facsimile of home in facilities that house the aged. Because a Green House must be fitted to a particular time and place, its specific dimensions and layouts can only be derived from the way elders live in a particular locale.

Green Houses will foster a new longevity. Elders who would otherwise be placed in an institution can make a home there. Senescents can choose to enter its intentional community and, once there, seek the meaning, beauty, and worth that are the proper gifts of old age.

Culture

One of the most insidious aspects of the old-age archipelago revolves around the ways in which residents are expected to surrender autonomy and personal dignity as payment for their reliance on the staff. Nursing home residents are removed from the sustaining power of human community and, as inmates of an institution, are made to suffer losses in privacy, freedom, and choice. Feelings of depression, isolation, and worthlessness are pervasive and well documented. The usual response to such an assault on one's personhood is to retreat into learned helplessness and induced disability.

Here's how it works in practice. Staff members tend to be generous, benevolent people and they are quick to identify situations that will allow them to be helpful to residents. The problem is that the more often these functions are taken over by the staff, the less likely the residents are to do such things for themselves—and the more helpless they become. The staff, always eager to help, thus tutor residents in the art of helplessness. Ever-rising levels of "assistance" progressively weaken the elder even as they reward the staff with feelings of accomplishment and generosity. The result is a remorseless downward spiral.

The Green House is based on a different self-reinforcing cycle. It begins with the belief that elderhood exists. It presumes a right to late-life development that is an essential component of the human life cycle. Such growth, while undoubtedly difficult, can also be understood to have worth and meaning. Those who live in, work in, and care about a Green House share the duty to foster the emergence of late-life development within the daily life they create together. Institutional language, roles, and culture are surrendered in favor of the logic of intentional community. Declinism, a staple of the old order, gives way to a more complex and nuanced understanding of aging. Illness, grief, and loss are reframed. They become elements of an ancient way of living that gradually brings emotions and relationships to the center of an elder's experience.

The words and ideas that surround the Green House have special importance. Culture is no accident and it never misses an opportunity to reinforce its shared beliefs with the power of habit. Because new ways of thinking demand a new lexicon, Green House language has been designed to match its culture. This vocabulary, some of which may sound strange at first hearing, helps protect the Green House from a thoughtless return to declinism.

> **intentional community** *noun* A group of unrelated people who come together in order to share the deliberate pursuit of some noble aim. (Many, but by no means all, such communities have revolved around religious beliefs.) Intentional communities avoid excessive hierarchy and have a history of accepting into their midst those who have been cast out of society.

> **Green House** *noun* An intentional community for elders built to a residential scale and devoted to the pursuit of the most positive elderhood possible. The value of clinical services is recognized and is then made part of a habilitative social framework that gives primacy to human development in late life.

> **habilitation** *noun* The effort to bring forth existing but latent potential within a person or group of people. It is distinguished from *rehabilitation*—a term that presumes a defect to be rectified or a brokenness that must be repaired, whereas *habilitation* presumes wholeness.

> **well-being** *noun* This is a much larger idea than either quality of life or customer satisfaction. It is based on a holistic understanding of human needs and capacities. Well-being is elusive, highly subjective, and the most valuable of all human possessions.

> **elder** *noun* A person who, by virtue of age or life experience, has transcended or has the potential to transcend the limitations and shortcomings of adulthood; a mature person who gives precedence to BEING-doing in daily life.

> **elderhood** *noun* The state of being and living as an elder. It is founded on the developmental potential that is latent in late life, and is as distinct from adulthood as adulthood is from childhood.

care *noun* The common use of this term in the language of the institution has perverted the word's true meaning. In the Green House, the universe of care is defined as those thoughts, words, and deeds that contribute to the growth of the people participating in its community. Care can include but is in no way limited to medical treatments.

treatment *noun* The provision of expert diagnostic and therapeutic interventions, which are all governed by credentialed medical and nursing professionals.

rhythm of daily life *noun* The pattern of behavior that best enhances the well-being of the people in the Green House. Because this pattern can be known only by paying attention to the needs and preferences of the people directly affected, the household does not operate on a predefined schedule. Elders eat meals, bathe, sleep, rest, and socialize at times they choose. Elders can, if they like, participate in homemaking, including meal planning and preparation, gardening, caring for household pets, cleaning, and doing laundry. This rhythm is created by and evolved through household decisions made jointly by people living and working in the Green House.

to welcome *verb* Intentional communities take great care to ensure that new members are properly welcomed into their midst. To be welcomed is to become known and to be accepted as a full member of the community, with a right to speak and be heard that is equal to that of every other member.

to befriend *verb* To pursue a knowing and affectionate relationship with others. This requires a deliberate commitment to make oneself known to others and to be known by others. To befriend is to allow for the possibility of cherishing others and being cherished by others in the ordinary manner of the everyday.

The Green House offers the roots of a language that is liberated from declinism and from the legacy of enforced dependency. It is not an attempt to change the culture of long-term care because it rejects the very idea of long-term care. It offers instead an intentional community that is devoted to fostering late-life development. The rewards and difficulties of elderhood are acknowledged and the people who work with the elders are given voice in the work of creating and sustaining the life of the Green House's intentional community.

Organization

Elders and senescents who choose to make their own Green Houses can learn much from those who create Green Houses for the most frail among us. The language of the institution typically paints these most-frail people as passive receivers of professional services. The Green House takes a different view. Elders whose health has declined to a substantial degree are the same people they have always been; what has changed is the manner in which they collaborate with others. Their longevity has changed the nature of their daily lives, making close cooperation essential. Because the person is the same and only the needs have changed, every Green House must do all that it can to see that no elder ever has to leave simply because of increasing frailty. This commitment to aging in place entails the coordination of priorities imposed by those who are paying for the care (in many cases a government agency) and the Green House's culture of word, thought, and deed.

Most of the people who are placed in nursing homes live there simply because their needs are greater than what their family or community can provide. In the later years of his life, Pope John Paul II was, medically speaking, eligible to be admitted to a nursing home. He remained in his own home only because the Holy See had the funds available to meet his needs. Few families, however, can match the resources of the Vatican. Our collective obsession with diagnosis and treatment notwithstanding, the real reason people go to live in a nursing home almost always relates to a mismatch between their needs and the resources available to the people who care most about them.

The typical resident in a nursing home receives only a couple of hours of hands-on care per day, and just a few minutes of attention from registered nursing personnel. From a practical point of view, it makes sense to organize the experience of daily life in the Green House around the daily affairs of eating, bathing, dressing, sleeping, celebrating when we can, and grieving when we must. The clinical needs of the people living in a Green House, while admittedly important and sometimes even urgent, should not be imagined to be more important or necessarily more urgent than the pursuit of well-being.

The Green House can be organized along one of two basic lines: elder-initiated or organization-initiated. The elder-initiated house grows from the desire of a group of individuals to share living arrangements and the pursuit of the BEING-doing of elderhood. These houses will take many forms. Most will be organized by small groups of friends who are determined to enter elderhood together. The people who create elder-initiated Green Houses are likely, in the beginning, at least, to have relatively few medical or care needs. A Green House must, however, make arrangements to ensure that elders never have to face losing their place due to ill health. Otherwise, it is not a Green House.

The organization-initiated house will be created mostly by those who have been involved in some aspect of institutional long-term care and are ready to leave that era behind. These houses will be home to people who are likely to be very old and perhaps very frail and ill as well.

Whatever their genesis, all Green Houses use a similar organizational strategy. The terms defined in table 11 on the next two pages present the essential elements.

Our present system of housing and caring for elders is declinist to the very marrow of its bones. It prides itself on providing options for people at every point on the "going, going, gone" continuum, never pausing to reflect on what this sequence says about aging itself. The Green House does not accept the idea of this continuum. It is an intentional community and thus can nurture people of all abilities and disabilities. There will be a temptation to force the Green House into the usual scheme, something along the lines of "Green Houses— aren't they those teeny little nursing homes?" Or, more unexpectedly, "Green Houses—aren't those the communes for old boomers?"

In fact, the Green House is always willing to fly the most convenient flag available. If the circumstances call for licensing Green Houses as skilled nursing facilities so that a nursing home can be closed—permanently—then such licensure should be sought. (That is what happened in Tupelo.) In other situations, it will be better to

Table 11

Green House Organizational Structure

Green House Term	Organization Initiated	Elder Initiated
sponsoring organization	A sophisticated health-care delivery network that can ensure quality, provide expertise, organize back-up staffing, and deliver back-office support (e.g., account billing).	A group of senescents and elders who choose to create and then inhabit the intentional community of a Green House. They may form a corporate structure for legal and tax reasons.
constellation	A group of Green Houses all under the umbrella of a shared sponsoring organization. A Green House cannot exist in isolation. It must be part of a constellation that is itself linked to a sponsoring organization.	A large collective of Green Houses that rely on each other. The constellation fosters the well-being of each house in its range and benefits from a voluntary peer-to-peer support network.
clinical support team	An interdisciplinary team that includes the physician, the registered and licensed practical nurses, the occupational therapist, the physical therapist, the recreational therapist, the social worker, the dietitian, the speech therapist, and any other professionals needed by one or more elders. They are employed by the sponsoring organization and come to the Green House as honored guests. They embrace and are guided by the practices of home health care.	An interdisciplinary team that includes all of the health professionals on whom the elders of the Green House depend. The membership of this team will change as the needs of the elders change. The elders pay for their services just as they would if they had continued to live in their own homes.
guide	An adult nonresident employee of the Green House and the guardian of the culture of the Green House. The guide is part teacher and part preacher, advocating for the habits, beliefs, and practices of the Green House and defending against the intrusion of the old-age archipelago.	An adult nonresident employee of the Green House who can help the elders create the intentional community they desire. The guide coaches and mentors the elders to keep them on track as they develop and live in their intentional community.

Green House Term	Organization Initiated	Elder Initiated
sage	An elder volunteer who is living in the broader community, who understands the ideals of the Green House, and who has experience in helping small groups of people work out conflicts and make decisions. The sage has no operational responsibilities but can and does listen to those who live and work within the Green House.	An elder who is not living in the Green House but who is invited to participate in the life of the community. This volunteer brings the perspective and influence of an elder and helps Green House residents fulfill the tasks of elderhood.
social membrane	A barrier that delineates the social space inside the group from the rest of society. Large, impersonal bureaucracies have thick social membranes and discourage the easy movement of people and ideas into and out of its interior. The Green House cultivates the thinnest membrane that is consistent with the safety and well-being of the people who live and work there.	A barrier that delineates the social space inside the group from the rest of society. The Green House is not meant to be a one-house ghetto for older people who are afraid to live alone. It cultivates meaningful relationships with neighbors of all ages. It does not become a social center but serves the community even as the Green House is served by the community. Elderhood that does not touch the lives of its neighbors is not a worthwhile elderhood.
shahbaz	A person who works in a Green House with elders and is dedicated to (1) the enlargement of the skills and capacities that are latent within the elders, and (2) the pursuit of the most positive elderhood possible. A shahbaz is the midwife of a new elderhood. *Plural:* shahbazim	A person who works with elders once the capacity for mutual caregiving within the house has been reached.

operate along the lines of assisted living. Many more Green Houses will take root in neighborhoods and apartment buildings brought to life by elders themselves and carrying (at least at first) no special licensure. With regard to licensure and organization, the Green House is agnostic: it uses the regulatory and economic system that is most congenial to its mission of creating a sanctuary for elderhood. But always remember . . .

- A Green House that is licensed as a skilled nursing home is not a nursing home—it is a Green House.
- A Green House that is licensed as an assisted living facility should not be confused with such a facility—it is a sanctuary for elderhood.
- A Green House that is licensed as an adult home cannot be defined in only those terms—it is first and always a Green House.
- An elder-initiated Green House that closely resembles a family dwelling is no such thing—it is an intentional community, dedicated to fostering the most positive elderhood possible.

Elderhood blooms or withers in the context of daily life. Conventional long-term care regularly dismisses bathing, eating, and dressing as necessary but labor-intensive tasks. In contrast, the Green House relies on these necessities as primary sources of meaning and worth. (I will say more about this later.) An African proverb holds that it takes a village to raise a child, and in that same spirit we could say that it takes a community to grow an elder. Whatever legal forms it may operate under, the Green House serves as a vessel for just such an intentional community.

Environment

There is a staggering sameness in the design of long-term care facilities all over the industrialized world. The similarity derives in large part from a nearly universal emphasis on operational efficiency. The financial and organizational power that accompanies that goal will always tempt those who create Green Houses with the siren song of size and economy. After all, we have spent four decades "perfecting" the design of long-term care facilities, and the consensus of most experts in long-term care is that small intentional communities for elders cannot be cost-effective. The design of the Green House must face up to the difficulties of creating operational efficiencies without resorting to the logic of a large institution. The legacy of the nursing home may not be able to tell us what a Green House should be, but it can show us what it must never become.

The architecture of long-term care facilities reflects—in steel, brick, and tile—their fundamentally medical intention. Though the term *homelike* is often invoked, nursing home design actually gives its most careful attention to maximizing the efficient use of labor. Owners and operators of new and refurbished nursing homes take great pride in their equipment and facilities and, when a staff member gives a tour to a family member, these features are highlighted. The people who work there—often overworked, usually underpaid—are given far less attention.

These buildings give those within their walls little reason to suspect that elderhood can be a rich, rewarding phase of human development. Long corridors disable frail people, forcing them into wheelchairs. Massive dining rooms are impersonal and intimidating and promote anxiety. There is limited access to outdoor space. Double rooms (laughably called "semiprivate" rooms) and shared bathrooms invade privacy. Furniture, floor coverings, and drapery are matched consistently throughout, as if the place were a chain hotel rather than the home it is meant to simulate. The grim institutional appearance damages the well-being of staff and residents alike.

Rural, suburban, or urban, Green Houses are dwellings that house six to ten people. They belong in residential settings and should be good architectural neighbors. Some will be built into high-rise apartment buildings; others will be free-standing houses. Whatever form they take, there should always be as little distinction as possible between a Green House and the other housing nearby. In an ideal situation, a person looking for a Green House might pass it by because it is so inconspicuous. Inside the building, furnishings and decorations reflect the preferences of the elders of that community.

Elders fill the house, to the greatest extent possible, with their own furniture, art, and decorations. At its best, the interior of a Green House closely resembles the homes of other elders in the vicinity.

We know that people find pleasure in the company of animals, the laughter of children, and the growth of green plants, so every Green House must offer elders opportunities to be in contact with the living world that surrounds us all. We also know that privacy is important to life satisfaction, and so the design of a Green House must ensure that privacy is plentiful. In fact, every elder must be able to have his or her own room. Because they are smart, these houses take full advantage of unobtrusive technology that promotes well-being. Ceiling-track lifts help create a safe environment that is good for elders and helps protect the people who work with them from injury. Communications technologies can improve health through tele-health and tele-nursing. The intelligent use of adaptive devices helps those living and working in a Green House be more at ease.

During the years I searched for the best design elements for a Green House, I visited many people and places. All of them influenced me. In Saskatoon I was fascinated by the Sherbrooke Community Center and inspired by its village model of community living. In Boston I toured the Hearthstone facilities created by John Zeisel. As we bumped and juddered over the city's back streets, he told me that *focus* was Latin for "hearth." When we focus on something, we make it the center of our attention. The hearth is the center of a home, the place around which we arrange our living. Every Green House must have a center, a hearth around which the affairs of daily living may be arranged. Our deepest cultural memories suffuse the hearth with the twin pleasures of food and fire. The hearth includes an open kitchen and a large table around which meals are shared. The importance of having such an arrangement is confirmed by research showing that people living with dementia benefit from taking their meals in communal settings. Because the hearth is the center of the design, each elder's room opens onto this space. There are no long corridors.

Professional nurses enter into and work within the Green House using the home health care metaphor and thus have no need for a fixed base of operations. Indeed, there is no evidence of the permanent presence of professional nurses. The nurses' station, long a fixture of the long-term care institution, has no place in a Green House. The medication cart is obsolete because elders' pills are kept in their rooms. There is no treatment cart and no chart rack because such things would be out of place in a private residence. The people of the Green House counter the tendency to medicalize their home by asking, "Can we find this in our neighbors' homes?" If not, then its use in the Green House must be seriously questioned. It is important to remember, though, that the Green House is not a private family home. Its design is meant to support a distinctive form of intentional community. It is a vessel that sails through time, taking the people who share its spaces ever further into the realm of elderhood.

A
WINK
and a
SMILE

*Our society must make it right and possible for old people not to fear
the young or be deserted by them, for the test of a civilization is the way
that it cares for its helpless members.*

Pearl Buck, *My Several Worlds*

MIDWIFE OF ELDERHOOD

The Possibilities of *And*

While I was homeschooling my oldest son, it came time to teach him about chemical reactions. He understood that elements were the building blocks of chemical compounds but found it hard to believe that an explosive metal (sodium) and a poisonous gas (chlorine) could unite to make the salt he sprinkled on his french fries. Even more amazing, the two elements themselves would remain unchanged. What is new is the bond they have created with each other. It seems like magic, but it is even better than that—it's chemistry.

Fortunately, the workings of miraculous combinations can be found in the social world as well. Think of the singer and the song. Each can exist without the other, but each is diminished without the other. The classic song "Summertime" has been performed by many great singers.

> Summertime,
> an' the living is easy.
> Fish are jumpin'
> an' the cotton is high.

What would this song be without its greatest singers? People such as Billie Holiday, Ella Fitzgerald, Al Green, and Janis Joplin took words and a tune, joined their voices together with them, and brought forth something new. Nor are they the only ones capable of such alchemy. These kinds of pairings are all around us when we know where to look. Think of the conductor and the score, the game and the player, the poet and the rhyme, the actor and the role. Neither is the miracle confined to the worlds of sports, art, and music. The mother brings forth the child; the child brings forth the mother. The teacher instructs the student; the student educates the teacher.

These pairs are sometimes mistaken for opposites. They are actually complements—they complete one another. The error of mistaking them for opposites is a function of our general preference for the simplicity of having either A *or* B. We find the clash of opposites much easier to understand than the complexities that arise when we combine A *and* B. Ideas, in particular, are apt to be transformed in surprising ways when they are set free from the limited logic of opposition. The Christian instruction to "turn the other cheek" comes to mind. It fuses the polarity of *love* and *enemy* with revolutionary consequences. Today we are struggling with the cult of adulthood's insistence that people must be *either* independent *or* dependent. This tyranny damages our longevity and constricts our imagination. There are other possibilities—much better ideas that are capable of transforming childhood, adulthood, and elderhood. To find them we need only open our minds to the possibilities of *and.*

Beyond Independence

A human being cast away from society is as frail and vulnerable as a honeybee separated from its hive. The pain and suffering that accompany forced isolation are well understood and have long been a subject for art and literature. One of the first novels to examine this form of grief was *Robinson Crusoe,* by Daniel Defoe. Published in 1694, it remains a frightening tale of life lived outside the embrace of human society. Washed ashore after his ship is broken on the rocks, Crusoe's joy at surviving soon gives way to a bottomless grief. He is alive but condemned to a wretched life of loneliness and longing. In his anguish he tears at his clothes, pulls out hanks of hair, and pleads with God to let him die.

But he does not die. His survival is ensured when he salvages a trove of ironwork, rope, planks, firearms, gunpowder, shot, canvas, seeds, and tools from the hold of the ship. Even though he is alone on the island, it is the work of the gunsmiths, smelters, carpenters, weavers, and loggers of his homeland that make his survival possible. If circumstances had denied him access to the fruits of their labors, *Robinson Crusoe* would have been a short story rather than a novel.

Defoe's novel reveals and then strips bare the mythology of independence. His Crusoe gives ceaseless attention (devotion that would put a colony of honeybees to shame) to the mundane work of repairing, strengthening, and expanding the delicate fabric of his existence. His struggle is plainly at odds with the cinematic myth of the mountain man who seeks, and is somehow sustained by, the shelter of having no shelter. Any island castaway would be enraged by the Hollywood hero's insistence that true independence is being able to leave society behind. In terms of that myth, Robinson Crusoe was as independent as any human is ever likely to be. Day and night for thirty years he dreamed of being rid of that terrible independence.

Myth: *Being independent means relying as little as possible on other people.*

Reality: *Being independent means being able to define the manner in which one cooperates with others.*

The myth of independence is dangerous because it leads away from the truth of life. As members of the human species, we must cooperate or die. Dismissing our genius for working together, and instead lauding the myth of independence, gives rise to a perverse fear of dependence. For those who spend time thinking about longevity, but especially for the aged themselves, *dependence* is a dirty ten-letter word. And, like the concept of independence, it is subject to deliberate distortion.

Myth: *To be dependent is to be compelled to rely on others for the most basic necessities of life.*

Reality: *To be dependent is to be human. We all rely on others for the necessities of life. The form this reliance takes adds to or detracts from our well-being.*

The myth of independence and the misconceptions it has spawned serve the cult of adulthood. After all, those who come to worship independence are certain to fear dependence. The myth conveniently highlights the strengths of adulthood, showing adults in a flattering light that gives them little cause to question its distortions. Meanwhile, the fear of dependence becomes a razor-wire fence. Our dread of becoming a burden to others does more than anything else to keep older people securely confined to the realm of adulthood. We can avoid being imprisoned by these ideas if we allow ourselves to acknowledge the simultaneous truths of our dependence *and* independence. The word that is usually used to signify such a unification is *interdependence*. As human beings, we live by and through ceaseless cooperation with others—it is our destiny. The nature of our cooperation with and relationship to others changes as we grow, mature, and then age.

Vigorous adults ordinarily give little thought to ideas of this kind. Instead, they pride themselves on not needing anything from anybody. Being needy as a result of economic or emotional poverty is the surest way of diminishing one's standing in adult society. The stigma attached to being needy has also laced our longevity with a poisonous distinction. The aged can be independent (which is very good) or dependent (which is very bad); there is no other choice. The maintenance of this duality damages people of all ages and is the foundation upon which the cult of adulthood rests.

Because the myth of independence plays to the strengths of fit and vigorous adults and seems to offer a perfect validation of the doctrine of youth's perfection, it can be very hard for adults to imagine beauty and fulfillment in any circumstance that renders people, even temporarily, dependent. Fortunately, though, there is a life passage, common in adulthood, that can illuminate the richness of interdependence. The drama of pregnancy and birth exposes the myth of independence, albeit temporarily, and allows us to glimpse both the folly of pure self-reliance and the virtues hidden inside our complete and inescapable dependence on others.

Waiting to Be Born

The fear, pain, and exertion that accompany childbirth should never be confronted and surmounted alone. Hollywood mythmakers will never green-light a film about a brave corporate executive who, seeking complete independence, treks high into the mountains so that she can give birth unaided. Pregnant women have little use for the rhetoric of independence. They and their children have always relied on others for their safety and well-being. During the twentieth century, the practice of obstetrics made childbirth much less dangerous and far less painful than it used to be. Still, as any mother can tell you, plenty of pain and risk remain. Strange as it may seem, a look back at the recent history of childbirth can help us develop a new approach to aging and elderhood.

By the middle of the last century, the advantages of an intensively medicalized approach to childbirth were thought to be so complete that traditional ideas about birthing were dismissed or even actively condemned. It seemed, for a time, that the ancient practice of midwifery might disappear entirely from modern industrial societies, leaving only the obstetricians and their gleaming metal instruments. Fortunately for us all, this did not happen.

I attended many births during my family practice residency in the 1980s. At that time, there was a running battle between the family physicians, with whom I was allied, and the obstetricians, who were in charge of the labor deck, as it was then known. Both groups of physicians agreed that labor and delivery should be safe and carefully monitored. The conflict revolved around what the *experience* of the childbirth should be like. The obstetricians looked at parturition (the fancy medical name for childbirth) and saw a specialized surgical procedure. The family doctors, not surprisingly, saw a potentially meaningful event in the development of the family. The basic standards of medical practice were settled; the dispute was one of emphasis.

The debate that raged within the medical staff of the hospital went something like this:

Family doctors: "Natural childbirth is a safe alternative to
    conventional obstetric practice."
Obstetricians: "Is not."
Family doctors: "Is so."
Obstetricians: "Is not."
Family doctors: "Is so."
Obstetricians: "Is not."
Family doctors: "Is so."
    Repeat *ad nauseam.*

To the surprise of many, this conflict was resolved not by the medical profession but by expectant mothers and their families. Social pressure for a safe but far less medicalized approach to childbirth overwhelmed the specialists. Now the birthing center has replaced the labor deck in every corner of the country. American mothers and their families no longer tolerate stirrups, leather restraints, glaring lights, and gleaming tile. Now hospitals and doctors boast of their ability to make childbirth a safe *and* richly rewarding experience.

Whenever we despair of the possibility of liberating our elders, we should remember that the forces of history tower over organizations like the American College of Obstetrics and Gynecology. The revolutionary changes that transformed childbirth during the last quarter century were the product of two distinct social trends. First, advances in medical technology improved obstetric safety and outcomes. This relative feeling of safety is an important part of what made the new emphasis on the quality of the birthing experience possible. Second, a new generation of women (many but not all of them members of the baby boom) began to challenge the authority of doctors and question their rigorously clinical approach to labor and delivery. They sought out ideas and practices that were in harmony with their own beliefs about childbirth. These changes sparked a revolution that catapulted an obscure French obstetrician named Fernand Lamaze to worldwide fame. No longer would women be forced to choose an emotionally fulfilling experience *or* the medically sophisticated safety of obstetrics. Families could have both.

Understanding the rise of natural childbirth can help us renew our longevity. All of the forms and practices of natural childbirth can best be understood as a reformulation of the millennia-old legacy of midwifery. Lamaze succeeded because he embraced traditional ideas about birthing *and* clinical obstetrics. In the process, he created something new. The renewal of midwifery in the late twentieth century did not seek to restore the birthing practices of long ago. Few would ever have accepted such a dangerous step backward. Instead, it became a hybrid of old and new, different from anything that had come before. We are now preparing for a similar revolution that will transform elderhood and the lives of elders the world over.

Because traditional aging has always placed responsibility for the aged inside the family, there is no direct old-age equivalent to the midwife. Mitigated aging—with its morbidly negative view of old age and its fixation on the brokenness of the elderly—has presumed to have all the answers the aged need. Represented at its extreme by the old-age archipelago, mitigated aging is marching us all toward an old age defined by disease, disability, and death. This orientation is responsible for much of the dark pessimism that currently surrounds the idea of growing old. Fortunately, we can find hope in social conditions that increasingly resemble those that inspired the revolution in childbirth. The pattern is eerily similar:

1. Advances in technology are shown to outperform traditional practices and beliefs.
2. Long-established habits are overthrown and replaced with a shiny new technocratic regime that is run by professionals.
3. Popular revulsion against the new order grows and eventually matures into a direct challenge to professional practice.
4. Advocates for change wisely reject a simple return to old ways. Instead, they seek a fusion of old and new. The result is transformational social change that alters the terrain of society as a whole, often in profound and unexpected ways.

Perhaps more than anything else, old age needs its own midwife, someone who is prepared to be with older people as the familiar terrain of adulthood recedes into the past. We need people who can guide others toward the best elderhood possible. Seen from the proper vantage point, the prospect of enduring the rigors of old age without such assistance can be as daunting as the experience of giving birth alone. After all, labor and delivery last only hours, whereas elderhood (which is much more dangerous) extends for years, even decades. Like the midwife of childbirth, the midwife of elderhood will be a person outside the family who earns the family's trust and respect. Old age is and will remain difficult. Given the complex dangers and opportunities that define elderhood, we would do well to cultivate people who can help elders negotiate its passages.

One Million Strong

In the past, the nearest our society has come to creating a midwife for elderhood has been the development of frontline workers in the long-term care industry. However, that experience has fallen far short of almost everyone's expectations. The low pay, low prestige, and difficult work that define this occupation have led millions of these people to seek employment in other fields. Staff turnover in the nursing home industry is a staggering problem, averaging about 100 percent yearly and running as high as 400 percent. Inadequate staffing is a constant problem.

Like mining, deep-sea fishing, and logging, the business of long-term care is an extractive industry. Whereas those other industries measure their success in tons of ore, tons of fish, or board feet of lumber, the success of long-term care comes from its ability to extract good will and generosity directly from its own employees. As with all extractive enterprises, there is a limit to what can be taken: the long-term care strip mine now yields much less of the human heart than it used to. Increasingly, people are saying no to work as low-paid functionaries in sterile, unfeeling institutions. The nursing home can no longer depend on a steady flow of undemanding, extremely generous nurse aides, housekeepers, and dietary workers. More and more people now enter into this work unwilling to freely offer the gifts of compassion and tenderness that have so often saved the nursing home from itself. Much has been made of the age and archaic nature of the buildings that are used for nursing homes. Far more important and much less well recognized is the corrosive nature of the industry's labor practices.

The workforce crisis is being blamed on the millions who, despite their affection for elders, are choosing not to work in the old-age archipelago. Foundations, governments, and corporations in the long-term care arena are all investing large sums in workforce recruitment and retention strategies, with few of those strategies showing any signs of success.

The problems of staff absenteeism and worker shortage and dissatisfaction persist even though we already know what people who feel a calling to be with elders need in their work. Research supports each of the following staff needs:

- Advanced training
- Permanent assignment
- Involvement in decision making
- Self-managed work teams
- Better pay

The industry has been trying to fill a sieve. It cannot bring itself to completely reconstruct the role given to those who have a hands-on relationship with elders because doing so would destroy the dependency-based management strategy that animates the old-age archipelago. The duality of "staff" and "resident," which is a cornerstone of the institution, must be dissolved before a twenty-first-century elderhood can come into existence. In its place we need a holistic concept that is large enough to contain both elders and the people with whom they cooperate.

For tens of thousands of years, children, adults, and elders were sustained by a complex multigenerational interchange that occurred predominantly within the context of the family. Despite the advantages of that tradition, we no longer have the luxury of fostering exchanges between young and old solely within the family. In its place, we must develop an approach that embraces midwifery's legacy of extrafamilial reciprocity. While the midwife helps bring forth the child, mothers and their children, over the decades, return the favor by leading the midwife toward mastery of her craft. In just this way, those who cooperate with elders as they negotiate the challenging passages of elderhood must, in turn, be nurtured by the elders with whom they work. They need each other. They complete each other. This approach goes far beyond rewriting job descriptions and instituting empowerment programs. It requires a revolution. We will be witness to the rise of a new pattern of collaboration in old age that will dwarf the changes we saw in childbirth in the twentieth century.

Our society needs a hundred thousand Green Houses, intentional communities within which the gifts of elderhood can be given and received. We must also bring forth, in the first half of this century, one million midwives of elderhood. This will be an epic effort, with its own stories and heroes.

The First Shahbaz

The Myth of Origin

I once had the opportunity to work with a small group of people who were interested in developing new programs and services in the field of aging. Over the course of several meetings, the participants laid out their projects, goals, and ambitions. In particular, I remember Nora Gibson. She told us of her dream of creating neighborhoods capable of keeping elders at home. Her ideas were just taking shape and she struggled with the definition of what a "neighborhood" is or should be. Near the end of our time together, it became clear that the words she was using to describe these neighborhoods were not conveying the richness and depth of what she had in mind. Her ideas needed to be clothed in narrative language. She needed a story that could explain exactly what she meant.

There was a lull in the conversation and an older woman, a Catholic nun who had said little up to that point, spoke up. She told the story of the founder of her order—how, more than a century earlier, this woman had been seized by a passion to serve others. She told the tale the way, I am sure, it had been told a hundred thousand times over the course of a century. When she finished, the group was silent. We had just received the very essence of the founding myth. The story was powerful because those who heard it understood at once the source of this woman's calling, her work, and her place in the world.

The story was a gift to us all but especially to Nora; she left the session with her energy renewed and a commitment to find and then tell her own story.

Those who would dedicate themselves to helping others grow into the most positive elderhood possible must have their own myth. I offer what follows as their story, the tale of the first Shahbaz.

SHAHBAZ THE FALCON

NOBODY GETS THROUGH LIFE WITHOUT TROUBLES, but there was once a king who got himself into a terrible fix. He wasn't bad, just a man who lost his way. Nothing new there. Plenty of people, kings and commoners alike, head straight into trouble—often without a single look back. This man did stop to think, and that made all the difference.

The land the king ruled was far from the sea, far from the overland trade routes, far, it seemed, from any place anyone wanted to be. Still, his subjects were a sturdy lot. They endured, meeting hardship with a laugh and a smile whenever they could. The people comforted each other with the old saying "A poor man living in peace is better off than a rich man in the midst of strife." Deep inside, they held the hope that someday things would get better.

Early in his reign, the king kept to his father's custom of moving among the people, listening to their stories, laughing at their jokes. He held court so that the people could seek justice from him. But the temptations of power proved too great. Gradually, he set the old ways aside. He began staying up all night, scheming with his ministers and playing the lords and ladies against each other. Heavy black curtains were hung over the windows in his room and he slept until noon. Every day, after lunch, he called for his falcon and went hunting. This he loved above all else. At dinner, his belly full of ale, he would often roar, "Shahbaz!" for that was the falcon's name. "Shahbaz has never failed, and that is more than I can say for any of you."

Life got worse, not better. The kingdom grew disorderly. Fights broke out. Bandits prowled the ridgetops and forests. Brother turned against brother, friend against friend. The people became afraid, and Shahbaz saw it all. Her keen eyes found a house in flames, a woman crying, a child dressed in rags. She returned each day with game for the king's table, but something was changing inside her.

One day as she wheeled through the deep blue sky, Shahbaz saw an old man stumbling in a thicket. He had been chased from the roadway by a band of brigands and now was lost. Shahbaz lifted her left wing and arced slowly toward him. As she drew closer, she could see that he was cowering in fear. A mountain lion had cornered him and was preparing to pounce.

Now, for the first time, the falcon's heart filled with compassion for a human being. This warm feeling melted all doubt. Shahbaz tucked her wings and dove. Streaking out of the sky like an angel of mercy, she thrust out her talons and buried them in the lion's neck. The beast roared as it struggled to free itself from the falcon's grip. Teeth, claws, beak, and talons whirled in a terrifying struggle until, at last, the lion surrendered. Shahbaz released her grip and took flight; the lion fled in terror. The man was bewildered by what he had seen but thankful for his safety. Shahbaz returned to the king but had no game for his table. He berated her, not noticing how worn and weary she appeared.

The next day the king went out to hunt with Shahbaz on his arm. In the midday heat, he released the tresses and the falcon took flight. Immediately, she set a course for the place where she had protected the old man. She found him even farther from the road. He had wandered into a ravine where there was no food or water. The afternoon sun beat down on him. Again Shahbaz brimmed with compassion. Putting aside the task the king had given her, she descended from the sky and landed in front of the astonished man. Shahbaz was made mighty by the power of her loving-kindness, and she knew just what to do. With a short hop, she came to a large stone. With her beak she struck the stone—once, twice, thrice. The rock split open and water—clean, cold water—flowed from its depth. The thirsty man drank.

Shahbaz took wing and hunted, returning to the old man with game. Then, before leaving, she approached a pile of brush, striking it with her beak once, twice, thrice. With that, it burst into flames. Having sustained the man with food, water, and fire, she took wing and returned to the waiting king, having once again failed to supply the king's table.

"Perhaps I have been feeding you too well," he snapped. "A night without supper might focus your mind."

The next day the king went as usual to the hunting grounds and released his falcon. She hurtled skyward and sought the lost man. The search was long and difficult, and she feared that he had died. At last, she glimpsed him in the distance. Weak with hunger, she made her way there. He was alone and in despair. As Shahbaz settled down on a branch, he looked up at her through tear-filled eyes. The remarkable creature who had fought off a mountain lion, fed him, and given him water and a fire had returned to him.

Thinking that perhaps this magical creature might understand his grief, he poured out his heart to Shahbaz. His brothers were dead, as were his wife and their children. He had been seeking his father's village when the bandits had attacked him. He and his family had suffered greatly in this time of violence and disorder, and it was all due to that fool of a king. As the great falcon listened, loving-kindness stirred once more within her breast.

Moved by the man's story, the falcon now found the gift of speech. She spoke of knowing love and loss. She spoke of all that she had seen in the many years she had soared above the kingdom. She told the man not to despair; she knew the way to his ancestral home. She stayed with him through the night, lulling him to sleep with stories of the great and noble people she had seen and known. When the morning dawned, she took flight and led the man to a stream that flowed into the river that lay beside the village of his father. This done, she returned to the king's castle.

Alighting on the castle wall, she found the king preparing for a hunt—with another falcon on his arm. As the hunting party went forth, Shahbaz moved to a low branch that hung over their path. The king saw her and condemned her loudly as an unworthy traitor. Shahbaz, he said, no longer deserved to be known as a royal falcon. Another bird could take her place—it did not matter to him. The king's fury was great, but Shahbaz did not stir. Instead, she fixed him in her gaze. Finally, his rage spent, the king turned away.

Then Shahbaz spoke: "I have watched you and I have watched your kingdom. You think highly of yourself, but you have ruled poorly. The people suffer; they cry out from fear, from hunger and thirst. They are lost, and yet you hear them not."

The king and his men listened in stunned silence. Then a royal counselor cried out, "This is an abomination. No such beast should have the power of speech; this is surely the work of an evil hand. I plead with your majesty to destroy this foul creature at once." At this, an archer drew his bow and aimed at the falcon.

Shahbaz did not flinch; she kept her keen, unwavering gaze upon the king. Silence hung in the air, and then she spoke again: "You are not a bad man. You could do much for the people of this land, even yet. But you must change."

Again the counselor cried out for permission to kill Shahbaz. The king waved him off. In the long, stony silence that followed, the king's mind returned to his youth. He remembered the peaceful days of his boyhood when he first went hunting with his grandfather and the great man's royal falcons. Soothed by these memories he, at last, allowed her words to enter his heart.

Shahbaz offered the king a partnership. She and her kind would sail the skies above this land, seeking always to protect, sustain, and nurture the people. The king would put down his scepter and his crown and become a royal falconer, devoting himself to the training and well-being of the royal falcons.

With time, the man who had been king became a skilled falconer. All of these great birds came to be known by the name of the first, each a shahbaz. This is how the people of this land found peace and comfort at last. Whenever they looked into the great blue sky, they could find a shahbaz there. The days of the king and his servants passed from memory and a new partnership—between the people and the royal falcons—came into being and endures even to this day. No one can remember a time when the morning light did not reveal a shahbaz circling high overhead.

Shahbazim

The conviction that we need a new framework around which to organize the experience of those who protect, sustain, and nurture our elders came to me early in my exploration of longevity. Much more challenging was the selection of a name for the people who would pursue these goals. I ransacked dictionaries in search of an English word or phrase that would convey the proper meaning. All of the words that might have served the purpose were tangled up with meanings that reinforced the tyranny of dependence and independence. I finally chose the word *shahbaz* precisely because it is unfamiliar. It is a Persian word that means, literally, "royal falcon." More than a few people have argued that the word is too strange, too foreign, and too unfamiliar. (This in spite of the fact that English has borrowed many words from Persian, including the very familiar *paradise* and *bazaar*.) While there is a price to be paid for such unfamiliarity, the word does free us from the sediment that has accumulated around English words such as *worker, assistant,* and *helper*.

The story of the original Shahbaz is the founding myth of a new way of being with and working with elders. The story dramatizes the transforming exchange that occurs between the old man and the falcon. The bird protects, sustains, and nurtures the elder even as the elder brings forth from the falcon new strengths, new powers, and new capacities. The result of this collaboration is the overthrow of a dysfunctional status quo. Together, the old man and the falcon bring about changes that make life better for all those in the kingdom—including the man who had been king.

In the modern industrial economy, the kinship group, in its stripped-down nuclear form, can no longer serve as the sole source of support for elders. Increasing numbers of families now rely on a non-familial system of therapists, services, and organizations. The people who work within this system are often generous and big-hearted, but the organizations themselves do not know love, cannot know love, and, indeed, reject the idea that love could form the basis for a reconsideration of our longevity. The rigorous application of professionalism and therapy expels love from the experience of elderhood.

The demand for what we now know as "paid caregivers for the elderly" exceeds the supply of people willing to do this work, and the imbalance is growing. This shortage is a direct consequence of the long-term care industry's perverse habit of confining good people within narrow task-driven jobs. They are asked to perform extremely challenging work at low pay and with little security. In exchange for a meager paycheck, they are expected to give themselves completely to their work and the people they serve. A shahbaz, in contrast, is a big person in a big job. Not only does a shahbaz protect, sustain, and nurture elders as individuals, a shahbaz also cooperates with elders to create a new society-wide understanding of elderhood. The elder and the shahbaz go together like a wink and a smile. Some of the people doing this work, like the falcon in the story, will begin as dutiful servants to an ungrateful king. The power of loving-kindness transformed a falcon into a mythic creature with the power to change its world. It will do the same for the people who choose the way of the first Shahbaz.

The plural of *shahbaz* is *shahbazim* (shah-bah-ZEEM). It, admittedly, sounds strange to the English speaker's ear. The *im* ending is drawn from Hebrew, whereas the root *(shahbaz)* is Persian. The mixing of these two languages is deliberate. The shahbazim are, themselves, something new. They draw on and contribute to many traditions, professions, and patterns of belief. They are allies of the new elderhood and will stand shoulder to shoulder with the nurses, doctors, and therapists whose skills also contribute to the well-being of elders. Their myth of origin makes their intention clear: They will "sail the skies above this land, seeking always to protect, sustain, and nurture the people."

THE PROBLEM OF PROTECTION

An Unpredictable Path

Becoming a midwife of elderhood is much more challenging than becoming a midwife for pregnant women, because old age is far more variable than pregnancy and childbirth. Thankfully, nearly all pregnancies follow a predictable pattern. The midwife understands and is well served by an in-depth knowledge of the stages of labor. Newborn babies are also very similar to one another (even if their parents don't see it that way). As a result, the midwife of childbirth nearly always walks away from a healthy baby and mother.

Becoming an elder, in contrast, is an extraordinarily diverse process. One woman will reach her eightieth year and remain spry, another will have lost her memory but be physically fit, still another will struggle to care for herself even as she works the *New York Times* crossword puzzle. In addition, the midwife of elderhood has little historical and cultural experience with extrafamilial support for people living in old age. Longevity offers us many paths, no two the same. But the outcome for the midwife of elderhood is always the same— different from that of the midwife of childbirth, but no less important.

The shahbazim go about the work of creating the most positive elderhood possible with three aims in mind. They, like the falcon of the story, are devoted to protecting, sustaining, and nurturing others.

The first of these three duties is the most controversial. The declinist vision of old age has too often transformed the noble idea of protection into a suffocating pattern of control. To understand why this is so, and how the "duty to protect" became a point of fierce dispute within the long-term care community, we need to revisit some important points in the history of protecting the old.

The Senior Citizen

Adults who deny the existence of elderhood actively oppose the concept of special rights for the old. Adulthood, with its attendant rights (and those rights are glorious), is said to offer sufficient protection for all adults no matter what their age. To think otherwise undermines the cherished "adulthood forever" fiction. Even so, age matters, and given the way declinism has been used against the aged, many older people have decided that the best defense against ageism is to deny that age is ever relevant. The idea of a vibrant elderhood as a *distinctive* continuation of a lifelong developmental process is but a murmur next to the extraordinary chorus of millions of older people proclaiming their devotion to permanent active adulthood.

The ancient idea of a community that *includes* elders conflicts with the modern vision of a society that happens to include people who, through no fault of their own, are "differently aged." Viewed from this perspective, the declaration that "the shahbazim have a duty to protect the elders with whom they work" seems demeaning and superfluous. Special treatment for elders, long a precious dividend of longevity, is being cast aside in favor of uniform treatment for all.

When the privileges of age are exchanged for a place at the adult bargaining table, older people must lobby ceaselessly for their fair share. To its credit, this strategy has ensured that the levers of a democratic society remain within their reach. The flaw, however, is fundamental and, I think, irremediable. It creates a ceaseless demand for civic engagement, lobbying, and competitive struggle. This necessity snares the old in the thicket of political struggle.

When the role of elders in society is converted into interest-group politics, the most frail, the most ill, and the most demented are also the most likely to lose. Whether they live in a remote tribal society or a modern nation-state, elders should be one step removed from the flying elbows, the cursing, and the struggle that accompanies adult politics. By driving people away from elderhood, contemporary society transforms our older people into just one of many competing special interest groups. All of them are eager to get their share—and more, if possible. The rules of the game require that they muster the greatest possible strength for the fight, and no quarter is given. Instead of an elderhood that is a source of cultural preservation and growth, the aged are reduced to the status of interest group.

As people, elders are best served when they are known as individuals. The problem is that no government can know each elder as a person. It can only respond to the aged as a class—in this case a class whose members qualify for predefined entitlements. Individuals seen in this way cannot be considered elders of their communities. Instead, they must settle for the role of "senior citizen."

Tie Your Mother Down

The advocacy-driven approach to aging forms an understandable but inadequate response to a ravaging ageism. This approach succeeds when it ensures that older people have at least as many rights as younger people but fails when it can't grasp the meaning and worth of what lies *beyond* adulthood. This focus is responsible for much of the harm that is being done to older people in contemporary society. Without a true elderhood to protect them, the rights of the aged can too easily be overwhelmed by the rights of more powerful groups. This injustice has played itself out with tragic consequences in the subjugation of the ill and frail by the medical and nursing professions. The relationship between the medical, nursing, and social work professions and the elderly is a tangled skein of good intentions gone bad.

To their credit, these professions have long recognized the special conditions of old age and the very real need for benevolent protection. Each discipline has carefully documented the limitations, impairments, and disabilities that come with advancing years. While their observations are surely correct, the conclusions they have drawn are terribly wrong.

That the "helping professions" have placed themselves above the community is evident from the language they use to describe their work. They serve the community the way a president serves the people. They *meet the needs of* the community. They *provide care to* the elderly members of the community. On first reading, this comes across as a dedication to service and the general betterment of society. Hidden in these sentences, though, is a proud insistence that professional techniques and technology exist outside the community and are thus to be governed only by the professionals themselves.

This distinction might seem to be nothing more than semantics until we look closely at a situation in which the ethic of professional autonomy played itself out with disastrous consequences for our elders. Exhibit One in the case against relying on professionals for the protection of elders is the not-yet-extinguished practice of tying older people to beds, chairs, and railings. For decades intelligent, empathetic professionals refined the bizarre logic of "physical restraint." Fancy vocabulary aside, their efforts amounted to the rationalization of bondage for the geriatric set.

Being restrained against one's will, even by a benevolent authority, violates a basic human right. This plain truth was papered over with the argument that, however unpleasant the locks and straps might be, they served the greater good of protecting older people from injuries related to falls. The concern was easily justified; a fall can be a serious, even fatal event. Hundreds of thousands of older people (possibly including someone you loved) have perished after falling. An ounce of prevention, the professionals argued, is better than a pound of cure, especially when the stakes rise to the level of life and death.

Professionals of all stripes came together in a common cause to persuade elders (along with their wives, husbands, brothers, sisters, sons, and daughters) that tying them to their beds was both right and necessary. I have been in many meetings in which well-trained, compassionate nurses soothed the qualms of family members with the honey of their professional authority. When that did not work, those who resisted the use of restraints were treated to a full measure of professional and organizational disapproval. Few could resist such power.

In the end, the argument for holding the elderly in physical bondage relied on the idea that the restraints protected older people from injury. A professional, hands on hips, would proclaim that restraint use was necessary because "my license is at stake if he falls and hurts himself." The professional duty to protect was given clear precedence over the patient's right to dignity and freedom of movement. The decision to use physical restraints was removed from the realm of personal choice and transferred to the standards of practice that every nurse and doctor was duty bound to uphold. Those standards were clear, and as onerous and undignified as the restraints might be, their use was justified by the "fact" that they saved lives. This placed families at a permanent disadvantage in any discussion about restraints. Lay people rarely prevail against the weight of professional opinion.

The argument for physical restraints crumbled as evidence accumulated that these devices killed, injured, and humiliated far more people than they helped. The professionals were wrong. Dead wrong. The result was a loud, angry, prolonged struggle that is not yet fully resolved. While the professionals debated the wisdom of retreating from their established position, thousands of people were strangled by restraints that were intended to protect them. Millions of others were stripped of their dignity as they pleaded with staff members to untie them and take them to the toilet. Still, committees parsed the language of new professional standards. The evidence accumulated, the body count rose, but many professionals continued to label the "restraint-free care" movement as a softheaded initiative led by uninformed and irresponsible laypeople.

The struggle over this question remains intense. Even after more than a decade of debate, people are still being confined against their will in nursing homes all across America. The numbers are decreasing, but restraints remain a fact of life in thousands of facilities. Given the intensity of the struggle and the fact that it is not yet won, it should not come as a surprise that the battle to eradicate restraint use by those who work with elders has created a stinging resentment of the supposedly benign protection afforded by "professional standards."

The shahbazim have a duty to protect the elders with whom they work. Now it might be easier to see why these words, spoken at a gathering of advocates for elders and elderhood, provoked angry dissent. People recoiled from the idea of giving any group a paternalistic license to protect and thereby govern the lives of elders. Like generals who always seem to fight the last war, we risk getting bogged down in past debates and losing sight of the essential truth that elders need and deserve our protection. The debate over physical restraints and the dominance of professional opinion has obscured the richness that does exist within the concept of protection. When understood correctly, protection can be an important part of fostering well-being and enriching the lives of those engaged in late-life development.

We do have access to another form of protection, one that is much more subtle. Protection can, in fact, be given and received among equals. This approach is founded on the principle of reciprocity rather than on the helplessness of the frail in the face of adult vigor. Human beings are easily moved to protect what they value and come freely to the defense of that which is dear to them. Millions have given their very lives for their faith, their rights, and their way of life. These intangibles are protected because they are cherished. We must employ this ethic as the basis of our own protection of the elders we cherish.

The contrast between the two forms of protection can be seen in the waiting room of any family doctor's office. Near the window sit an aging mother and her daughter. The daughter is at ease and takes pleasure in her mother's company. The ravages of age and disease are acknowledged and accepted for what they are. The daughter anticipates and moves to meet her mother's needs quietly and unobtrusively. Protection is offered and received subtly and with grace. This makes the exchange easy to overlook.

By the door, and hard to miss, are a querulous daughter and her agitated mother. The daughter makes note of and then broadcasts each of her mother's failings. She deliberately draws attention to the burden she has shouldered and seeks approval for the difficult work of contending with her mother's decrepitude. This display is deliberately made public because it reinforces their change in status. The daughter is in charge now and no one (least of all her mother) will be allowed to forget that.

Coming to the aid of a person as an equal ennobles both parties. The crucial difference, and the one that cleaves the issue plainly for the shahbazim, is the difference between doing something *with* another person and doing something *to* that person. We are entitled to do things *to* those who are subordinate to us, while we are obliged to collaborate *with* those who are our equals. As adults, the shahbazim are very different from the elders with whom they work. That difference is the basis for a rich collaboration—not a rationale for control.

Living in the Real World

With this distinction in mind, how should a shahbaz use the "duty to protect"? Elders should be protected from unnecessary illness and injury, but such efforts must be limited to practices that dignify both the elder and the shahbaz. Two questions must be asked and answered over and over again:

- Does this protection enlarge the capacity of the elder to experience the richness of elderhood?
- Does this protection promote the development of the shahbaz?

These are not difficult concepts. When we encounter them in the context of childhood education, they have the ring of common sense. Just imagine what would become of a teacher who protected children from playground injuries and taunting by tying them to their desks during recess. The scandal would make headlines. It is the very fact that children are cherished that protects them from such degradation. The shahbazim give protection and are repaid in the currency of human growth and well-being—the elders' and their own. *Shahbazim have a duty to protect the elders with whom they work.*

Convivium

Wants Versus Needs

The elements required for human survival are simple and few. A person can get along with a couple thousand calories a day, a liter of water, a sprinkling of vitamins and minerals, and a steady supply of air to breathe. Shelter that offers protection from the extremes of the weather and predatory activity (human and animal) is important as well. More than we might suppose, though, human life also depends on easy access to affection. It is affection that brings meaning and purpose to the mundane affairs of daily life.

Even after many years of working with older people, I continue to be amazed at the way advanced age prunes the overgrown wants and desires of adulthood. Very old people rarely, if ever, covet material symbols of status, rank, and wealth. Chasing after the totems of adulthood grows wearisome with age and is often given up entirely. Those living in the late decades of life are not like the young. They can easily be content with far less than what the average adult demands. Still, we hear the constant and often bitter complaint that the needs of the elderly are bound to bankrupt us. The old, some say, are a luxury the young can ill afford.

Ageist rhetoric aside, what can we say about sustaining our elders? This is a question that a shahbaz studies carefully. The second duty of the shahbazim (the first being to protect) is to sustain the elders with whom they work. Fulfillment of this duty requires an understanding of what makes life worth living.

Food

Some people eat to live. Others live to eat. Those in the first group regard food as fuel; those in the second group know better than that. Good food has always offered people much more than just calories, fat, carbohydrates, and protein. At its best, food nourishes us—body and soul. A meal can embody powerful symbols of love and acceptance. The bond between comfort and food, which begins at the breast, is fortified throughout childhood and gains renewed strength in the late decades of life. Properly prepared, the meals we cook and serve to our elders should be drenched in memory, ritual, and culture.

Reacting to case reports of actual starvation among nursing home residents, the government has established significant penalties for facilities that allow residents to lose weight "unexpectedly." As a result, nursing homes struggle constantly to increase the dietary intake of their residents. Just how challenging a task they have undertaken becomes obvious when you look at how these facilities prepare and serve food.

They shop from industrial food catalogues and unload the groceries from a tractor trailer parked at the loading dock. Meals are prepared in vast industrial kitchens that are deliberately isolated from the people who will eat what they produce. Some long-term care facilities, like airlines, outsource food production entirely and take delivery of dinners by the truckload. In a down-to-the-minute ballet, food is rushed upstairs in huge rumbling carts. Staff members distribute it to waiting residents as quickly as they can. It is a never-ending challenge to serve hot food when it is still hot and cold food when it is still cold.

The people involved do their best. The realities of large-scale food service demand, however, that the material characteristics of the food—its color, viscosity, temperature, and nutritional content—become its most important descriptors. The emphasis on consistency and low cost is constant. Food is shorn of meaning, leaving only numerical measurements. The lifelong rhythm of good food shared within the circle of family life is absent. It is just not possible to imbue six hundred meals a day with the essence of love.

The Romans had a special term for the particular pleasure that accompanies sharing good food with people we know well. They called this experience *convivium*. The word has enjoyed a revival recently. The "slow food" (an alternative to fast food) movement has seized on the word as a way of describing dining experiences that are rich in meaning. Fresh, local ingredients prepared according to authentic regional recipes are served to people eager to share. They use smell, taste, and texture as a springboard to good conversation and vital relationships. The shahbazim foster a convivium that enriches the lives of elder and shahbaz alike.

The relationship between people and the food that sustains them begins with the planning that by necessity must precede each meal. The idea that meals can and should be planned with loving care and then prepared with loving hands will strike the typical food service manager as little more than wishful thinking. For the rest of us, it is simple common sense confirmed by our own experiences in our own homes. The suffering created by the industrialization of food in long-term care institutions deserves more than passing attention. Nursing homes are canaries in the mine, warning us of the assembly-line approach to food that is spreading across our social landscape. We are all losing our grip on convivium. Institutions may be able to blame their mechanical approach to food on their own gigantic size, but we can see the erosion of convivium all around us, even in our own lives.

The ability to create and maintain convivium demands an appreciation of the long, languorous meal and is one of the core competencies of a shahbaz. Time must be taken because food tastes better when it is soaked in anticipation. Elsewhere, soup may be purchased in bulk, heated, and then served. The shahbaz insists that soup be made fresh and be allowed to simmer all morning long with ingredients added slowly as the hours pass. In an institution, mealtime is a mad rush. For the shahbaz it is an opportunity to create and then deepen meaning. The spirit of convivium calls upon us to linger, to savor, and to draw strength not just from the food we are blessed to eat but also from the people with whom we are blessed to share our meal.

Shelter

The conventional long-term care facility has struggled with, but never satisfactorily resolved, its split personality. As Mr. Hyde, it poses as a home. In its propaganda, the long-term care facility tells its staff members that "this is the residents' home; we just work here." Meanwhile, Dr. Jekyll maintains, with full professional authority, that the facility is actually a "health care services workplace." Despite the rhetoric about home, Dr. Jekyll rules this roost. The proof is easy to come by. Just watch the employees and note the way they control space, time, and people in their building. Imagine a similar group of well-meaning professionals entering your bedroom while you are sleeping and carrying on their work without regard for your desire for privacy or rest. Staff rules.

I highlight this conflict because in a time when protecting people from wind, rain, snow, and the heat of the summer sun poses little challenge, the real difficulty lies with creating an effective social shelter. In an affluent society, housing is available to all but the most unfortunate (and could be made available to them as well). A social shelter, though, is much more difficult to come by. The tension between the formality of the institution and the ease of a home is familiar to a shahbaz. Just as the shahbaz transcends "food service," choosing to practice convivium in its place, the shahbaz has a similar devotion to the art of homemaking.

Few social institutions have fallen as far and fast as homemaking. Once the object of glorification (as a female pursuit), homemaking is now belittled. Many no longer regard it as a legitimate pursuit for skillful people. The identification of homemaking with unpaid female labor inside the nuclear family too often served as a prop for the sexist denial of equal rights for women in the workplace. The sustained attack on homemaking as an unnatural sexist institution has created its own collateral damage. It has obscured some of the craft's very real virtues. There is much to be gained by retrieving homemaking from the ash heap of history (or at least popular opinion), dusting it off, and putting it to a new use.

Affection

By medicalizing old age, the cult of adulthood has degraded an ancient commitment to sustaining elders. The injection of massive government funding into the field of aging has benefited millions but has also forever altered the family's relationship with its elders. Long-term care's obsessive concern with medical treatment springs from society's deliberate equation of aging with illness. In the early 1960s, advocates for the elderly faced a situation in which millions of older people were both poor and sick. They made a strategic decision to channel needed resources through the health care system rather than the welfare system. Medicare and Medicaid were given dominion over the care of the aged, and these programs pumped trillions of dollars into improving the health of older Americans.

Along the way, a powerful industry has grown up around these programs. Being fed by health care dollars, this industry has little reason to imagine that the most important aspects of elderhood might have little to do with medical and surgical therapies. So complete is the medical-industrial domination of aging that people who need long-term assistance can be compelled, for purely economic and political reasons, to live out their lives within the sick role, tended to in medical facilities.

This is how the concept of "professional distance" came to be injected into the lives of millions of elders. An unquestioned assumption held by millions of professionals, this idea holds that unnecessary closeness and undue affection for patients is to be avoided. Doctors and nurses have long held that personal attachment to a patient could cloud one's thinking and lead, at a critical moment, to an error of judgment. This logic continues to reign, virtually unquestioned, in the acute care and hospital sectors of our health care system. Even so, it is spectacularly ill suited to the needs of our elders and those who work with them.

Rightly claiming that the aged are much more likely than the young to fall ill, health care professionals continue to perpetuate the fallacy that old age is mostly a medical problem. The need for medical and nursing services is assessed with precision and then used to justify payments made by the government to the long-term care facility. As I have noted, the need for health care services is rarely if ever the only reason an elder is made to leave home and enter an institution. The old, like the young, do fall ill. But, unlike the young, the old can be compelled to make illness the center point of their lives. Old age, like all the other phases of our lives, should be about life and living.

Treating aging as a medical condition that must be managed with the professional distance prescribed by the medical model is wrong and leads to terrible suffering. Virginia Bell and David Troxel have written powerfully about this in their book *The Best Friend's Approach to Alzheimer's Care.* They argue persuasively that the proper metaphor for organizing our thinking in this area is not the distant clinical reserve of the professional but the open and engaged warmth of a best friend.

Shahbazim develop their relationships with elders within the distinctly nonmedical framework of befriending. This perspective creates daunting challenges that require both skill and maturity to overcome. The idea of befriending elders is sure to raise the hackles of medical professionals. They can object, with some justification, that encouraging the bond of friendship between elders and shahbazim opens a door to abuse and manipulation. Preventing "overinvolvement" and manipulation of residents by facility staff members is one of the primary aims of the medical model of care. Anyone who has worked, even briefly, in a long-term care facility knows how diligently the boundary between staff and residents is patrolled.

Even so, the deliberate separation of residents from the staff creates its own brand of suffering. Imagine yourself surrounded by people ostensibly pledged to care for you but discouraged from knowing you as a person. Nor are they permitted to share their humanity, their story, with you. Imagine living with a burning thirst and being denied the crisp, cool water that is kept intentionally just beyond your reach.

There is one other objection that can be raised against befriending as an organizing concept for the shahbazim. Getting close to elders who are, admittedly, themselves close to the end of their lives is said to be a prescription for burnout. Professionals tell us that, as much as they might like to do so, they cannot afford the luxury of having deep feelings for people under their care. Because this work demands that they spend a great deal of time with frail and elderly people, having emotional attachments to patients could lead to a paralyzing grief with each death. This notion turns the "It is better to have loved and lost" adage on its head and concludes, quite forcefully, that it is better not to have loved at all.

Recent surveys of people who work with elders have found that the number one reason people stay in the field is the opportunity to create and sustain meaningful relationships with elders. This is a remarkable finding, considering that the weight of professional practice and regulatory enforcement is balanced against this tendency. It hurts to lose a friend, but the pain of not befriending is even greater. The true cause of burnout is the deadening effect of closing one's emotions to people who are in obvious need of a human connection. Human life is sustained by affection.

The purest form of friendship is found among equals. So it is with the shahbazim. They leave the cloak of professional authority and distance for others to wear, knowing that they are and will remain the equals of the elders. *Shahbazim have a duty to sustain the elders with whom they work through the practices of convivium, home-making, and befriending.*

THE TWOFOLD PATH

Self-Actualization

The psychologist Abraham Maslow's gift was explaining clearly what we all know intuitively. A person does not live on bread alone, not even when it is fortified with vitamins and iron. It is the fulfillment of needs for food and water that call forth a desire for safety. The person who feels free from danger yearns for love and affection. The person who knows love pines for the fulfillment of his or her truest self. This makes a tidy package that, while powerful in its simplicity, overlooks an important element of a life well lived.

Life, as it is lived by the elders I have known, reveals a different dynamic. While the basic human need for food, water, and shelter can be met in innumerable ways, it is *how* these needs are met that determines the quality of one's life. Imagine two women, each of whom consumes the same number of calories, grams of fat, and milligrams of vitamins. The first is fed under the supervision of a registered dietitian in the large dining room of a local nursing home. The second eats at the table with her family and chooses among her favorite foods at each meal. Scientifically speaking, their intake is the same. Spiritually, there is no contest. The second woman is nourished not just by the food but, much more importantly, by the way that food is prepared, presented, and consumed.

Maslow contends, rightly, that basic needs must be met before other needs can emerge. Elders teach us that, at least in an affluent society, it matters a great deal how those most basic needs are met. This relationship is strongest for those in their last years of life. People hurry through the tasks of helping elders bathe and dress, eat and drink, with the hope (usually unfulfilled) that, at the end of the day, there will be time for meaningful, enriching activity. Lost in the rush is the idea that bathing, dressing, eating, and drinking can themselves become instruments of self-actualization. They are not, as they are often imagined to be, time-wasting necessities. Buddhists claim that chopping wood and carrying water can transport one to enlightenment. A shahbaz knows that meaning and worth can be found within the most basic routines of everyday life.

Most adults find it difficult to think of self-actualization as a relevant goal for older people in general, let alone for those who are struggling with disease, dementia, or frailty. Old people can do so much less than they could when they were young, and these changes lead easily to the misconception that the potential for growth has disappeared as well. In fact, the development that is characteristic of elderhood relies on the virtues of BEING-doing rather than the frenetic activity of DOING-being. Adult preoccupations make it difficult for many to appreciate the contribution that BEING-doing makes to well-being.

Shared Development

A shahbaz recognizes that a healthy human community needs both DOING-being *and* BEING-doing. The merging of these forms of experience is healthy, and every shahbaz needs to develop the skill in their Green House. The true value of BEING-doing can be learned from the elders themselves if the shahbazim pay close attention to the lives the elders are living in the Green House. Even people living with advanced memory loss and physical decline retain a surprisingly robust capacity to experience the world through being. The busy shahbazim serve as beacons for the elders—reminding them, through their actions, that all of us must continue to value the doing that living requires. Elders and shahbazim have within their relationship a shared opportunity for growth, satisfaction, and even self-actualization.

Though we like to suppose otherwise, the richest forms of human development are most available to those willing and able to interweave their needs and their potential with the needs and potentials of others. The oldest of the old have always been our most important teachers. They instruct us not with words or memories of times long ago; they teach us with their selves. As time leads them to rely ever more closely on others, they offer us the opportunity to care for them. They bring into our lives the realization that all life is precious. Through them, we begin to understand how caregiving makes us human. We remember, generation after generation, that there is a vital and never-to-be-forgotten distinction between the withered husk of the body and the beauty of the human being that body still shelters.

I delved into the question of a midwife for elderhood because elders and elderhood cannot and should not be considered in isolation. It is true that most older people manage well enough on their own, content with their waning independence and not needing or wanting help from others on a day-to-day basis. But this book is not about individual satisfaction. It is about our society, the lives we make with and for each other, and the direction we are moving as a people. It is about human liberation.

We know that the old way of being old is passing away. Ancient understandings about elderhood are crumbling under the assault of adulthood. At the same time, we are being tempted by a new faith in medical technology and pharmaceutical laboratories. The most disastrous conclusion we could reach would be that our longevity can be embraced as an individual phenomenon—a race against time that must be run, and lost, alone. There are, all around us, enlightened adults who are eager to remind others that elderhood (and with it, true longevity) can only exist as an active exchange between generations. Any consideration of aging that does not include all parties to those transactions is doomed to failure. *Shahbazim have a duty to nurture the elders with whom they work.* The shahbazim need the elders. The elders need the shahbazim. Together they can renew the ancient virtues of elderhood.

The adults who choose to enter actively into this exchange should be precious to us. We honor those who teach children even though nurturing the young is an ordinary act, common throughout the animal kingdom. Nurturing elders is an extraordinary achievement. Alone among all the species that live or ever have lived on Earth, *Homo sapiens* nurtures its elders. This work is the source of our finest achievements. More than anything else, it is what makes us humans.

The Work of Shahbazim

Shahbazim have a duty to protect the elders with whom they work. They always ask, "Does the protection that I am offering—
- enlarge the capacity of the elder to experience the richness of elderhood and
- promote the development of the shahbaz?

Shahbazim have a duty to sustain the elders with whom they work. A shahbaz—
- practices the art of convivium,
- values the craft of homemaking, and
- honors the act of befriending.

Shahbazim have a duty to nurture the elders with whom they work. They know that—
- fulfillment can be found within the most basic routines of everyday life,
- the shahbazim need the elders and the elders need the shahbazim, and
- together they can help renew the ancient virtues of elderhood.

The
RIPENING

Ripeness is all . . .

William Shakespeare, *King Lear*

Elderhood Reborn

Choosing Elderhood

Our culture declares that adulthood is forever, that old age means decline, and that perfection is lodged in remaining young. These great lies stand behind all the propaganda against aging and longevity. The truth is that old age is difficult, but it is essential because it teaches us how to live like human beings.

Our society needs a reconstructed elderhood that can serve as an effective alternative to the conspiracy of adulthood. We cannot return to the old age of the hunter-gatherers, and we are especially ill served by the nostalgic haze that surrounds our views of traditional aging in agricultural and pastoral societies. Mitigated aging has done much to lessen pain and suffering in old age, but as the inspiration for institutional long-term care, its defects have been made plain in the bleakness of the nursing home and the dread that fills all who enter there. Clearly, an elderhood that is capable of saving our future and our world must transcend the limits that have defined aging in the past.

Fortunately, art and imagination have been preparing the way for historic change. For well over a century, poets and sages have reflected on what old age could be and have dared to imagine a new old age. Together they have prepared a vision of aging as a *continuation* of human development. We can trace this vision from Alfred, Lord Tennyson to Barry Barkan to today's writers and researchers.

Tennyson's "Ulysses"

In his poem "Ulysses," written in 1842, Alfred Tennyson presents a new kind of elderhood. A complex work with many classical allusions, "Ulysses" explores two related themes. The first stanzas consider the turbulence created by the emerging industrial economy. The last half of the work addresses the question of old age. Tennyson's linkage of these two themes showed extraordinary foresight. He understood that modern society could both shatter tradition and create the possibility of something entirely new. Through him, and for the first time, we can see an elderhood that goes well beyond the pale shadow of an uncomplaining grandfather.

> . . . I will drink
> Life to the lees: All times I have enjoy'd
> Greatly, have suffer'd greatly, both with those
> That loved me, and alone, . . .

This poem imagines and offers us something we could not have anticipated—an old age with its own claim on greatness, an elderhood kindled by the spark of a life lived. What, after all, could mere youth know of passions savored, of possibilities examined, explored, and now remembered? This is greatness founded on decades of experience with both joy and sorrow. This is the taste of life drunk to the lees.

> Little remains: but every hour is saved
> From that eternal silence, something more,
> A bringer of new things; and vile it were
> For some three suns to store and hoard myself,
> And this gray spirit yearning in desire
> To follow knowledge like a sinking star

It is the fact that the end of life is near that makes time so precious. "This gray spirit yearning in desire" links old age with its own pursuits. Here, at last, we savor knowledge and knowing without the adulterations that spring from youth. Tennyson celebrates a passion that only a dawning sense of mortality can awaken.

> Old age hath yet his honor and his toil;
> Death closes all: but something ere the end,

Some work of noble note, may yet be done,
Not unbecoming men that strove with Gods.

Old age makes its own demands on us, which should not be confused with the work of youth. This work may be noble and befitting "men that strove with Gods." Time takes much from us, but it also presents us with new paths to greatness.

. . . Come, my friends,
'Tis not too late to seek a newer world.
Push off, and sitting well in order smite
The sounding furrows; for my purpose holds
To sail beyond the sunset . . .

This impulse to seek a newer world is part of a larger faith in progress and in human development. Tennyson asserts that such progress is not only possible but also essential in the last years of life. The evening of a life worth living reveals many things, few of which youth can know. There is much to learn beyond the sunset.

Tho' much is taken, much abides; and tho'
We are not now that strength which in old days
Moved earth and heaven, that which we are, we are;
One equal temper of heroic hearts,
Made weak by time and fate, but strong in will
To strive, to seek, to find, and not to yield.

"That which we are, we are" is a perfect expression of the dualistic nature of elderhood. It is heroic in ways that Achilles (who craved glory but was ignorant of life's true depth) could never understand. An elderhood so full of passion must be yoked to new ends. It transcends the worn husk of adulthood and searches out new ways of knowing, being, and feeling. The goal may not be, should not be, to move heaven and earth. The struggle is to move the self. It is to plumb the depths of the old in search of the new.

Barkan's Definition

One hundred forty-four years after Tennyson published "Ulysses," Barry Barkan wrote "The Live Oak Definition of an Elder." I do not know what inspired Tennyson to write his poem, but I do know how Barkan found his definition of an elder. Born in Brooklyn in 1942, Barkan was, at first, an unlikely candidate for sage of a new elderhood. He got his start as a journalist working the civil rights beat, first for UPI and then for the Richmond, Virginia, *Afro-American* newspaper. He left the paper in the late 1960s to devote himself to "The Egg Cream Coliseum," a drug and alcohol rehabilitation program he created that was housed in a soda fountain shop. By 1972, Barkan had moved to Berkeley, taking with him a deep faith in two ideas: first, that people in need must be a vital part of any attempt to meet those needs, and second, that the creation of an intentional community is a powerful tool for the regeneration of the human spirit.

Fortune favored us all when Barkan brought these ideas to the world of aging. He committed himself to the work of restoring to the aged a meaningful role in our society and our communities. He foresaw that the people of his generation would, in the decades to come, form the largest and most influential group of elders the world has ever seen. In 1976, Barkan imagined that this age boom could be instrumental in creating regenerative communities on a vast scale. Such communities would serve all people, regardless of their age. One day, after a long sojourn in Live Oak Park, he composed "The Live Oak Definition of an Elder." The words remain fresh and insightful more than a quarter century after they were first written.

> An elder is a person
> Who is still growing,
> Still a learner
> Still with potential and
> Whose life continues to have within it
> Promise for and connection to the future.

Barkan begins by restoring elderhood to its rightful place in the human life cycle. Longevity, far from diminishing a person, gives forth its own promise and potential. He then confronts the declinist interpretation of aging. Elderhood creates a new potential for growth that must be declared and then protected. The last line uses the language of commencement. Because healthy beginnings always draw on the goodness of what came before, Barkan repeats the word *still*.

All that was, remains; still there is more to be experienced, more to be known, more to be felt.

> An elder is still in pursuit of happiness,
> Joy and pleasure
> And her or his birthright to these
> Remains intact.

The definition moves on to the political realm, echoing the Declaration of Independence and the powerful heritage of natural rights. Barkan proclaims that the elder retains, in full measure, all of these rights. The body, in old age, will be transformed. The force of time is sure to batter and break the powers of youth. The inalienable rights of the elder, however, remain undimmed. The human being possesses a sacred nature that is not weakened, not harmed, not marred in the slightest degree, no matter what age may do to the body. Happiness, joy, and pleasure, Barkan astutely observes, can be made available to all of us no matter how tired or worn the body and mind might become. The importance of this claim needs to be emphasized in a time when science provides the means to extend life despite advanced age and physical infirmity.

> Moreover, an elder is a person
> Who deserves respect
> And honor
> And whose work it is
> To synthesize wisdom from long life experience and
> Formulate this into a legacy
> For future generations.

The definition closes with a summary of the ancient transaction that lies at the root of elderhood—passing on a legacy. Barkan restates the declaration of personhood and then turns to what is due to the elder. He advocates a respect for elders that is active rather than passive. These are not good manners or, heaven forbid, good customer service. Instead, he presents the vibrant, living transaction that has been part of the human experience for millennia. Elders have a role to play, one that is centered on the legacy they will leave for future generations. The experience of a life lived provides the raw material for a legacy of wisdom that can benefit future generations. Barkan deftly rescues elderhood from the realm of charity and forbearance and restores it to its rightful place as the greatest of all human achievements.

Barry Barkan has devoted his life to bringing this definition of an elder to life in the context of something he calls "regenerative community." An elder himself now, his definition rings with integrity just as it did the first time he formulated it under the spreading branches of a live oak tree.

Developmental Aging

Our attitudes about and approaches to longevity reflect a jumble of conflicting and overlapping ideas and beliefs. I wouldn't have it any other way. Old age is the time of life when similarly aged people are most different. Aging in modern society is not one thing; it is many things, many beliefs, many practices. Any single theory of aging is sure to be flawed because the phenomenon it seeks to describe is so diverse. That said, it seems possible to offer a unifying theme that allows us to examine critically the many different ways of understanding our longevity.

The concept of developmental aging allows us to see old age as part of the ongoing miracle of human development. It offers a perspective that connects all elements of the human life span from birth to death. The fetus becomes the newborn, the infant becomes the girl, the girl becomes the mother, the mother becomes the grandmother, the grandmother becomes the elder of her family and community. For tens of thousands of years, our mastery of age and aging has enabled the human species to reach beyond its grasp. Aging has propelled the development of the human being from the beginning.

Unexpected Insights

This sequence is being threatened now by an out-of-control adulthood's assault on childhood and elderhood. However, conditions for the overthrow of the cult of adulthood have never been more favorable. Each and every day we are cultivating the potential for the greatest generation of elders the world has ever known. Helping these millions recognize the possibilities of life beyond adulthood will not be easy. Sadly, many will cling to adulthood for the rest of their lives. I believe many more will come to see themselves as elders and accept the crucial role that elderhood must play in a truly just society.

A society that cultivates the ability to bring a life worth living to the least among us enriches itself beyond measure. When we honor those who can do nothing for others, we enlarge a capacity for compassion that serves all people. A person who willingly sets aside the clatter of adulthood and enters deliberately and specifically into a life beyond adulthood becomes a beacon of hope to others.

It is relatively easy to imagine a growing cadre of socially engaged older people who are willing and able to dedicate time, money, and energy to leading positive social change in our society. The fog of declinism, however, makes it much more difficult to see how people who have been labeled "old" and "frail" could contribute to this effort. Any honest accounting of the potential influence of elders and elderhood must also address the contributions that people who are weak, ill, infirm, dependent, demented, disabled, and dying can make to this struggle.

The old and frail are able to surmount the dizzy bustle that clings to the young—to enter a time and place in which the spiritual and emotional dimensions of human life are wholly precedent over the humdrum workings (and failings) of organs, tissues, and systems. This is among the most admirable of all human endeavors. What the old and frail do is show us the way and provide us with greater insight into and a clearer perspective on the human condition.

I remember giving a speech about new perspectives in aging and long-term care in Anchorage, Alaska, one snowy January afternoon. I had worked my way through the ideas and projects I was engaged with at that time and, near the end of my presentation, made the observation that "Alzheimer's dementia is a tragedy." After I finished, I was approached by a young woman who wanted a word with me. She thanked me for my remarks and went on to say that among her people (she was a native Alaskan) dementia was viewed as a gift rather than a tragedy. This observation rocked me. She said that when an elder living with dementia made reference to seeing and speaking with long-dead relatives, it was taken as proof that the elder had been gifted with the ability to have "one foot in this world and one foot in the spirit world."

As a physician, I had been accustomed to thinking of Alzheimer's dementia as a severe and ultimately fatal degenerative brain disease. This assumption can be shown to be accurate and even useful (for example, when searching for new drugs). It is not, however, the *only* way to see people living in this way. After I returned home from my trip, I began asking a question that was new to me. What if the people living with dementia were actually experiencing an unusual (and admittedly abnormal) form of development?

This line of thinking led me to see people living with dementia in new ways. What I had understood as a "progressive decline" in memory could also be defined as rapid rise in the power of forgetting. Older people, much more than the young, recognize that the ability to forget can bring us just as much happiness as remembering ever will. People living with dementia (who are supposed to have memory defects) actually soar over those of us who lack their power to forget. Perhaps not coincidentally, they also inhabit the state of BEING-doing much more comfortably than those who still treasure doing, getting, and having. It is possible to reinterpret the experience of living with dementia as an unusual form of accelerated development (something like the fifth-grade boy who is six feet tall) that propels people toward a state of being that few of us will ever live long enough to achieve on our own.

The point is not that people should aspire to a diagnosis of dementia; the normal course of aging is surely preferable to such a life. Instead, we should use this example as a reminder of how easy it is to dismiss the oldest of the old as having little or nothing to contribute to our understanding of life. The belief that a particular group is worthless and lacks a full measure of humanity has proven to be exceptionally dangerous in the past and could lead to tragedy in the future if we are not careful. In fact, rather than dismiss the oldest of the old, it is our duty to open ourselves to the diverse forms their wisdom takes.

Advocates of antiaging would likely shrug off my reinterpretation of dementia as being beside the point. After all, there is no need to bother with such questions when technology is close to rendering aging itself obsolete. Antiaging promises us the precise opposite of human development; it offers a longevity that is divorced from aging. Eager to believe that technology can strip old age from human existence, antiaging cares little for the consequences of such an act.

Science has long proven its ability to turn the seemingly impossible into a daily reality. Who knows? Perhaps someday we will stumble onto a twenty-first-century fountain of youth. Such a success would come, however, at a price far greater than we could afford. In destroying elderhood, we would discard the truth of fifty thousand years of human experience. In contrast, developmental aging seeks the unification of aging and longevity, understanding that each needs the other, each enriches and informs the other. Our longevity grants us a magnificent opportunity to age. Aging brings depth, richness, and meaning to our longevity. Together, they are humanity's most treasured possessions.

Table 12
The Triumph of Aging

Traditional Aging	Mitigated Aging	Antiaging	Developmental Aging
Old age is both a blessing and a burden.	Old age brings mental and physical decline.	Old age is unnecessary.	Elderhood is difficult (but so is all of life).
The aged should be respected.	The aged are entitled to high-quality medical and surgical treatment.	The young should resist old age with all means possible.	Elderhood is a vital and necessary part of the human life cycle.
The aged should be stoic.	The aged should lobby for access to resources.	Technology has or will have the means to conquer old age.	Elders need the highest possible level of health in order to develop properly.
Care for the aged is a family responsibility.	The obligation to care for the aged is shared by the family and the government.	Perpetual youth will eliminate the problem of caring for the aged.	There is an ancient and dynamic exchange that goes on between elders and their families and communities.

On Being an Elder

Late-Life Developmental Tasks

The idea that elderhood should have developmental tasks would seem to contradict the very idea of an old age rich in *being*. In fact, *doing* is and must remain (until the last breath is drawn) an element of every human life. For adults, the idea of putting *being* first in daily life seems an unlikely route to gaining influence in the world. Some would argue that the measurable decline that accompanies aging obviously and permanently disqualifies the old from playing an important role in society. The book you hold in your hands disproves any such claims.

Although it was written by an adult, the elders who have touched my life inspired and guided this book's development and final form. From my great-grandmother Georgiana Williams to my grandparents, Durwood and Olive Saxon and William and Vivian Thomas, to my parents, William and Sandra Thomas, I have been molded, shaped, influenced, and educated by my elders. Even as an adult physician (and specialist in aging), my elder mentors Frank and Carter Williams, along with thousands of patients and their families, continue to lead me toward a deeper understanding of age and aging. The hands of an adult may have typed the words on these pages, but elders provided any and all of the truths they contain.

For as long as I remain an adult I will be ignorant of the lived experience offered to elders by their longevity. Despite this limitation, my practice as a physician and an ingrained habit of observation lead me to ask: What does it mean to live as an elder? How can elderhood shape the future we all share? What are its most important functions? What does it offer us—young and old alike?

Decades from now, when I am at last prepared to lay down the work of adulthood, I will begin my own life as an elder. When that happens I hope to be prepared for the historic, *being*-rich responsibilities of making peace, giving wisdom, and creating a legacy.

Peacemaker

Human elders have long been known as peacemakers, and for good reason. The physical changes that accompany advancing age make conflict, armed and otherwise, worthless to the old. They simply cannot prevail against the young. While this transition can be painful on a personal level (and is usually painted as a form of failure), it serves society as a whole by preparing older people for life outside the adult hierarchy. Over time, the action-oriented strategies of DOING-being give way to the indirect and subtle influence of BEING-doing. Age may remove elders from power, but they remain a part of society. Longevity loosens the grip of the ego but also grants elders a new perspective on self and society. Together, these trends prepare elders for the singular role of peacemaker.

Tennyson, Tornstam, and Carstensen are right: the awareness of one's mortality that normally arises in late life—and so terrifies adults—opens new perspectives on the world in which elders live. Like statesmen serving their final terms in office, elders are freed from the tactical maneuvering that defines the struggle for adult rank and prestige. It is this freedom that allows them to put forth unique interpretations of the problems faced by their families and communities and to take on the role of peacemaker.

Elders' position outside the hierarchy is made secure by the changes age brings to the mind and body. Adults can accept elders as peacemakers because age ensures that elders will not use their new role to gain unfair advantage—elders simply cannot overpower the adults around them. (It is true that a small number of extraordinary older people are able to exert power in the fashion of adults even into the last decades of life. They are the exceptions that prove the rule.)

The idea that elders' influence is actually ensured by their loss of vitality runs contrary to the beliefs of senior citizen lobbying and action groups. These groups hold that the well-being of the elderly depends largely on the skill and aggressiveness of their political strategists. There is some truth to that, and I would not want these groups to be excluded from political deliberations. Still, there are other more essential functions—making peace, giving wisdom, creating a legacy—that only elders can fulfill.

Peacemaking is a delicate craft that can be mastered only through practice. Little in contemporary adulthood prepares one to become an elder, but even less attention is given to developing, learning, and practicing the art of the peacemaker. Those who would accept this role must be willing to leave adulthood behind and enter into the world of the human elder.

Making Peace with the Self

I remember being at work in a nursing home one day when I was called on to do a history and physical examination of an elder recently admitted to the facility. I sat down with the woman and ran through the usual topics related to her diagnoses and medical history. Then I questioned her about her family. Quite unexpectedly, her eyes welled with tears. She told me that her mother had died when she was five years old. In those days, people believed that a widower should not be entrusted with the care of young children and so, following the custom of the time, she and her younger brother were sent to live with relatives. In order to distribute the burden, she was sent to live with one family and her brother was sent to another. Over time, they lost contact. Now she lay in a bed in a nursing home, still grieving the loss of a mother, brother, and father seventy-five years before.

Rarely have I felt so inadequate. My education and training had given very little attention to such difficulties. How could I hope to help her find peace within herself? The institution I worked in was well prepared to deal with depression, psychosis, and dementia but had next to nothing to offer to those struggling with guilt and grief three-quarters of a century in the making. Even these limitations might have been overcome if this woman had believed that old age was a time for healing and making peace. Instead, she despaired of ever finding relief this side of the grave.

Inspired by Tennyson and Barkan, and working from a developmental approach to aging, I see now what I could not see then. I can imagine an alternative wherein this gentle soul could be received warmly as the newest member of an intentional community. Surely, the elders of such a community could have done much to bind up her wounds. Instead, she found herself confined to an institution, attended by an ill-prepared physician, with the means of her healing nearby but completely unavailable.

The difficult work of making peace with one's self can begin at any time and is an essential first step in the much longer journey toward becoming a peacemaker.

Making Peace in the Family

Every family is a civilization. It proclaims its achievements to the world, hides its secrets and shames, and struggles with the passage of time. My work as a physician has given me many opportunities to observe how families behave when they are confronted with the greatest calamity, the death of a loved one. Too often, their fumbling attempts at making peace in the moment of crisis fail because the effort is too little and has come too late. The prodigal daughter returns at the last moment but cannot receive her mother's forgiveness. She can only weep at the bedside, opening her heart but never knowing if she is being heard. A family, long splintered, worries together, all in the same room, for the first time in years. Old animosities are submerged, obscured, and sometimes surrendered in a last effort to "do what's right for Mom."

I am suggesting a vision of elderhood that does not delay peacemaking until this late date. It is the place of the elder to tend to the wounds of the family sooner rather than later. Where does the courage to take such action come from? Tennyson tells us:

Old age hath yet his honor and his toil.
Death closes all; but something ere the end,

Some work of noble note may yet be done, . . .

The courage to do the noble work of deliberately bringing peace to a family is, today, beyond all but a few exceptional elders. This will change, and in the not-too-distant future we will come to see skill at making peace as a normal part of late-life development, just as we now recognize mastery of letters and numbers as an ordinary step in early childhood development. In time, I expect to see fewer anguished deathbed reconciliations. As elders come to understand the nature of nonadult influence and the importance of their obligation to serve as peacemakers in their families, many wounded hearts will be cleansed, dressed, and healed. The good that comes of this healing will extend beyond those immediately involved, touching the members of every generation, even those yet to be born.

Making Peace in the World

We live in a world made by and for adults—a world wherein elders and elderhood are pushed to the margins of society. Mass society is, itself, the creation of adulthood and is compelled to serve the needs of adults. Not surprisingly, it has little use for the guiding hand of elderhood.

It is important to distinguish between a society guided by elders and a society governed by elders. The technical term for the latter is *gerontocracy*, and that form of government is particularly offensive to the modern individualistic sensibility. Gerontocracies have proven, throughout history, to be sclerotic, risk averse, and largely incapable of the kind of vibrant creativity essential to healthy human communities. Although it is known best for its military prowess, Sparta was first and foremost a gerontocracy. While Athenians clearly did not share the Spartans' special reverence for the aged, they did possess a freedom to think, to question, and to challenge the status quo that has echoed through the centuries.

The elder-guided society is and should be run by the vigorous adults of the time. Elders should intervene at critical points to ensure that the adults take into account perspectives that are too easily ignored by those gripped by the fever of rank and wealth. This form of cultural guidance has long proven its worth. The hilltop on which

I now live was, for thousands of years, considered to be part of the Iroquois Confederacy. Even today, the elder-guided form of governance is practiced in the longhouse of the Onondoga Nation. The voice of the elders is received with respect by the chiefs who administer the daily affairs of the nation.

Modern industrial society would be well served by the restoration of the elder's voice in public life. While the prototypical beauty pageant contestant espouses world peace, it is an old woman who has the experience, the voice, and the insights needed to pursue that lofty goal. The peace activists of the 1960s may now return to this work informed by a life lived—by experiences that, over the decades, have prepared them to do the real work of making peace.

Wisdom Giver

The Uses of Wisdom

Adulthood never stops whispering in our ears, never stops reminding us, "Doing is more important than being." Accustomed to valuing that which can be touched, or at least counted, we are often confused by the indistinct nature of being. We are taught not to rely on the pillars of emotion, affection, and love as the basis for understanding self and society. Society is especially eager to inflict these doubts on the aged. Few escape its ceaseless propaganda in favor of doing. The idea that being has virtues of its own is routinely undermined. The result is a stunted form of aging that subsists on the thin gruel of long-ago victories.

I remember visiting a retirement community in California in the late 1990s. I presented a lecture on the Eden Alternative to the leadership and then met privately with the organization's executive director. She was articulate and highly experienced. As our conversation progressed, she worked her way around to a frustration that she was reluctant to admit aloud. Every morning before she arrived at work, a handful of the men who lived in the complex lined up outside her office. Each man was eager to present a complaint or criticism relating to the physical plant or grounds, always making sure to emphasize his credentials while making his point. The issues were always highly technical: "I was an engineer for John Deere for forty-five years, and I am telling you that the backup generator is too small for the demand; if there is ever a blackout, there'll be hell to pay." And so it went.

The source of her frustration, though she would not have put it this way, lay in the demand that these men were making that she readmit them to the society of adults. They yearned to be respected experts, restored to the technical problem-solving work of the adult.

As I came to know this woman better, I learned that she was facing a heavy burden of her own. Her adolescent daughter was struggling with a serious chronic disease. The girl's illness repeatedly plunged this woman into a whirlpool of grief and anger. On the flight home it occurred to me that the men of the retirement community and the executive director were like ships passing in the night. She had a crying need for the very life-wisdom that these men had spent decades acquiring. Despite this, she could see them only as nit-picking fault finders. The way she rolled her eyes when she talked about them revealed how deeply she resented their constant questioning of her abilities. For their part, they could have become wise men, the elders of this community. Instead, they chose to depend solely on the residual value of their increasingly outmoded stock of technical expertise. The desire to be recognized and respected as adults closed elderhood to them. Not surprisingly, they remained completely ignorant of this woman's grief. Meanwhile, she suffered the consequences of her failure to understand that she spent each workday in a building full of people who had struggled and overcome life challenges equal to or greater than what she was facing.

This dynamic is played out a million times over every day. Adults and elders alike confuse expertise and information with wisdom and stories. It would be better to live in a world that made appropriate use of each. The information glut has all too often drowned out the stories we need. In the life of a healthy community, stories actually matter more than information. They are also far more durable. Stories are told only when they can be heard, heard only when they are told. They come to life in the moment of their telling and then make a place in our memories. Contrast this with the daily table of stock price quotations. Those who prepare them care little about how they are used. They know that the next day's prices will make that day's information instantly obsolete, forgettable, and forgotten.

Mechanical Stories

Everyone knows that elders like and use stories. Storytelling is one of the pleasures of life, its sweetness enhanced when the story is used to transmit a bit of wisdom. Muriel Rukeyser once wrote that "the universe is made of stories, not of atoms." I would like to add a corollary: "Stories make the best wrapping for any gift of wisdom." When a thought is easily translatable into a story, it probably holds a good bit of wisdom. Technical information, useful as it is, has little or no wisdom in it. This is why computer-programming manuals are never made into feature films.

Elders' stories can be imbued with great value because the stories emerge from a life and a nature that give precedence to being. A lifetime in the making, the wisdom of elders is a subtle thing, too easily overlooked. We may be witnessing a worldwide triumph of longevity, but our society is dangerously ill prepared to receive the bounty of stories that our elders have to offer. Increasingly, our society resembles a country that has built the world's best libraries but whose citizens cannot read.

This is not to say that we are without stories of any kind. In place of the ordinary stories of the everyday, of people who will vanish from human memory if their lives are not recalled for us, we have raised up a vast mechanized storytelling industry. This entertainment business specializes in action, adventure, romance, drama, and comedy, all acted out by people we do not know and can never know. Like brightly colored cotton candy, these confections are tasty but offer little or no nutrition. The cult of adulthood has aggressively mechanized the telling of stories, confusing technical sophistication with wisdom and making an industry of the finest human art. What we need is the real life wisdom of the elders in our lives. Listening to and reflecting on their stories can bring us insights that the dramatic exploits of action heroes can never hope to inspire. Best of all, no special-effects budget is needed.

Stories that remind us to be kind to one another, stories that tell us to be wary of strangers, stories that prod us to welcome strangers, stories that reveal dimensions of good and evil—these are the instruments of a culture, not the culture itself. For millennia, elders have been the repositories of their people's lore. They have stored our most cherished beliefs and then transmitted them to the young. The legacy of the elder by the fire recounting tales to a circle of children has a powerful pull on us and, indeed, is a function of elderhood that has been endangered by the vast and growing entertainment industry.

We are, in these days, much more likely to get our stories from corporate conglomerates and much less likely to get them from people we know, people who have lived life long and well. This must change. The rebirth of elderhood must include the concept of elders telling and others receiving the wisdom that only stories can hold. Why do I say this? Because, at the very least, making this reconstructed elderhood available to the old men of the retirement community that I mentioned above would allow them to finally let go of their obsession with pipes, conduits, and fittings and, hopefully, reach for something larger, better, and vastly more important. Storytelling could help them become the elders they were meant to be.

The wisdom of elders is most available to those who are willing to acknowledge that they no longer possess (or need to possess) "that strength which in old days moved earth and heaven." It comes to those whose longevity has taught them to embrace being "made weak by time and fate." The elders among us are meant "to strive, to seek, to find, and not to yield." What is little recognized in our time is that, for elders, striving need not be yoked to doing, getting, and having. An elderhood that understood its own story would be well suited to passing on just the right bit of wisdom to a grieving mother. It would be delivered, as wisdom always is, in the form of a story told by one person to another.

Legacy Creator

I grew up in a small town on the New York banks of the Susquehanna River. My family had been part of the community since the late

1700s. In fact, one of my great-great-grandfathers is listed as the first recorded death in the town. For better and worse, everyone knew everyone else; it could hardly be otherwise. As an adolescent, I had very mixed feelings about being so well known. One day I decided to hitchhike to a nearby town to see my girlfriend, despite the fact that I had been forbidden to do so. I stuck out my thumb and soon was on my way to her house. After a pleasant visit, I returned home. Whistling innocently as I entered the house, I was immediately informed that I was grounded. Someone had seen me hitchhiking and had called my parents to tell them what I was up to. The small-town grapevine is fast and efficient, with a bandwidth that puts the Internet to shame.

As a boy living in a small town, I had little use for being so well known that passersby would not only recognize me but also know my family and know what kind of conduct my parents expected of me. I lived with the knowledge that my neighbors felt perfectly comfortable calling my parents and telling them that I was, at that very minute, violating their expectations of me. For elders, though, the issue cuts in an entirely different direction.

Old age is increasingly being defined in terms of the dangers of being *unknown*. Instead of living in the warm embrace of others, the aged increasingly occupy a twilight zone outside the whirl inspired by the cult of adulthood. The dangers of being unknown were brought home to me when Nancy Fox, the executive director of the Eden Alternative, wrote to me about an experience she had while on vacation in Florida:

> The problems of aging and long-term care seemed a million miles away on this beautiful island, but I should have known better. Friday morning I was walking down to the beach when I came upon an older man, standing beside the road. As I got closer I could see that something was wrong. He was trembling with fear as he summoned me closer. I had to lean close to hear, as his voice was barely above a whisper. He told me that his wife had fallen and that he could not help her up. I told him that I could help and he led me slowly back to his house.
>
> I could hear her moaning even before we entered the house. We found her on the floor in the kitchen. Even slighter in build than her

husband, she was lying on her side on the hard linoleum floor. Her light, cotton housecoat barely covered her thin legs. The breakfast dishes, still unwashed, sat on the counter above her. And she was in pain. I had to step over her to reach the phone. I called 911. As the phone rang, I asked the man his address. His wife responded, "218 Oakwood Lane." I asked his name and she responded, between cries of pain, "Hammond with an H. Katharine and Henry." I asked her if there was a daughter or son I could call. Katharine said, "None." Any family? "None." Anyone I could call—a neighbor, a friend, clergy, anyone? "There is no one," Katharine answered.

She began to cry. Although her hip was surely broken, there was much greater pain in her heart. She knew only too well that the life she had known was over. These would likely be their last moments together as a couple in their own home.

Her grief moved me to tears.

Contrast Katharine's confession that "there is no one" with my friend Bernard Mambo's belief that "the death of an old person is like the loss of a library." We live in a time and place that allows older people to disappear from view and then leave this life without being known by others. Every human life has or should have a legacy. William Tyndale called this the "message wherefore I am sent into the world." Barry Barkan, five hundred years later, declared that an elder is a person:

> . . . whose work it is
> To synthesize wisdom from long life experience and
> Formulate this into a legacy
> For future generations.

The final task of elderhood is the creation of a legacy that can serve others and, later, be handed down to those who have yet to be born. This work is easily accomplished in a settled traditional community and terribly difficult in a highly mobile industrial society.

I grew to maturity knowing not only my own elders but also the elders of the community: Burtis Everett, the town historian, who worked for years as a railroad stationmaster—he and his wife, Laura, were devoted to the Methodist church. Jack Klausner never married but loved children—he sat on the steps of the post office and handed out Tootsie Rolls to the children who came by. Louise Barton knew my parents well and, when my father was out of work, saved our home by paying the taxes on our property. Marjorie Lee taught school and made quilts, which she gave away to her neighbors. I mention them now not only to honor their memory but also as proof that these men and women were able to live and die as well-known members of the community.

Their legacies were handed down informally in the casual manner of the everyday. Living as we do now, we will need to be much more explicit and methodical in our effort to capture and then share the legacies of our elders. The legacies that I have in mind are part life story, part simple biography, and part gift—in the form of a poem, a drawing, a letter, or a piece of hard-won wisdom. Taken together, these elements can become much more than the sum of their parts. The creation of such a legacy requires a cooperative journey of discovery to capture the essence of a life lived. Ideally, this life review process should take place in partnership with members of several generations. A grandfather may wish to gather up his mother's legacy and encourage his grandson to be part of the process. Members of a faith community may create their own intergenerational teams and prepare them to capture the legacies of older members of the congregation. As our understanding of elderhood and its rightful place in our society grows, the creation and sharing of legacy will come to be seen as an essential part of late life. This is more than an idle wish. Our society needs these legacies and, day by day, grows less and less able to gain access to them. We need them because they can—

- foster gerotranscendence by encouraging the rethinking of an elder's life,
- fulfill our duty to honor elders by creating opportunities for elders to give as well as receive,
- create and strengthen the intergenerational bonds of affection on which every healthy human community depends,
- answer important questions about our own lives and locate our own experiences within the vast terrain of human experience, and

- serve as an ongoing reminder of the value and importance of elderhood, when rightly understood.

Although this idea would have seemed stranger than any science fiction to the elders I knew as a child, life in the twenty-first century requires us to make smart use of information technology that can help us record, store, and share the legacies of our elders. Many Web sites have begun to document the legacies of elders. Some give advice to those who would join with elders in the work of creating legacies. In the years to come, the library of online legacies will grow to include the stories of millions of lives. The ability to search this archive will allow users to locate legacies that are likely to touch on the challenges in their own lives. Imagine a young couple faced with the heartbreak of a seriously ill child. Searching among the legacies of elders, these parents might be able to find the wisdom that only long decades of reflection on a life lived can provide. This is something neither the expert counsel of a credentialed professional nor the real-time empathy that a support group of peers offers. It provides access to that most authentically human of all possessions: knowledge of the "message wherefore I am sent into the world."

Eldertopia

Old Age in a New World

Throughout this book I have argued that our longevity is both ancient and a vital contemporary presence. We are headed into the most elder-rich era of human existence and should be celebrating our good fortune at every turn. Instead, we are in danger of squandering this historic windfall. Human elderhood was created, protected, sustained, and nurtured because it serves vital human interests. It can continue to do so if we understand it properly and provide for its continued development.

The cult of adulthood promotes the misconception that old age is an appendage to both human life and human society. The cult bemoans the vast expense associated with our growing longevity but also congratulates itself on its marvelous generosity toward the survivors. Our popular culture offers little or nothing that can lead us toward a deep understanding of elders and elderhood. Instead, we are tutored, day and night, in the virtues of youthful vigor. Advocates who currently lobby for the aged work toward a society in which the aged are given protection and respect equal to that accorded to the young. They forget that the virtue of elderhood lies in how stunningly different from either childhood or adulthood it is. Those who would dismiss elderhood might as well also surrender fire-making and the wheel. Our longevity is a gift greater than either of these; it is the invention that made all inventions possible.

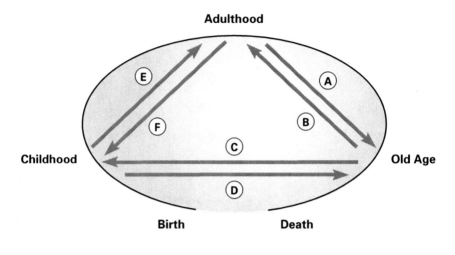

Adulthood

Childhood

Old Age

Birth   **Death**

A Support adults provide to elders

B Assistance elders give to adults

C Gentling and acculturation of children by elders

D Assistance and affection given to elders by children

E Participation in work of adults by children

F Food, shelter, clothing, and affection provided to children by adults

The cycle of cultural evolution

The diagram reminds us that the relationships that have powered human cultural advancement for tens of thousands of years are a complex set of intergenerational interactions. Taken together, they form the engine that has shaped us, served us, blunted our worst tendencies, and magnified our best. Given the terrible might of modern industrial society, we need this engine more than ever before. The cult of adulthood is insistent in its claims that old age is irrelevant and possibly on the edge of its own extinction (given sufficient progress in pharmaceutical laboratories). Though few actually believe that old age can be vanquished, it is easy to wish that it were so. Many find refuge in treasured illusions about traditional aging. In truth, the old way of growing old was never as good as we like to remember it being and is especially ill suited to the society in which we live today. We really have no choice but to look ahead. The times demand that we create a new elderhood—one that fits the way we live now. We need this new elderhood not only for ourselves (we all deserve a better, richer, more meaningful old age) but for people of all ages.

Public discourse, however, operates from very different assumptions. Within its realm, longevity is imagined to be of concern solely to the aged, those who care for them, and those who pay for that care. We are constantly reminded of how expensive this is, and like the miser who feels he may have been cheated, we expect a precise accounting of what has been paid and what has been delivered. Former Colorado governor Richard Lamm begins his essay "The Moral Imperative of Limiting Elderly Health Entitlements" by noting that "one of the great challenges in America's future is to retire the baby boomers without bankrupting the country or unduly burdening future generations . . . Age could well be as divisive in the next forty years as race and sex have been for the last forty years."

Given the sums involved and the potentially devastating consequences of mismanagement, much of this concern is warranted. What is missing from the debate, however, is a proper accounting of what elderhood can contribute to society. This side of the ledger is given scant attention by those who can see only the wealth and vigor of adults and the potentially ruinous burden imposed by the aged. Lamm goes on to point out that, regardless of how it may make us feel, decisions will have to be made: "We are a compassionate society and can afford a lot, but we cannot afford everything. No publicly financed health system can ignore the law of diminishing returns . . . It is necessary to find, among the myriad of things we can do, what practically in a budget we ought to do."

The worldview that former governor Lamm represents places old age outside the pale of productive, contributing adults. They are expensive accessories and, while we may be a "compassionate society," there is a limit to what *we* can do for *them*. I am arguing for a very different conception of elders and elderhood—one that places them (and their needs) within rather than outside the central purposes of our society. What we need is a holistic perspective that appreciates and respects the contributions that people of all ages have made and are now making to the pursuit of happiness and our collective well-being. It should not come as a surprise that our language lacks a word that describes the interdependence that joins young and old. Instead, we have "entitlements" and "cross-generational wealth transfers." The wisdom of living in a multigenerational social structure is ancient, undeniable, and deserving of a word of its own. I like *Eldertopia:*

> **Eldertopia** *noun* A community that improves the quality of life for people of all ages by strengthening and improving the means by which (1) the community protects, sustains, and nurtures its elders, and (2) the elders contribute to the well-being and foresight of the community. An Eldertopia that is blessed with a large number of older people is acknowledged to be "elder-rich" and uses this human capital to the advantage of all.

Earlier in this book, in the chapter "The Way We Live Now," I presented a map of life that I think can help us make sense of life as it is lived in modern industrial societies. An understanding of the role BEING-doing plays in childhood and elderhood, and the virtues that DOING-being brings to adulthood can help us find our place within the lives we are living today and might well be living in the future. Such a map can be helpful as we explore longevity; it very usefully highlights the danger of confusing our longevity with the perpetuation of youth. Eldertopia goes even further by showing us why we live so long. Our longevity exists, has meaning, and creates value because it provides human beings with a mechanism for improving the lives of people *of all ages.* That mechanism is a pattern of reciprocal relationships that unite the generations. Far from being society's expensive leftovers, elders and the elderhood they inhabit are crucial to the well-being of all.

This assessment highlights the flaws inherent in the accounting systems of the "old-age welfare state." Conventional practice tabulates to the penny the money spent serving the elderly, even as it ignores the vital contributions that our longevity makes to society as a whole. We need a new and much more realistic set of accounting books.

Fortunately, Eldertopia can lead us to a deeper and far more accurate understanding of how longevity completes us. For a start it can shed light on the complex and easily overlooked intergenerational transfers that are essential to people of all ages. The idea of the "greedy geezer" is the product of a society that counts only what the young pay to the old. Becoming more conscious of the contributions that elders make to the young is a good first step in correcting the bias against the old. Fully developed, this more balanced approach can document in black and white why our longevity is a solid investment.

Mapping Eldertopia

Eldertopia supposes that human communities rely heavily on reciprocal altruism and calls for a detailed accounting of all sides of these exchanges. In its most basic form, such a chart of accounts would include answers to the following questions:

- In what ways and to what extent do elders receive support from adults?
- In what ways do elders contribute ongoing assistance to the adults of the community?
- How are we to recognize and properly value the gentling and acculturation of children by elders?
- In what ways and to what extent do we acknowledge the ongoing assistance and affection given to elders by the children in their lives?

Some of these contributions can be reduced to numerical terms; others cannot. The current public debate surrounding aging and its entitlements is distorted by the nearly exclusive emphasis that is placed on the financial cost of publicly funded programs and the pitiful lack of attention that is paid to the more qualitative elements of the ongoing exchange between young and old.

It is easy to obtain figures on the cost of government programs that support the aged. We know exactly what our society spends to finance worthy programs such as Medicare, Meals on Wheels, Aging Resource Centers, home health care, transportation, prescription drugs, Area Agencies on Aging, and Adult Protective Services. Much more valuable, however, than all these programs and much harder to reduce to fiscal terms is the support that family and friends offer to older relatives and neighbors. What is the value of an attentive and loving daughter-in-law? What value should society place on all those trips to the doctor, the shopping, the meals prepared, the checkbooks balanced not for money but for love? In fact, we do not know and perhaps will never know the answer to such questions. What we should acknowledge is that these contributions dwarf the expenditures made by publicly financed programs. The sum of our investment in old age (public and private) is said to be large and growing, but it is already much larger than we suppose, and it is growing faster than we think.

In order for any exchange to be fair and just, both parties must fully understand the value of what is being given and received. Alarmist rhetoric of the "plague of locusts" variety becomes shrill precisely because it fails to acknowledge the value of what elders have done, do now, and will continue to contribute to the young. Public officials and academic experts have surprisingly little to say on the subject of how the aged help sustain their families and communities. Studies of volunteerism have lauded the work that senescents and elders do within faith-based and community organizations, and a few studies have even attempted to put a price tag on those contributions. Far greater, though, is the commitment that the aged make to the people they love. Most people suppose that adults support their aged parents with material resources (and many do), but taken as a whole, the elders of our society give more to their children and their children's families than they receive from them.

Perhaps the most endangered and least appreciated element of the ancient exchange between young and old is the gentling and acculturation of children by elders. Historically, this has taken place exclusively within the family and kinship group. Life in modern society has, of course, disrupted many of these arrangements. Children are increasingly confined to and molded by large, professionally run educational institutions. Elders are segregated, by choice and by fiat, within their own age-specific institutions, facilities, and housing developments. The result is a generation of young unlike any before it, a generation that is growing to maturity without the guiding hand

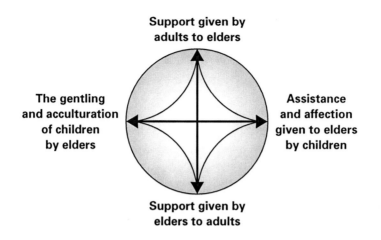

The four dimensions of Eldertopia

of elders and elderhood. This arrangement penalizes elders as well. Many must live and die without knowing the tender embrace of the very young in their daily lives.

A full accounting of these exchanges, even one that lacked precise values, would alter public policy and reshape public opinion. The material aspect of such an exchange—goods and services—is the easiest to document and can usually be tallied in dollars and cents. But we must also make the informal and private dimensions of the exchange known, and give them their due. Eldertopia is, at its most fundamental level, a path to a new consciousness of age and aging. It sets aside incomplete ideas about dependency and decline and presents instead the dynamic image of an active and ongoing exchange between the generations. Taken seriously, it can help us document the staggering value contained within the global age boom. It can change how we live together. Consider the following Eldertopian possibilities.

Elders Giving Warmth Elders have always made important contributions to the young of their families and communities. For thousands of years, relationships created between young and old have made life better for both groups. In Eldertopia, all school construction and remodeling projects would include housing and community services for elders. The idea of isolating one group from the other would be seen as the ridiculous waste that it is. Those who sought to provide care and services for the elders would take care to integrate their offerings with the routines and needs of the young. In Eldertopia the wall that separates young and old would have to come down.

Elders Receiving Warmth The myth of independence has led millions of elders to prefer living alone to any form of communal life. This is in spite of the fact that old age, like childbirth, was never meant to be confronted alone. The Meals on Wheels program is intended to improve life for elders living at home by delivering meals to their homes. Because of the expense involved, some programs have turned to weekly deliveries of frozen food instead of daily deliveries of hot meals. Of course, the daily delivery of meals offers much more than food. It also provides what one elder calls "a face at the door." In the future, daily meal deliveries will be difficult to sustain unless there is a community-wide awareness of the value of bringing human warmth into elders' lives. In Eldertopia, community leaders would acknowledge that elders cannot live on frozen food alone.

Elders Giving Wisdom Many traditional societies maintain mechanisms whereby the wisdom of elders can be communicated to the leaders of the day. Elder councils, for example, provide a balancing perspective that considers the long-term consequences of any proposed action. Too often in our society, the perspective of elderhood is reduced to just one of many competing interest groups. Eldertopia encourages the formation of elder councils that meet regularly and offer their views on the challenges and opportunities facing the community. The topics addressed might well include matters that the conventional political system would rather sweep under the rug. The media can and should cover the elder council and its deliberations. In Eldertopia, the community as a whole would no longer be deaf to the voices of it elders.

Elders Receiving the Benefits of Technology Advances in technology have done much to improve the well-being of older people, but so much more could be done. There is a tremendous potential for using ordinary off-the-shelf technology to help elders do more themselves, expand their potential to live independently and in dignity, and maintain vital connections to their community and people they love. We can and should embrace a smart technology that fuses an accurate understanding of the challenges of old age with the best tools that our industrial society has to offer. Eldertopia would ensure that the elders had access to technology capable of aiding the pursuit of the best elderhood possible.

Elderhood's Commitment to Stewardship Elders have long been critical of the adult's desire to get, have, and take all that he or she is capable of getting, having, and taking. The consequences of such avarice can be found in our dirty air and water and the mass extinction of species that is currently in progress. Elders have long spoken for Earth, its living creatures, and the children who are yet to be born. They have not always prevailed, nor should they, but a society that marginalizes elders and the value of their lived experience endangers us all because it removes their concerns from our thoughts. There is much to be done if we are to repair the damage that has been done to the living world that sustains us. Eldertopia would have an Elder Environmental Conservation Corps that would tackle projects that would strengthen the health and vitality of the natural world. In Eldertopia, nature would have an influential new ally.

Elders Receiving Well-Being from Nature There is a dawning awareness that nature should be an important part of any setting intended to improve health or assist in healing. Eventually, the inclusion of nature in plans for these environments will seem as essential and ordinary as planning for doors and windows. In Eldertopia, the community would organize itself to see that the healing effect that comes with a connection to nature is made available to every elder.

Eldertopia is a useful concept because we can use it to improve the well-being of all members of society. It makes explicit the ancient patterns of exchange between the young and the old. We all benefit when these connections are strengthened and enriched, just as we all suffer when they are ignored or trampled. The most elder-rich period of human history is upon us. How we regard and make use of this windfall of elders will define the world in which we live. When the woodcutter returned his father to the family table, he made life better not just for his father but for the whole family. Eldertopia restores aging to longevity and returns the aged to a worthy elderhood. Even more than that, it restores elderhood to its rightful place in the human life cycle. In this way, it creates the possibility of a better life for us all.

New Directions

The word *Eldertopia* is tinged with impossibility. Sophisticated adults, after all, feel that they have outgrown utopias—left them behind on their journey into the future. We should not be so hasty. The utopian ideal has long served to reveal the gap between what is and what ought to be. At its best, it is distilled imagination placed into the service of everyday life. Utopias have the power to change how we think about our times and our selves. Eldertopia is notable because it offers not the violent disruption of revolution but a patient, gentle return to an evolutionary process that began long ago and that is already deep in our bones. Because it is founded on millennia of human experience, Eldertopia requires neither federal legislation nor a court order in order to come to life. In fact, we can begin creating Eldertopia today.

Marcel Proust observed, "The real voyage of discovery consists not in seeking new landscapes but in having new eyes." This is the challenge of Eldertopia. How can we convert ordinary situations and daily decisions into extraordinary opportunities to explore a new way of seeing, thinking, and acting? How do we bring the complex web of interdependencies that define a healthy community out into the open? How can we cope with the grinding efficiency of the cult of adulthood, which is, increasingly, putting the true nature of our longevity beyond our reach?

This alienation is not inevitable. Not a day, not a moment passes when we do not have the opportunity to move our society toward the ideals of Eldertopia. The importance of this idea grows with the gathering power of adulthood and the distortions that come of living in a world run by and for adults. There is a limit to how long we can continue to discount and dismiss the guiding intelligence of elders and elderhood. How does society acknowledge the bilateral nature of the community's relationship with its elders? How do our decisions and priorities enlarge or diminish our ability to sustain this exchange? Does the item you are hearing about at a meeting, reading about in the newspaper, or discussing within your family aid in the rebirth of elderhood, or does it simply extend the power of adults and adulthood?

Consider the following situations according to how well or poorly they bring forth the possibility of Eldertopia:

- A local nursing home is requesting approval for an addition to its existing facility. This move simply strengthens the grip that the old-age archipelago has over the aged and offers the community little or nothing in return. **Rating: Poor**
- A local senior center announces that it is hosting a "brown bag" evaluation of local elders' prescribed medication regimens. A licensed pharmacist tours local communities, helping elders avoid the perils of polypharmacy and drug interactions. The elders who attend save money by eliminating unnecessary medications and reduce their exposure to unpleasant medication side effects. **Rating: Good**
- A coalition of organizations serving the young and the old creates a summer camp that accommodates and integrates the needs of older people (including people currently confined to nursing homes) and local children. Such an intergenerational summer camp strengthens the community by enriching the bond between young and old. **Rating: Excellent**

Does the change actively recognize that elders are a vital resource in the community and that the community is, in fact, elder-rich? How is that richness integrated into innovation?

- Nursing homes lobby for increased funding for the services they provide, and the dollars needed to fund the increase are taken from programs that provide home- and community-based services. This outcome reflects the political strength of an industry rather than the preferences of community elders. It fails us because it slows the move away from institutional long-term care. **Rating: Poor**

- A local school initiates a program that connects elders with latchkey children. A participating elder makes regular daily phone contact with a child and provides a reliable source of interest and concern. This reduces loneliness among both groups and teaches children about the meaning and worth of elderhood. **Rating: Good**

- A newspaper article announces the creation of a local chapter of the Elder Environmental Conservation Corps. The Corps recruits members and organizes projects with a special emphasis on bringing young and old together. The Corps also reaches out to those who have been removed from the community by taking an active role in the "greening" of local long-term care environments. This work provides visible proof of the value of stewardship and creates opportunities for the young to share the company of the old. **Rating: Excellent**

To what degree does the project or service demonstrate a commitment to improving the quality of life for people of all ages? Healthy communities rely heavily on the virtues of reciprocal altruism; we can guide social change by favoring innovations that foster reciprocity and by discouraging changes that rely solely on the movement of material resources from one group to another.

- A local agency seeks funding to extend its Meals on Wheels service area. It supports its request by emphasizing the number of people who will be served and the number of meals that will be prepared and delivered. **Rating: Poor**

- The request is revised. This time the funding is justified both in terms of the number of people served and a promised increase in participation by volunteers of all ages. The desired outcome is evaluated in terms of a combined measure of service delivered and growth of the volunteer effort. **Rating: Good**

- Another revision is submitted. This time the envisioned outcomes include the number of meals delivered, diversity in the age and background of volunteers, the variety of efforts contributed, and the impact of an outreach effort to communicate Eldertopian ideas to elders, volunteers, and community members in the new service area. **Rating: Excellent**

The need for human warmth touches people of all ages. Eldertopia is dedicated to creating human warmth for young and old alike. In fact, it leverages the ancient virtues that have held the generations together for millennia. In our families, in our jobs, in our thoughts and conversations, we can dedicate ourselves to the creation of a community with greater warmth for everyone. Human warmth is associated with optimism, trust, and generosity. How does what we do create or destroy human warmth?

- The local Area Agency on Aging announces the creation of a geriatric case management system for frail elders living in the community. This worthy goal is presented solely in terms of cost control and the arm's-length delivery of professional services. **Rating: Poor**
- A group of community and faith-based organizations begins to teach its members how to advocate for people they care about. This unites young and old and enables people to demonstrate their commitment to the elders in their lives in an effective new way. **Rating: Good**
- A United Way agency announces its intention to evaluate all requests for funding in terms of the precepts of Eldertopia. This does not mean that it will fund only "services for the elderly." In fact, it is just the opposite. The United Way will back efforts that can demonstrate how they intend to improve the quality of life for people of all ages by strengthening and improving the means by which (1) the community protects, sustains, and nurtures its elders and (2) the elders contribute to the well-being and foresight of the community. **Rating: Excellent**

How can our mastery of tools and technologies be used in support of elders and elderhood? Smart technology acknowledges the human dimension of the tools we use and is conscious of how those tools shape the communities in which we live.

- A local senior center installs Internet-ready computers for use by the elderly. **Rating: Poor**
- The school district arranges for elders to use the school's equipment and staff for computer technology education. **Rating: Good**
- Senior centers match children with elders so that each can teach the other about computers and the uses of the Internet. Simultaneously, elders are encouraged to go to schools to learn and share computer skills. Children and elders act as both teachers and students as time and circumstances dictate. Eldertopia cultivates a growing awareness of the bilateral nature of the exchange between generations—each gives, each receives. The key variable is enlarging the bilateral exchange of skills and abilities. The temptation to pigeonhole either group according to stereotyped attitudes is resisted. **Rating: Excellent**

In what ways does society acknowledge the importance of nature and contact with the living world?

- A nursing home establishes a pet visitation program. While it is better than doing nothing, this type of intervention medicalizes the joys we associate with the human-animal bond. **Rating: Poor**
- Local gardening clubs (whose members are mostly older) actively recruit school children into their ranks. **Rating: Good**
- Your local Elder Environmental Conservation Corps announces its first meeting. You and your grandchildren decide to attend and mark the date on your calendars. **Rating: Excellent**

One of the advantages of a concept like Eldertopia is that it weaves a concern for our elders together with the interests and desires of people of all ages. In the context of Eldertopia, groups that support children, refugees, women, education, entrepreneurship, and ecology can all find reasons to be enthused about bringing elders into their own work.

This idea of bringing elders into the work of various groups provides a powerful opportunity to spread the concept of Eldertopia and leverage the power of social change across a wide range of community agencies and organizations. A similar strategy was employed with respect to public art in the city of San Francisco. In the 1990s, a small group of people were intent on seeing a wider array of art become available to the public outside of museums. Though their funds were limited, they saw value in sharing their ideals with many other stakeholders, including architects, developers, neighborhood associations, and community groups. The result is that many of these other entities included public art in their own projects and initiatives. The impact ultimately went far beyond anything they could have done on their own.

~

I have devoted these last pages to practicalities because the consciousness of elderhood that I have been arguing for matters little unless we also challenge the cult of adulthood and its campaigns against both youth and old age. We are not prisoners of this social order; we can confront its beliefs. We can rethink the approach we are taking toward our own longevity. A life centered on BEING-doing, once embraced, can be made very sweet indeed. We can begin to look at the older people we know not as potential burdens but as elders in the making. Political debate can be steered away from the looming war between young and old, fit and frail, and toward policies that are dedicated to the good of people of all ages and abilities.

The ideas of Eldertopia show how our commitment to the elders of our community can lead us to better ways of living together. Eldertopia rejects the zero-sum game of interest-group politics and embraces instead a fount of human wisdom fifty thousand years in the making. It is true that we are living in a time of crisis, and it is also true that this crisis carries with it the seeds of our personal, social, and cultural renewal. We are living in a historic moment. Decisions we make now can either ensure or destroy the prospects for our own longevity and the elderhood of those yet to be born.

What we need most of all, what we must never lose sight of, is the truth of our human heritage. Old age is not the source of our problems; it is where we will find the answers we need. Indeed, it has been the source of all our answers from the moment we first learned to grow old.

Acknowledgments

The generous support provided by the Robert Wood Johnson Foundation (RWJF) made this work possible. I am enormously grateful for the opportunity the foundation gave me. As a visionary in his own right, David Colby saw what few others could see and advocated for these ideas early in their development. As a respected RWJF program officer, he guided the project from the beginning. My relationship with the RWJF deepened with time, and I came to appreciate the comments and insights of Jim Knickman and Jane Lough, especially their feedback on the Green House Project in Tupelo, Mississippi.

Dr. Mary Jane Koren has been my guardian angel for more than a decade, first in her role at the New York State Department of Health and later at the Samuels Foundation and the Commonwealth Fund. Mary Jane has supported the development of many of the ideas in this book. The Green House, in particular, owes much to a nearly daylong conversation in her office. She pushed me to express my ideas more clearly, always seeming to ask the perfect question that could open my eyes just a little bit wider.

Robert Mayer read an early version of the manuscript and provided written comments that proved very valuable to me. He has supported the work of the Eden Alternative for years, and for that I am very thankful. His dedication to positive social change has also led him to support the Green House. With his help, we were able to gain Rothschild Foundation funding for the Green House Project film. This film has aided our educational efforts immensely. As the producer of the Green House film, Dale Bell (of Wiland-Bell Productions) created a visual representation of important parts of this book and did so with his customary brilliance.

When I was writing this book, I was named an Ashoka Fellow. Ashoka is dedicated to promoting social change by fostering the practice of social entrepreneurship. The fellowship has allowed me to strengthen my ability to lead reform in the field of aging. The best part of being an Ashoka Fellow has been the rich interchange with other Fellows. My conversations with Marc Freedman, in particular, have been very useful to me.

Since the very beginning of my work in the field of aging, Danny Siegel, Naomi Eisenberg, and the Ziv Tzedaka Fund have been a constant source of encouragement and support. Danny helped me clarify many of the ideas in the "Old Maps" chapter. Best of all, he took the time to read a nearly complete version of the manuscript and offer his thoughts on it to me.

The Community Foundation of Oneida and Herkimer Counties, with the encouragement of Peggy O'Shea, supported the early work on the concept of Eldertopia. The assistance that Peggy and the foundation provided enabled me to spend time thinking deeply about the true nature of the intergenerational exchange that sustains human society. The general concepts in the chapter "Eldertopia" grew out of specific recommendations I made to the foundation regarding their ongoing work in the community.

John Zeisel gave me the gift of a careful and highly constructive reading of a draft manuscript. He offered just the right blend of praise and criticism and led me to reorganize and substantially rewrite major sections of the book. I hope, someday, to be able to return the favor.

I have been blessed with the opportunity to participate in a years-long, ongoing, three-way conversation about many of these issues. Bill (Liam) Keene and Wendy Lustbader have sustained me with the nectar of true friendship and a thoughtful, reflective consideration of how to develop a "new culture of aging."

Lynn Morris, a gifted technical writer with the eye of an editor, was my partner as we worked through dozens of versions and revisions. Lynn somehow made sense of the comments I scrawled on printed sections of the text, incorporated those changes into the manuscript, and advised me on where the argument continued to be unclear. She stuck with me as a ragged series of incomplete chapters gradually became a book.

Barry and Debbie Barkan have also contributed much to this work. Barry paid me the honor of advising me on the social structure and priorities of the shahbaz and helped me think through the idea of radical alternative to the dependency-based system of workforce organization that currently prevails in long-term care. Barry continues to innovate, write persuasively, and organize his own fresh new approaches to age and aging in contemporary society.

I have benefited enormously from the opportunity to work with AARP and to participate in the evolution of its social-impact agenda. Bill Novelli read an early version of the manuscript and his thoughts on it helped me revise the book, especially the last half. I am also thankful for the advice and counsel of Lisa Davis, Marty Davis, Kevin Donellen, Christine Donohoo, Bonniebeth Foltz, Chris Hansen, Nancy Leamond, Barb Quaintance, and Kirsten Sloan. Each has helped me better understand the complex relationships among policy, advocacy, and social change.

Since its founding in the early 1990s, the Eden Alternative has grown into a healthy and vibrant international movement. Its most recent successes are due in large part to the inspired work of its executive director, Nancy Fox. Nancy read and reread early drafts of this book and provided me with especially valuable guidance on the chapters relating to the Eden Alternative and the Green House. We reviewed many of those changes during the long hours we spent flying home from an Eden training in Australia. She is leading the Eden Alternative with grace and dignity and will, in years to come, bring the movement to heights we can only dream of today.

A terrific advisory board has guided the evolution of the Green House. Meeting on an occasional basis since 2001, these advisors have always maintained that the Green House be more than an attractive idea. They have insisted that it be a viable, self-sustaining alternative to the long-term care institution. I am pleased to acknowledge the contributions of Bill Benson, Ira Byock, Sheldon Goldberg, Robert Kane, and Robyn Stone.

Part of what makes this book useful is the fact that its ideas are, even now, being placed into practice. A nursing home in Mississippi has been closed and the elders who lived there are now living in the world's first Green Houses. This great leap never would have been possible without the visionary leadership and personal courage of Steve McAlilly. He and his leadership team have worked tirelessly to turn a dream into a reality. The board of directors of the Mississippi Methodist Senior Services organization blessed and supported every effort, and much of the success is due to their imagination and courage.

Thank you and congratulations to the first shahbazim: Matilda L. Belue, Tomeka R. Blackmon, Jennie L. Buchanan, Bridget L. Bumphis, Gennie Anne Butler, Ida Mae Cummings, Jacky Lee Davis, Maggie C. Doss, Samantha Fullilove, Callie R. Gates, Tarlyn K. Gates, Gina A. Goff, Doreen A. Guinn, Emma Marie Hankins, Shelia D. Harkness, Peggy Johnson, Lisa L. Jones, Bobbie Dale Letson, Everetta Torrane Mabry, Latanya D. Mayfield, Shirley Jean McCrady, Ana R. McDowell, Martha W. Miller, Inita G. Pannell, Anita M. Perry, Eric J. Poole, Reena Reid, Mary L. Richardson, Cheryl Denise Richey, Henry Santana, Kathy W. Santana, Angie Mae Berry Shannon, Natasha S. Smith, Cathy Jean Swingrum, Gwendolyn Niki Thompson, Ruthie Mae Wade, Stephanie Rena Wilson.

There are many people who have helped me in so many ways, often when they were unaware of how valuable their assistance would be. Gloria Cavanaugh, Dale Danefer, Nora Gibson, Sarah Greene, Elma Holder, Gail Kass, Paul Kleyman, Susan Misorski, Rick Moody, Laverne Norton, Anna Otigara, Joanne Rader, Sandy Ransom, Steve Shields, Jerry Smart, Debbie VanStratten, Carter and Frank Williams, and Tom Zwicker among many others have all contributed something to this work; they deserve a share of any credit given to this book.

The writing of a book involves every member of a household. All my children have contributed to the creation of this work. They have watched as the book went through countless rounds of revision and rewriting, and each inspired me in his or her own way. Thank you, Zachary, Virgil, Haleigh Jane, Hannah, and Caleb.

It is said that a good marriage is the most precious possession any man can have, and by that standard I am a very wealthy man. The wife of an author must not only tolerate a rival for her husband's attention but encourage him to fall in love with his creation as well. That is asking much, and my wife, Judith Meyers-Thomas, has supported this work in every way possible. As a reader, she prodded me to be clearer. As a friend, she encouraged me in my lowest moments. I cannot thank her enough.

The skilled professionals who share in the care of Haleigh and Hannah (and care for us as well)—Kathy Bohndorf, Jennifer Bono, Sue Caraher, Mary Cook, Francie Goff, Jan Jerabek, Amy Pinney, Jody Stage, Sarah Stewart, Jane Swingle, Barb Taskey, and Joan Tomaselli—all influenced me as well. Our farm and retreat center, where we do much of our teaching, would not be able to operate (and I would be unable to write) if it were not for the skill and dedication of Jerry Alverman, Jason Morgan, Jeff Price, and Mike Squires. My partners and staff at my medical practice carried on through the long ordeal of creating this book and made sure that every patient received superb care, even when I was immersed in writing. Dr. Upinder Singh and Lynn Paquette read and commented on chapters, especially "Navigating Life." Carol Ende and Diane Urtz helped keep me organized so that I could fulfill all my obligations and neglect none.

There is a great tradition of authors writing in public, and much of this book was written at the corner table of the D and D Diner in my hometown. The entire staff became accustomed to seeing me sitting there, hour after hour, tapping away on my computer. They watched over me and cared for me with great warmth and affection. Their consistent generosity sustained me through many difficult passages. I must acknowledge Kelly Abdul, Richard Ackerman, Thomas Ackerman, Jill Ayers, Ronald Baker, Brian Button, Jerry Cappadonia, Amanda Carpenter, Roberta Kerwin, Laurie Knochenmus, Kelly Manwarren, Nathan Manwarren, Gina Merritt, Kandi Monroe, Kelly Page, Vern Palmiter, Kitty Ray, Maria Searles, Bobbi Jo Showens, Allen Summers, Debbie Sutherland, Mari Underwood, and Diane Weinheimer.

In the end, Pat Moore, my editor at VanderWyk & Burnham, did more than anyone else to bring this work to fruition. She helped me to finish what I had started and made this work much more consistent, accurate, and well written than it would have been without her contribution. A thousand thank yous would not be enough to express my gratitude.

APPENDIX

As hard as it is to write about new ways of thinking about aging, it is far more difficult to place any such ideas into daily practice. Still, the true test of any theory is its ability to solve ordinary problems. Our society has had a particularly hard time providing a life worth living for those elders whose circumstances require them to leave their own homes and begin living with others. The nursing home has failed us, but we have yet to clearly define an acceptable alternative to mass institutionalization. Thankfully, the Robert Wood Johnson Foundation and the Mississippi Methodist Senior Services decided to cooperate in a test of the Green House model. What follows are the reflections of Steve McAlilly, the president of MMSS. He discusses the challenges that come with leaving the institutional model behind and the early results of their experience with the Green House model.

The First Green Houses

The story of the development of the quartz watch is frequently told to illustrate the concept that new ideas are often best developed by those on the fringe. A team of researchers employed by a Swiss watch manufacturer invented the quartz movement. When they unveiled their discovery, the management could not see any merit in it. Watches were supposed to have springs, gears, and hands that move. So, the quartz movement was shelved by the Swiss and only emerged after a Japanese company embraced it. Unencumbered by the watchmaker's common sense, this company brought an inexpensive, all-digital quartz-movement watch to market. Within five years, the centuries-old Swiss watchmaking industry was fighting for survival.

The watchmaker's dilemma provides a good analogy for the difficulties (and revolutionary potential) that attend the development of the Green House. The conventional long-term care industry possesses an especially resilient common sense. The way things are blinds us to what could be. The long arm of the status quo quickly lays hold of those who dare to stray from standard practices. It is in the context of this reality that we began our long and convoluted passage to providing a radically different kind of environment for the elders of our community. These notes trace the journey as we have moved fitfully toward our goal of making life better for elders, whose needs and gifts are so great. The quest has been a continuous battle against the power of established paradigms.

United Methodist Senior Services of Mississippi Inc. (UMSSM) is a not-for-profit corporation affiliated with the Mississippi Annual Conference of the United Methodist Church. Its home base is in Tupelo,

Mississippi. There are ten retirement campuses within the organization, located from the Mississippi Gulf Coast to the Tennessee state line. Among its 1,550 units are independent living apartments and cottages, and assisted-living facilities. In addition, three campuses provide skilled nursing care to 260 residents. UMSSM is fortunate to have a governing board committed to providing the most innovative care available. It takes its mission—serving older adults in the spirit of Christian love—seriously.

UMSSM is a pioneer and innovator in providing housing and services to elders in Mississippi. It opened one of the first HUD Section 202 apartment complexes for low-income elders in Mississippi. It started one of the first assisted-living apartment complexes in Mississippi. It formed one of the first Alzheimer units in the state. Recognizing the need to serve elders who live in their homes, it developed relationships that provide homemaker services and Meals on Wheels to many who do not live on its campuses.

The Tupelo campus of UMSSM, Traceway Retirement Community, opened in 1966 and today provides three levels of care: independent living, assisted living, and skilled nursing care. The skilled nursing unit, Cedars, opened in 1978. It is a 140-bed, semiprivate nursing home that participates in Medicaid. Traceway is a subsidiary, not-for-profit corporation with its own governing board whose members are from the Tupelo area. Cedars generates revenue from Medicaid reimbursement, private pay, and gift income. Without gift income, private pay rates would be substantially higher than they are.

Our journey toward the Green House started in the fall of 1993. The Traceway directors identified a need for a freestanding thirty-bed Alzheimer's unit. Preliminary estimates suggested that five hundred thousand dollars in donations would be needed to complete the project. True to its nature, the organization launched a comprehensive review of the state of the art in Alzheimer's care. Central to the vision was the idea that each elder deserved a private room and a private bath.

In order to increase operational efficiency, the initial design called for the unit to be attached to the existing Cedars skilled-care facility. The next iteration envisioned a new, attached Alzheimer's unit and the complete renovation of the existing Cedars nursing home. Cost estimates put that project near ten million dollars. That was a very big price tag for a project that would still leave us with a freshly renovated, increasingly antiquated medical-model nursing home. We also began to see that all of the design elements that were thought to be beneficial to elders living with dementia could be of great benefit to elders without dementia. This led us to the idea of replacing the entire Cedars building.

After reviewing several different design drawings, we settled on a replacement facility that came with a twelve-million-dollar price tag. It featured seven twenty-bed "neighborhoods," all with private rooms and private baths, and a central "great room" area where the elders in each neighborhood would socialize and dine. We were proud of what we had come up with, but the price was too high and it was a massive structure. Five years had passed and we felt a growing need to get started. The board of directors launched a capital fund-raising campaign to provide the up-front money for the project and pledged to continue working with the architects to find ways to bring the cost down.

In one of the many twists of fate that brought us to the Green House, the fund-raising campaign got off to a slower than expected start. If it had been an immediate success, we would have made a twelve-million-dollar mistake. Thankfully, it took years rather than months to raise the $2.7 million we needed to get started.

We have worked with the same architectural firm, McCarty and Associates of Tupelo, Mississippi, throughout this journey. Many architectural firms are not inclined to reinvent the wheel. They will actively resist new, unfamiliar approaches to established design problems. In the end, though, Richard McCarty "got it" and embraced the concept of the Green House. He has been a driving force in helping us make the Green Houses what they should be. McCarty's firm had extensive experience with hospital and physician clinic design. I remember an early discussion with the architects about the feel we were striving for. We were talking about the elders having enough space for their own furniture so they could bring their own chest of drawers and use it as a television stand, for example. One of the architects shook his head and asked, "You mean the televisions won't be attached high on the wall?"

Overcoming the inertia created by ordinary thinking takes extraordinary perseverance and a solid commitment to principles. As the fund-raising campaign lagged on, I began learning about the Eden Alternative.

I heard Dr. Bill Thomas make a three-hour presentation at a national conference. He gave me the words to articulate many of my feelings about long-term care. Having come from the "fringes" (I practiced law for fourteen years before coming to work for UMSSM), I had never been satisfied with what we were doing in our skilled-care facilities. Measured by objective standards, the care was better than average, but we struggled with mediocre survey results and elder/family complaints were the norm. What disturbed me more than that was the fact that our leaders found this situation acceptable. The prevailing view seemed to be: "Like it or not, this is how it is in nursing homes." I challenged them to reject mediocrity and reach beyond the usual.

As I've learned more about what is wrong with the current system and what I believe the answers are, I can see that the administrators really were doing the best they could with a very flawed model. The results we were getting were the best results possible in a large medical-model nursing home. But this was unacceptable. I believed the answers lay in the Eden Alternative principles and promised myself that I would work the rest of my life to see that every elder in Mississippi had the chance to live in a nursing home that practiced the Eden principles.

I still believed that our new design, together with the Eden principles, would do the trick. The first step of the transformation of elder care in Mississippi was up to us. We brought the Eden regional coordinator in for a daylong presentation of the Eden Alternative concepts to our executive directors and management team. In the end, we decided that we should implement the Eden principles on all our campuses. To help make that happen, in August 1999 I invited Bill Thomas to come down and address a statewide meeting of our directors and trustees, with as many of our employees as we could spare. On the ride from the airport to the meeting, I excitedly told Bill of the great new nursing home we were building. He made the comment, almost as an aside, that he wasn't sure that kind of home was what elders really needed. This thought stayed with me and I reflected on it for a long time. If not that, then what?

In 2000 our fund-raising total climbed to about $2.5 million but we were still far short of the money needed to build the nursing home. We continued to do our best to make the Eden Alternative come alive in our existing facilities and nursed the dream of building something new, something boldly original and ideally suited to the lives our elders wanted to live. The construction of a conventional (though innovative) facility remained well beyond our budget.

It was in the fall of 2000 that I first heard of the Green House concept. It seemed to me as I played with sketches and numbers that such an idea would be within our financial capacity and that life in such an environment might be much better than in our proposed institutional neighborhoods.

Looking back, I can see how tightly conventional wisdom still gripped us. We had much more to learn. After discussing the Green House idea with our staff and leadership, in early 2001 we asked our architects to begin preliminary design work. The extent of our Green House knowledge was limited to what was posted on the Green House Web site. This is where the lure of the usual almost trapped us. The architects presented us with a twenty-bed miniature nursing home. The project was more affordable because residential construction is less expensive than steel and concrete institutional construction, but the design was far from ideal.

Our own team had enormous difficulty seeing this project as something distinctively new. All of our systems were designed to maximize economies of scale and operational efficiency. We struggled to identify and maximize the economies of smallness. The blame for these difficulties is best laid at the doorstep of the long-term care industry. We are, more than we know, creatures of habit. It is the human way: we do what we know. When I expressed my concern that the Green House was too big for the type of living it was supposed to support, I was told that the financials and operations would be unsustainable if the houses were made any smaller. This was a critical point in our journey. The Green Houses had to be residential in size, and we had to find a way to make them work in the context of existing funding and regulations.

Despite the hard and fast cautionary advice of our best people, I knew that I had to go to our board of directors with a request for their support as we tried to push through this barrier. I believed that they would support the effort if we could help them understand the reasons for it. And they did, totally. With the board's solid support, we took on another major potential obstacle to building the Green Houses as Dr. Thomas had imagined them —the regulators.

As a person who canoes frequently, I've found that if you work with the river, you make it safely to your destination. People get into trouble on the river when they fight the current—no human being has enough strength to win such a battle. In contrast, those who surrender to the river can only go where the current takes them, which is usually into the rocks. The best course is set by using the paddle to take advantage of the current; doing so, canoeists can move the boat anywhere they need it to go, usually fairly easily. That was the way we approached the regulators.

With solid board support and the financial numbers finally looking good, we went to the State Department of Health to talk about redefining long-term care in Mississippi. We wanted to model a new way of working with the state, one based on collaboration, not conflict. We asked that all the persons who would be involved in regulatory approval be in attendance so that we could present the Green House concepts to them as a group. We told them that we were committed to the value and importance of the regulations and that we would seek to uphold every last one of them, but not necessarily in ways they were accustomed to. For instance, we would provide the functions of a nurses' station, but we would not build a nurses' station. The regulators were surprisingly receptive and took their part of the partnership seriously. I believe that government regulators recognize, as we do, that the system is broken. Fighting that system is as fruitful as fighting the river's current—none of us have the strength. Ignoring the system won't work either. Those who do so are bound to wind up on the rocks. The best course is to work as a partner with the system. Outside a state of revolution, this is how the most important changes are made.

In February 2002 the Cedars administrator took our floor plans to a national Eden meeting and showed them to Dr. Thomas. The next week Dr. Thomas called me to offer us the support and resources of the Green House Project. We had just finished a board meeting, and the board was anxious to get started with our twenty-unit project; we had donors who were wondering if we were ever going to do anything. Dr. Thomas wanted us to bring our architect and four staff members to Summer Hill to meet with his team. I told Bill that was great, but we really needed to get moving; he responded, "What about this weekend?" (It was a Wednesday.) I told him we would be there.

Our architect, chief operating officer, campus executive director, nursing home administrator, and a certified nurse's aid spent three days with Bill and his team and three other organizations working on Green Houses. They began fleshing out the details of the building and, more importantly, the concepts of living in the house. Our architect finally and totally got it!

We left with a new understanding: this was not only about a building that is warm, smart, and green; this was about a sanctuary for elderhood that rises and falls according to the relationships formed there. We learned so much and continue to learn much. We began thinking about the house as a home—the home of the elders who would live there. We began thinking about putting decisions in their hands about what and when to eat, about what furniture would go in the house, about what colors the rooms would be—little things to us, but big things they had lost. We began thinking about how to make elderhood the most meaningful and significant passage in a person's life. We began thinking about helping the elders seek peace, provide wisdom, and prepare a legacy.

We are trying to put our major focus on the front-line staff, formerly certified nurse's assistants, and make their jobs the most important jobs we have. We know that we have to have special people—ones who understand and have the heart required for this new work. We are trying to leave behind as much of the old as possible—everything from the way we organize work to what we call people. The person who works in the Green House with the elders is known as a shahbaz, from a story Bill Thomas tells about a Persian royal falcon. The story teaches the way of the worker in a Green House: a person with a heart who is focused on building a relationship with the elders and who protects, sustains, and nurtures them. The shahbaz will guide the elder through the challenging passages of late life.

But, the paradigms . . . just when you think everybody understands it, something comes up or a new person joins the team. I'd be a rich man if I had a dollar for every time I've said to an architect, "Think of home. You wouldn't have that in your home, would you?" It has been so hard to keep people from being pulled back to the safety and convenience of the way things have always been done.

So, we went to the state and worked through more than one hundred potential points of conflict with the regulations and solved all of them within two weeks. This effort is a testament to the power of people working together in good faith for the well-being of the elders. The state regulators have been great to work with—they've fulfilled their responsibility but have been flexible about new ways of meeting the regulations.

Every day a new question or concern comes up. Many times the root of the concern can be traced back to the anxiety produced by leaving the old paradigm behind. Such a journey can be frightening at times, because human beings like the comfort and security of black-and-white issues and answers to questions. That may be one of the hardest leadership issues involved in doing something like this—helping people find the courage to move forward. The path that lies at our feet is only dimly lit. We have far more questions than answers. What gives me the courage to press on is the knowledge that the current system is broken beyond repair; the life a Green House can offer is what our elders need. As difficult as it may be to achieve, it's the right thing to do.

I have learned so much and have much more to learn. For those of you about to embark on this journey, I would remind you to watch for the tendency to lapse back into familiar ways of thinking. Also, expect a steady stream of difficulties and barriers. Remember the river: work with the current, not against it. Finally, learn to be patient with people when they don't yet understand what the Green House means. Return again and again to the worthiness of the mission and vision. Try to find an architect who understands in his or her heart what you're trying to do (ours does!). Strong leadership throughout the organization is needed for such a shift in thought and practice. If I had not come from the fringes, I wonder if I would have been able to make the necessary paradigm shift, or even been able to see that such a shift was necessary. Be patient with those outside your organization who are having a hard time seeing the goal. Keep working with them and help them along in any way you can.

Yesterday I went over to one of the Green Houses that is six weeks from completion. The kitchen cabinets were being installed. The painters were at work. The fireplace was taking shape. I was more excited than I have been yet (and I've been pretty excited). We are going to make a difference. We really are going to put an end to the institutionalization of Mississippi's elders. And that is just the beginning.

Stephen L. McAlilly
September 2003

NOTES

TRUE LONGEVITY

3 A New Wrinkle
Information about wrinkles embodies the full range of society's conflicted attitudes about aging. For the most part, books and articles on the subject hold that wrinkles are very bad indeed. The mainstream view is that technology will, ultimately, provide a cure to this ill. Voices willing to proclaim that wrinkles are actually irrelevant are seldom heard. The idea that wrinkles should be welcomed as a positive sign of continuing development are virtually absent. A beautiful exception to the conventional wisdom is provided by James Hillman in *The Force of Character*. His book offers a highly evolved vision of the dynamics of aging in modern society. For a more academic look at the larger question of ageism, the best source I have found is *Ageism: Negative and Positive* by Erdman Palmore.

3 Reader Looks Younger . . . Now Dating Again! . . . , author's local paper, the *Evening Sun*, 2001.

7 "Wrinkled, sagging skin . . . ," Perricone, *The Wrinkle Cure*, 1.

8 In its pure form, a single gram . . . , Council on Foreign Relations, *Terrorism: Questions & Answers*.

9 "Because Botox wears off . . . ," Kuczynski, *New York Times*, February 7, 2002.

9 "If you imagine your face as a phenomenon . . . ," Hillman, *The Forces of Character*, 148.

9 "I want to grow old without facelifts . . . ," Hillman, 136.

9 "When they [dermatologists] have a product they can sell . . . ," Wilson, *Off the Record Research*, 3.

12 The Doctrine of Youth's Perfection
Research in the field of aging has yet to rival astrophysics as the leading frontier of human understanding. Mostly, this is due to the field's inability to rid itself of outmoded and unwarranted assumptions

about aging. It is as if cartographers simply refused to give up their faith in the flatness of Earth. I have more than a little sympathy for them, though, because old age is a social construct, not an objective reality. Those who choose to study aging are themselves the products of an ageist, declinist society. Our collective equation of aging and decline and our blind faith in the virtues of youth are on display everywhere. From dusty tomes of academic publications to the birth-day card rack at the local drugstore we are never far away from the idea that youth is perfect.

13 **Ripe 1. Fully developed; mature:** *ripe peaches* . . . , *The American Heritage Dictionary,* 1503.

16 **They included a graph . . . ,"** see graph (below) Human Mortality Rate, drawn from data in Strehler and Mildvan, "General Theory of Mortality and Aging," 15.

16 **They described vitality as "the capacity . . . ,"** Strehler and Mildvan, "General Theory of Mortality and Aging," 15.

16 **. . . every "organism consists of a number of subsystems . . . ,"** Strehler and Mildvan, 15.

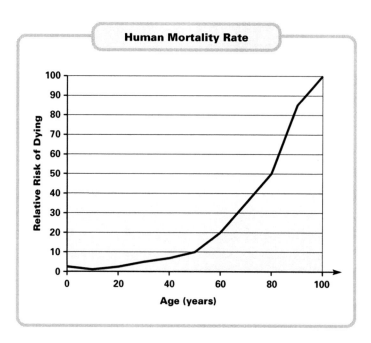

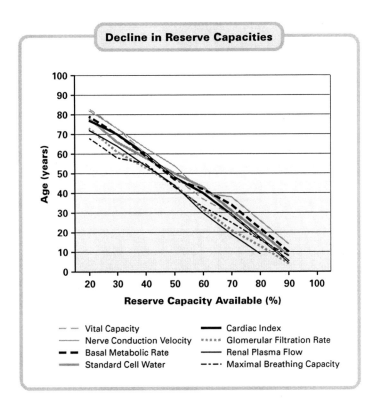

Decline in Reserve Capacities

Age (years) / Reserve Capacity Available (%)

- – – Vital Capacity
- —— Nerve Conduction Velocity
- ▪ ▪ Basal Metabolic Rate
- —— Standard Cell Water
- ▬▬ Cardiac Index
- ∗∗∗∗ Glomerular Filtration Rate
- —— Renal Plasma Flow
- —·—· Maximal Breathing Capacity

18 **The researchers' bias can be seen . . .** , see graph (above) Decline in Reserve Capacities, redrawn from Strehler and Mildvan, 16.

19 **They are growth in head circumference, . . .** , see graph (next page) Head Circumference, from Public Health Group of the Victorian State Government Department of Human Services, http://www.dhs.vic.gov.au/phd/childhealthrecord/growth/chart_boys1.htm.

20 **"a gradual change in . . . physical, chemical, or . . . ,"** Strehler and Mildvan, 15.

20 **Decade after decade that amount . . .** , see graph (next page) Change in Reserve Capacities, drawn from data in Strehler and Mildvan, 14–21.

22 <u>The Hidden Powers of Age</u>

The main idea that drives research on aging in a declinist society is that we can all benefit from the most detailed possible description of

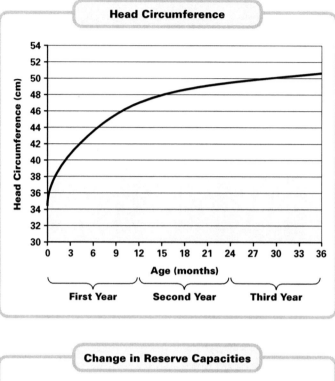

Head Circumference

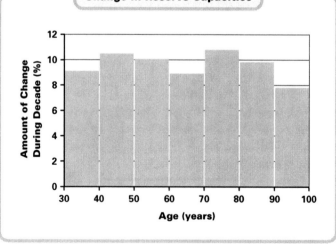

Change in Reserve Capacities

the gradual descent into oblivion that we assume aging to be. Old age is a complex and little understood interaction between aging and longevity. One of the first books that showed me the richness that could come from understanding the relationship between these two ideas was Betty Friedan's *The Fountain of Age.* That book startled me with its persistent reinterpretation of what I had assumed were settled matters. In particular, I found her discussion of age-related changes in thought, memory, and problem-solving to be brilliant. Those who want to delve even more deeply into the thoughtless ageism that defines our times should read Beauvoir's *The Coming of Age*. It should come as no surprise that two of the best critical evaluations of aging to be developed in the last 40 years come from feminist authors. The consequences of our mis-measure of aging fall predominantly on women.

22 "As Gregor Samsa awoke one morning . . . ," Kafka, *The Metamorphosis*, 1.

23 [He] "swung himself out of bed . . . ," Kafka,, 5.

25 "improvements in emotional functioning may continue . . . ," Carstensen et al., "Emotional Experience in Everyday Life Across the Adult Life Span," 644.

26 "Not even at the oldest ages did the frequency . . . ," Carstensen et al., 644.

26 "were more likely to maintain . . . ," Carstensen et al., 650.

26 Age was associated with greater complexity . . . , see graph (below) Differentiation of Emotional Experience, drawn from data in Carstensen et al., 644–655.

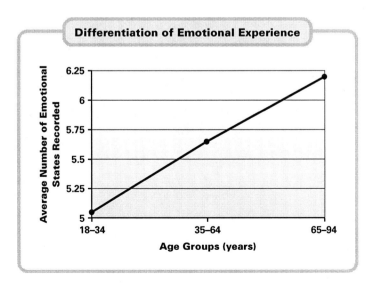

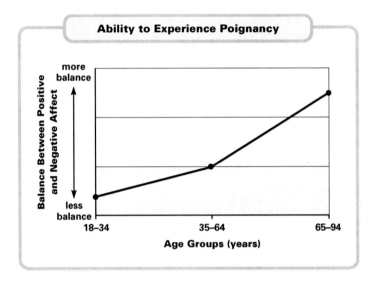

Ability to Experience Poignancy

Balance Between Positive and Negative Affect

more balance

less balance

18–34   35–64   65–94

Age Groups (years)

26 **Older people were more able to . . .** , see graph (above) Ability to Experience Poignancy, drawn from data in Carstensen et al., 644–655.

27 **Development brings increasing. . .** , Carstensen et al., 653.

28 **In his analysis, Tornstam groups these experiences . . .** , Tornstam, "Gerotranscendence: The Contemplative Dimension of Aging," 143–154.

32 <u>Myths and Other Theories</u>
The Greeks have one other story of aging that deserves notice. On his long voyage home, Ulysses was held on the island of an enchantress who had fallen in love with him. She offered him a magic potion that would give him eternal youth and swore to him that he could live together with her for all time. Ulysses turned her down, preferring to grow old with Penelope, his wife, and thus tasted the bitter fruit of mortality, his and hers. The story suggests that his decision was wise in that it was human. The Greeks knew both how difficult old age could be and how quintessentially human aging is. As I was writing the book, I quickly found that scientific understandings of aging were especially unhelpful to me. Being obsessed with the *how* of aging (as the scientists are) they paid little heed to the *why* of aging. Folklore, in contrast, has much to say on the latter question, and one subgenre that readers may want to explore further consists of stories that explain the origins of aging and of death. Such

stories frequently place the blame for these ills on an old and foolish woman. Other stories highlight pettiness and greed among older people. All of these stories are worth exploring because they make it clear that human aging is a complex and contradictory phenomenon. Sadly, such complexity is almost entirely missing in our attempts to assemble a modern and frighteningly mechanistic explanation of aging.

33 "of one so gifted . . . ," Bullfinch, *Mythology*, 164.

BECOMING HUMAN

41 A Matter of Life and Death
Evolution allows useful traits to evolve. Aging has evolved and evidence of that evolution can be used to support the novel idea that aging is a useful trait. While this argument does not lead to an immediately testable hypothesis, it does provide a strategy for confronting the basic declinist argument. If we are willing to see a pattern of development in the long line of adaptations that gradually allowed sea creatures to live on land, how can we not be open to the idea that the life cycle of such creatures might also be open to adaptation and change? The caterpillar becomes the butterfly. Who is to say which form is superior? Each has its own strengths and weaknesses. Just so, the child becomes the parent, and the parent becomes the grandparent. These forms were developed and remain available to us because they have value. For those who wish to delve further into the imprint that evolution has left on our being, I recommend Carl Sagan's highly readable, Pulitzer Prize–winning book *The Dragons of Eden*.

42 "Why, if man can by patience select variations . . . ," Darwin, *The Origin of Species*, vii.

50 Necessity's Virtue
The idea that the contribution of food made by the old to the young was a crucial factor in the development of the modern human is delightfully counterintuitive. Adult society is much more attracted to the idea of old age as the product of a peculiar form of noblesse oblige. Making old age central to the human story helps counter the declinism of contemporary society. Proof of that centrality will remain hard to come by. In fact, rereading older speculations on the roots of our humanity quickly reveals how easily such arguments can

be shaped by the social milieu of the writer, rather than the objective facts on hand. I think that academic research related to grandmothering, the grandmother hypothesis, and the grandmother effect is worthy of our respect, but it is important for another reason as well. Because the truth in this area will never be known with certainty, ideas about our origins have come to represent an acceptable form of modern-day mythology. With this in mind, it is hardly surprising that a rapidly aging society (such as our own) would be attracted to the idea that it is old age that made us what we are today.

51 **Lions and tigers are evolutionary cousins . . .** , see table (first below) Lion and Tiger as Closely Related Species.

51 **among all primates we are most closely related to chimpanzees,** see table Differences and Similarities in Chimp and Human Life Cycles.

Table: **Lion and Tiger as Closely Related Species**

Life Cycle	Lion	Tiger	Percent Variance
Gestation	110 days	103 days	6.4
Litter size	2–3	2–3	nil
Weaning	16–18 m	16–18 m	nil
Life span	18 y	16 y	11

Table: **Differences and Similarities in Chimp and Human Life Cycles**

Life Cycle	Chimp	Human	Percent Variance
Gestation	8 m	9 m	12.5
Lactation*	6 y	2 y	300
Litter size	1	1 (rarely >1)	minimal
Onset of fertility	12–15 y	12–15 y	minimal
Span of fertility	30–40 y	35–50 y	minimal
Maximum life span	55 y	110 y	100
Postfertility life span	1–5 y	30–50 y	1000

* Weaning ages for human infants range from zero (bottle fed) to six years. Most human infants are weaned in the second year of life.

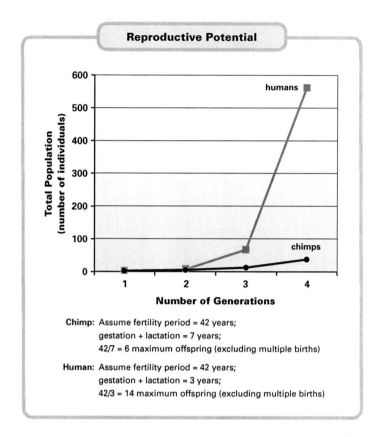

Reproductive Potential

Chimp: Assume fertility period = 42 years;
gestation + lactation = 7 years;
42/7 = 6 maximum offspring (excluding multiple births)

Human: Assume fertility period = 42 years;
gestation + lactation = 3 years;
42/3 = 14 maximum offspring (excluding multiple births)

51 **Our postreproductive longevity . . . ,** see graph (above) Reproductive Potential

53 **From birth to the teenage years . . . ,** Johnson, "Functional Brain Development in Humans," 475–483.

53 It is worth noting that primatologists have identified grandparenting behavior in other primates. The existence of this behavior can be seen as supporting my core argument, which is that humans are distinguishable from other primates in large part because of their emphasis on and refinement of grandparenting in particular and of eldering in general. Humans deploy the virtues of aging in ways that are distinct from what has been observed in other primate populations.

56 **"If the grandmother dies, you notice it . . . ,"** Sear et al., "Maternal grandmothers improve nutritional status and survival of children in rural Gambia," 1641–1647.

56 **When female rats are handled gently . . .**, "Gentling," *Encyclopedia Britannica*, 1979.

59 **An African proverb says . . .**, Mambo, *private communication*, 2002.

THE RISE OF ELDERHOOD

67 <u>Old Age Long Ago</u>
I was able to make several visits to Australia during the writing of this book. In particular, I found my visits to the Queensland State Library to be very helpful. Their collection of works related to paleo-anthropology and studies of pre-European contact with Aboriginal society were very useful to me. Much of the material I gathered there helped me shape the argument in this chapter. The most important idea is that investment in old age and the well-being of old people is, most of all, the product of a calculated weighting of risk and benefit. Just as evolution promotes or retards the spread of specific genetic traits, human culture accepts or rejects specific patterns of thought, belief, and practice. The global distribution of old age and social mechanisms for the protection and nurturance of the old is a power-ful testament to the value of these innovations. The best book I know that examines the power and utility of this kind of cultural evolution is Robert Wright's *Non-Zero*. Although the book has little to say on the subject of aging and longevity per se, it does provide a convincing description of the process through which aging might have been refined as an important cultural tool.

68 **[The day before the tribe was set to move] . . .**, Beauvoir, *The Coming of Age*, 47.

69 **[Those] who lived . . .**, Beauvoir, 51.

72 **"My Spirit will not . . .**, Gen. 6:3.

74 **Once there was an old man of considerable means . . .**, Hassidic folktale, as remembered by author.

76 **A woodcutter lived with his wife, his son, and his father . . .**, author's retelling based on the tale as translated by Varecha, *Grimms' Fairy*, 145.

79 <u>Industrial-Strength Aging</u>
   The old age that we take for granted today, is actually a recent invention. It grew out of the collapse of the feudal order and the rise of industrialization. For the most part, these changes have been bad news for older people. At the start of the twentieth century older people were, as a group, the poorest people in American society. The Great Depression set into motion a series of changes that, taken together, made older people into the wealthiest age group in the nation. When I was researching this book, I studied Arthur Schlesinger's two-volume history of the Depression. *The Crisis of the Old Order* was useful to me on two levels. First, it described, in scrupulous detail, capitalism's failure to protect the weak, the frail, and the ill. Second, it told the story of the collapse of a deeply entrenched social system. This interested me because I foresee a breakdown in the contemporary understanding of age and aging; indeed that crisis is already upon us. As its title suggests, the second volume details *The Coming of the New Deal* and presents an especially interesting review of the birth of Social Security. Those who have an interest in the emergence of a new kind of old age will be well served by reading both volumes.

80 " . . . the door flew open and Athelstane . . . ," Scott, *Ivanhoe*, 487.

82 . . . among the oldest long-term care organizations in the nation, see table (below) The Rise of Out-of-Home Care for the Aged.

Table: The Rise of Out-of-Home Care for the Aged

Current Name	Founded As	Location	Date
United Presbyterian Residence	Graham House	Brooklyn, NY	1885
Masonic Home of New Jersey	—	Burlington, NJ	1897
Hebrew Rehabilitation Center for the Aged	Hebrew Ladies Home for the Aged	Boston, MA	1903
National Lutheran Home	—	Rockville, MD	1905
Hebrew Home for the Aged of New York City	—	Bronx, NY	1917

88 **A 2001 survey of the American public . . .** , *The NewsHour with Jim Lehrer*/Kaiser Family Foundation, *National Survey on Nursing Homes*, 4.

91 <u>Victory</u>

I have made a habit of collecting aging-related "plague of locusts" news items. The topic seems to have become what journalists call an "evergreen." Such stories are deemed to always be pertinent and can be run in any season. It seems to be an article of faith that aging is a calamity that will lead us all to the poor house, or worse. At their most optimistic, reporters and commentators are sometimes able to assert that the age boom, while certainly a great peril, may not be as bad as some have feared. Conspicuously missing is any voice that is willing to proclaim that the age boom is actually an age boon. In my mind the person who has brought that argument forward with the greatest force and credibility is Theodore Roszak. Best known as the person who coined the term "counter-culture," Roszak has made a career of observing American society and offering careful critiques of what he sees. His book *America the Wise* is an inspired work in that tradition and has much to offer to those willing to consider the aging of our society as a windfall, perhaps the greatest windfall it has ever been our good fortune to receive. I have also benefited from reading *The Voice of the Earth*, also by Roszak.

93 **. . . a net social and economic gain for communities . . .** , see table (below) Trends in Federal Spending on People 65 and Over.

93 **. . . "social capital,"** Putnam, *Bowling Alone*, 18, 19.

Table: Trends in Federal Spending on People 65 and Over

Measurement	1971	1980	1990	2000	2010 *
Budget outlays (fiscal year in billions)	$46	$144	$360	$615	$1,050
Percentage of budget	22	24	29	35	43
Percentage of GDP	4.2	5.3	6.3	6.4	7.1
Outlay per elderly person (year 2000 dollars)	$8,896	$11,839	$15,192	$17,688	$21,122

Source: *Based on Congressional Budget Office 2001 data*   *Projected

99 Living on the Edge of the World

Some may wonder why this section begins with a lengthy review of the markings on a headstone. Certainly there is no standard footnote format for gravestones. This one stands where it has long stood, alongside East River Road just north of the village of Oxford, New York, and within sight of the veterans' nursing home. I devoted so much attention to the story of the Packer family because sometimes a thing is best revealed by studying the contours of its opposite. This family had remarkably little experience with either aging or longevity. Its members' lives may not have been nasty or brutish, but they certainly were short. Cemeteries are open books that reveal, to the curious, an almost infinite variety of experience with birth, life, growth, and death. It remains a useful thing to wander among the gravestones of strangers, and such an exercise is especially useful for those who choose to study aging.

NAVIGATING LIFE

106 Old Maps

The challenge in this chapter was to decide what to include and what to leave out. Each society, present and past, has its own map of life. In the end I chose to concentrate on the mainline of development in Western society. This decision excluded the richness I found in the maps of life created in non-Western and Aboriginal societies, and the reader would do well to dip a toe into this literature with *The Human Cycle* by Colin Turnbull being an excellent starting point. Overall, it is my view that human societies have moved gradually toward life cycles that are less tightly defined. The trend is toward more flexibility, more choice, and, truth be told, far more uncertainty. The evolution of the human life cycle, especially in the last 200 years or so, has been a major contributor to the overall increase in human freedom we have witnessed in that time. A clear sign of this trend can be found in the emergence of contemporary childhood. The book *Centuries of Childhood* by Philippe Ariès traces this development beautifully and, though some scholars have objected to his conclusions, the source material he draws on is fascinating, and the book has much to offer anyone interested in how the map of life changes over time.

106 Since 1900, the percentage of Americans over the age of 65 . . . ,
U.S. Dept. of Health and Human Services, *A Profile of Older Americans: 2000*, 2.

109 Sons were also born to Shem . . . , Gen. 10:21–24.

115 <u>The Way We Live Now</u>
The duality of doing and being represents nearly universal human understanding. The conflict between *vita activa* and *vita contempletiva* was well known to the ancients. Even today, the relationship between being and doing forms a conscious part of the daily lives of billions of people. Given all this it might seem odd and quite unoriginal to use these ideas as the starting point for a map of life. In fact, I think their ubiquity forms the highest recommendation for employing them in this way. My work in this area is based first and foremost on the principle of direct observation. I am disposed to watch people and organizations closely. I do my best to understand why they choose to embrace some things and forego others. I am content to let others use such observations to form carefully developed models. In a sense, the difference between my academic friends and me is the same as that which separates the classically trained violinist from the folk musician. Both can rightfully be called musicians, but they understand music in very different ways. Among my academic friends, Dale Dannefer has written most insightfully about the human life cycle from the point of view of a rigorous and carefully developed theoretical model. Conversations with him have brought me many insights into this problem and I recommend his work to any who seek a deeper understanding of the arc that stretches from birth to death.

121 <u>Five Ages</u>
I love medicine because it is an intensely practical thing. I did my residency in Family Medicine and supposed at the time that I would spend my career in an office practice in a small town. During my training, I was well aware of the long-standing argument between generalists and specialists. The former have to contend with knowing less and less about more and more—until they know nothing about everything. The latter seek to know more and more about less and less—until they know everything about nothing. I have always sided with the generalists in this matter, but I am also aware that this chapter will expose me to criticism from those who know much more than I do about the particular aspects of the life cycle I propose. Such criticism can be useful and ought to be received with respect but does not itself invalidate the whole fabric of what I am proposing. Our society needs generalists, especially today, because generalism offers us the only opportunity we have to cavort wantonly across

the boundaries set by disciplines and experts. This annoys the specialists (and there are few things I enjoy more) but, in the end, even the dedicated generalist must submit his/her insights to the one test that matters most, "Do they yield useful results?" I am ready for such a test as long as we remember that the Five Ages I have proposed are offered as a useful way of thinking about the life cycle in contemporary society and not as an objective description of how life is actually being lived. This is the difference between a written review of a symphony's performance and the musical score that was actually performed.

TRAGEDY

131 <u>The Cult of Adulthood</u>

I have found that offering useful criticism of one's contemporary society is harder than it seems. On the one hand, there is a temptation to avoid unpleasant conclusions: no one really wants to be the bearer of bad news. Shying away from the harshness of reality, however, disqualifies one from being able to say anything new or valuable. The status quo has plenty of spokespeople who are willing to apologize for anything and everything that it might carry off. On the other hand, those willing to attack the conventional wisdom of their time risk being dismissed for being unfair, biased, emotionally overinvolved, or just thick-headed. The explicit comparison of adulthood with a society-wide cult is likely to upset many readers. I am willing to take my lumps for this mainly because (a) I think the analysis holds up well under close inspection and (b) I have long been inspired by the writings of a large number of cultural critics.

Among my favorites are Christopher Lasch for his dense, carefully argued analysis of the most ordinary arrangements of daily life. I particularly like his *Haven in a Heartless World*, which traces his views on the American family. I would also recommend *The Death and Life of Great American Cities* by Jane Jacobs. The book is as fresh, insightful, and worthy of attention as it was when it was published more than 40 years ago. Jacobs provided us all with a penetrating critique of the school of urban planning then in vogue. Her devastatingly accurate assessment of the movement's weaknesses would, by itself, be enough to recommend her book, but she went much further than that. The book also opens our eyes to how cities actually work, and how they can be made to work even better.

131 "no social study that does not come back to the problems . . . ,"
Mills, *The Sociological Imagination*, 6.

132 What is the structure of this particular society . . . , Mills, 6, 7.

139 "The ego is voracious and continually wants to . . . ," Armstrong,
Buddha, 74.

140 <u>The Assault on Childhood</u>
In my view, the human life cycle is a highly flexible and adaptive creation. Other creatures have the arc of their lives written into their
DNA. One controversial but highly readable exploration of the
creation and evolution of childhood is Philippe Ariès's *Centuries of
Childhood*. In its pages, the author traces the growth of childhood as
a unique and clearly identifiable portion of the life cycle during the
middle centuries of the last millennium. Even though the story he
tells continues to provoke objections from other experts in this area,
the basic idea (that we can invent and discard ways of living according to their usefulness to us) is useful to those who care about the
future of aging.

A realistic assessment of the recent history of childhood can be quite
chilling. Early drafts of this chapter included a lengthy list of outra-
geous examples of adulthood infringing on childhood. Ultimately,
the list was shortened substantially because I began finding examples
of the destruction of childhood in so many places that it seemed best
to give a handful of examples and then help the reader recognize this
trend in his/her own family and community. The strongest support
for this change came from speeches I gave where I talked about
changes in contemporary childhood. Listeners not only nodded with
recognition, they volunteered many persuasive examples drawn from
their own lives.

140 In cultures such as those of the Ituri villages . . . , Turnbull, *The
Human Cycle*, 83.

143 . . . to fashion a common national culture out of a far-flung . . . ,
Ivins and Dubose, *Bushwhacked*, 82.

143 self-governance through self-respect . . . , Ivins and Dubose,
Bushwhacked, 82.

144 "A generation ago, the latchkey child . . . ," McKee, *New York Times*, September 25, 2003.

144 . . . an exciting new volume filled with stories . . . , Amazon.com editorial review, *A Taste-Berry Teen's Guide to Setting and Achieving Goals*, 2002.

146 According to a study published in *The Lancet* . . . , van Heteren et al., "Fetal learning and memory," 1169–1170.

148 <u>Adult Forever</u>
Gluttony is the act of eating more than is necessary or even healthy. It implies a disregard for what food is for—the nourishment of our bodies and minds—and focuses instead on maximizing the pleasurable sensations of taste and satiety. This disconnection of hedonism and utility is also at the root of our contemporary overindulgence in adulthood. Society heaps the best of what it can offer on those who reach this status the soonest and hold it the longest. This, too, is a form of gluttony. The difference is that those who overeat (and are overweight) are exposed to a prejudice against obesity while those who cling to adulthood are given all possible praise. Our society is being placed in peril by a two-headed monster. The assault on childhood threatens our development as young people but, even more frighteningly, the gluttonous pursuit of adulthood places our elderhood at risk. I look forward to the emergence of a new social consciousness, one that inveighs against the refusal to acknowledge the passage of time to prepare oneself for the further development that accompanies one's passage into elderhood.

149 "I find these concepts . . . ," de Magalhães, "A Vision for senescence.info," 1997–2001.

150 "First, [we must] stop thinking about health . . . ," Roizen, *RealAge*, 5.

150 "The better condition you are in . . . ," Roizen, 5.

151 "I was so inspired by Oprah's show . . . ," Amazon.com editorial reviews, *RealAge*, 4.

152 This book supports the method of using biostasis . . . ,
Amazon.com customer reviews, *The Baby Boomers' Guide to Living Forever*, 3.

152 **Clearly written and well organized** . . . , Amazon.com customer reviews, *Look and Feel Fabulous Forever*, 6.

157 <u>**The Old-Age Archipelago**</u>
I had an interesting age-related experience of my own while I was developing this book. While I was working out the ideas contained in this chapter, I had a chance to present my arguments to a group of thoughtful people who happened to range widely in age. As I presented my contention that the contemporary system of institutional long-term care was, in many important ways, analogous to the gulag archipelago described by Aleksandr Solzhenitsyn, listeners over a certain age nodded with understanding if not with agreement. Those under a certain age gave me a puzzled look. Finally, one of the younger audience members asked, "What is the gulag? What is an archipelago?" It amazed me that terms that were commonly understood in my youth had vanished in the course of a single generation. Fortunately (or perhaps unfortunately), there is a deep and broad literature of totalitarianism that can easily refresh our memories. Most recently, Anne Applebaum published *Gulag* (and won the Pulitzer for nonfiction). Her book provides a scrupulous review of the anatomy and physiology of Stalin's Siberian concentration camps.

I fully expect many people who work in long-term care institutions, feel loyal toward them, or profit from them to be upset by the claim that nursing homes are "instruments of coercion." It could hardly be otherwise. Those closest to and most dependent on any given social system are the least likely to see its dark side plainly. In contrast, members of the public who have heard me review this argument have voiced their strong support for my conclusions. In fact, many times I have been asked why I have not been more negative about nursing homes. Such negativity is surely tempting. There is much that is wrong with that system and the harm it does is easily measured. Still, I believe that we should be sure to give credit where it is due. While my positive statements about what we have learned from institutionalizing older people are unlikely to mollify my critics, I think they are valid and worth mentioning.

158 **I recently returned from "rehabilitation care"** . . . , letter to author from a nursing home resident, date unknown.

159 **I too am very concerned about the way** . . . , letter to author from a prisoner, October 24, 2002.

162 **Deficiencies in Nursing Homes,** Charlene Harrington, PhD, RN, 1996.

167 <u>Private Grief, Public Tragedy</u>
I was born near the tail-end of the baby boom, in the midst of the Cold War, and took my place in a working class family living in a rural community. It was not until I entered college that I came to know the work of C. Wright Mills. I loved sociology, read all of Mills's books, and came to appreciate the depth of his insights. He helped me understand why I had always gone to school in recently constructed buildings. The greatest mass of the boomer generation was a few years ahead of me and their passage had led the school system to enlarge its capacity to meet their demand. A defense contractor had a plant in my county, and my parents had been fortunate enough to find work in it. As a result, my upbringing was financed in large part by the federal government's long struggle against communism. The point is that Mills showed me how to connect my personal memories and the events of my private life to history, society, demography, and the economy. His insight into the connections between biography and history continue to shape my view of the world. I continue to follow behind the great mass of the boomer generation, though they are now hurtling into old age. True to form, they are seeking some new secret, some special attribute that will allow them to perceive the lives they are living in some new way. They will search until they find a flickering light within the glowering darkness that lies ahead. This book is meant to assist in that search. However imperfect it might be, it offers readers a vision of a new kind of old age, one that can transcend both private grief and public tragedy.

167 **Riley Housewright, Microbiologist . . . ,** Martin, *New York Times,* January 16, 2003.

DISTANT THUNDER

179 <u>The Eden Alternative</u>
The Eden Alternative is, and is meant to be, an evolving set of practices that answer back to a consistent set of principles. Over the years I have written several books about this movement, and the nature of these books helps illustrate the twists and turns that make up its course to date. In 1994, the University of Missouri published *The*

Eden Alternative: Nature, Hope and Nursing Homes. That book emphasized the changes in the physical environment that accompany the adoption of the Eden Alternative. Two years (and an enormous amount of experience) later, VanderWyk and Burnham published *Life Worth Living: How Someone You Love Can Still Enjoy Life in a Nursing Home.* This book explored the organizational, cultural, and management challenges of Edenizing in far greater detail. In 1999, I wrote *Learning from Hannah: Secrets of a Life Worth Living* (VanderWyk and Burnham). The book was released in the summer of that year and in order to bring it to wider attention, my family and I went on a 10,000 mile bus tour to promote the book. In more than two dozen cities and in the space of one month we performed a two-act stage adaptation of the book's stories. In 2001 I self-published *The Eden Alternative Handbook: Building Human Habitats.* That book was written to support those people and organizations who were requesting a pathway for Edenizing. It offers a clear set of steps and recommended organizations that choose to embrace this philosophy.

I should also note that Christa Monkhouse published Über-Morgen (in German) in Zurich in 2004. Also that year Yuki Nakajima published in Japanese in Tokyo. Our goal is to ensure that these books are just the beginning of a long exploration of the ideas of the Eden Alternative in books, films, and articles. Those seeking a current picture of the movement should go to www.edenalt.com. We work hard to see that the site is up-to-date with news, information, and resources.

187 **Some examples of this trend at work . . . ,** see tables (next page) Eden-Related Outcome Data (Lakeland Specialty Hospital) and Eden-Related Outcome Date (Lenawee CMCF).

191 <u>Resistance</u>
In preparing for this chapter I spent a fair amount of time reading accounts of the French Resistance. In many ways the stories of those men and women provide a parallel with the struggles of those who would confront the cult of adulthood. Before exploring this idea in depth, it is important to remember that members of the resistance against Nazi power faced the prospect of imprisonment, torture, and even death. They risked everything in their campaign for freedom. Those who would challenge the current overwhelming authority of the institution of adulthood are confronted only by the potential of

Table: Eden-Related Outcome Data (Lakeland Specialty Hospital)

Lakeland Quality Indicators	1999	2001
Family Satisfaction	86%	92%
Federal-State Inspection Deficiencies	13	7
Prevalence of Weight Loss	11%	5%
Prevalence of Bedfast Elders	15%	14%
Prevalence of Depression	19%	9%
Prevalence of Psychotropic Medications	15%	7%

Table: Eden-Related Outcome Data (Lenawee CMCF)

Lenawee Quality Indicators	1998	2001
Prevalence of Falls	94%	41%
Prevalence of Weight Loss	81%	68%
Prevalence of Bedfast Elders	95%	79%
Prevalence of Pressure Ulcers	81%	72%

embarrassment, frustration, and failure. Given these relatively minor risks one would suppose that millions would swarm to the banner of resistance to the cult of adulthood. In fact, the opposite is true.

The reason for the relative lack of interest in this endeavor is that adulthood reinforces rather than violates our most deeply held beliefs. It speaks in our own voice and in our native tongue. Adulthood never disturbs us with the equivalent of a coarse-throated soldier in uniform. We have yet to develop a consciousness that fully supports the idea of a meaningful life beyond adulthood. Lacking such a vision, we find little cause to resist. This is why I find the literature of the resistance in World War II to be so useful. My favorite book is *A Test of Courage* by Christopher Robbins. The book tells the story of one man's relentless fight to find freedom, for himself and his nation. It is useful for those who would oppose the status quo to be reminded of the sacrifices that the truly courageous were willing to make in the face of what was truly evil. The example of their courage comforts us by showing us how small the effort needed to resist the cult of adulthood really is.

202 **Place and No Place**

The title of this chapter makes use of a play on words. "Utopia," which literally means that "no place" usually thought of as an ideal circumstance, is something so right and good that it could not possibly exist in the real world. This cynicism is encouraged by the prevailing social structure because it reduces the possibility that people will begin to take such an alternative seriously. I am interested here in the more literal meaning of "no place." To be human and to be made to live a life without having the comfort of place in one's life is exceptionally harmful. Seen this way, "no place" represents the polar opposite of a utopia. America has, in my opinion, produced one great writer on the question of place. Wendell Berry, poet, essayist, and novelist, has explored the terrain of place in the land and in the mind for decades. Among his many insightful books, I must recommend *The Unsettling of America, The Gift of Good Land, What Are People For?* and *A Continuous Harmony.* For Berry, place matters greatly because it is the single greatest source of meaning. Rural or urban, valley or mountain, temperate or tropical, the land we come from molds the culture we are nurtured within and, ultimately, shapes our lives. Except, when it doesn't. To be torn from those roots, especially in old age, and being made to seek meaning as an unknown person in an unknown place is a great tragedy.

204 **First, all aspects of life are conducted in the same place . . . ,** Goffman, *Asylums,* 6.

205 **A sage took a young man . . . ,** Japanese folktale as remembered by author.

208 **Elderhood's Sanctuary**

Human warmth is an inherently subjective thing. Our sense of safety and well-being varies from moment to moment and can never be fully known by another person. Even so, the idea of a safe harbor, a haven from every storm, has nearly universal appeal. The desire to create a sanctuary of any kind or for any reason implies a faith in the essential sacredness of what is being protected. It is for this reason that the notion of a sanctuary for elders and elderhood can seem somewhat odd and out of place. After all, no one would ever look at a landfill and see it as a sanctuary for solid waste. A prison bulging with inmates would never be confused with a place of refuge. The first step, then, is to be willing to see elders and elderhood as precious, even sacred things that are worthy of the highest form of protection that society has to offer. Such a leap is a challenge for those reared in a society that equates aging with decline. Pervasive ageism tempts people to blend the virtue of protection with the vice of reform. Those who would create a sanctuary for elderhood must resist the temptation to offer shelter in order to repair, restore, or rehabilitate elders. Any true sanctuary accepts people as they are. This acceptance is the foundation for a habilitative approach to elders and elderhood. Our goal is to help elders be elders, to cherish and be cherished. Folklore (I especially like *The Complete Grimm's Fairy Tales)* is full of examples where a magical spell is cast over a beautiful young man or woman, transforming them into a repulsive creature. The enchantment endures until some person offers unconditional love. The gift of being loved in this way unlocks the enchantment and the true form of the person is revealed. The same can be said of our work with elders: it is the act of accepting them as they are that releases their potential to become, fully, the people they are destined to become.

208 "It's a big change here . . . ," Kleiner, *Where River Turns to Sky*, 190.

210 What I wish to emphasize . . . , Schumacher, *Small Is Beautiful*, 65–66.

222 The Green House

The greatest part of human experience has been lived within the confines of family, tribe, and clan. The great innovation that is at the heart of modern society is not, as is often supposed, the great rise in the power of our tools but rather the even greater faith we place in living life as individuals. No matter how storm-tossed contemporary society may make us feel, there are few among us who would wish for a return to traditional forms of social organization with their strictly enforced role definitions. The irony is that for thousands of years, some people have chosen to leave society-at-large and enter into intentional communities. These small communities did for social structure what user-defined architecture has done for the physical spaces we inhabit. For most of human history nearly all people have lived in buildings that were designed and constructed by their occupants. Professional architecture is a relative newcomer to society and, on the whole, its contributions to social well-being have been mixed. The best, most comprehensive, and most persuasive argument in favor of indigenous, user-defined design is *A Pattern Language* by Christopher Alexander, et al. Over the course of a thousand pages, the authors show how people faced with common design problems tend to rely on a consistent pattern of design responses. It is an easy argument to follow because the results are evident in the still significant part of the built environment that is still user designed. What is more difficult to grasp is the idea that people might be able to create user-defined *social* structures that help them cope with common problems of living. The Green House makes the best use it can of enhancements in the design of the physical and cyber spaces it provides for elders, but those features are actually secondary to its most important innovation. Most of all the Green House represents a new pattern language for addressing the social and cultural challenges that arise from growing old in a viciously ageist society. Those who seek a deeper understanding of what the Green House means should read Alexander's book while keeping in mind that it is possible for people to be as intentional about the communities they create as they are about the buildings they construct. It is the combination of both those perspectives that makes a revolution in late-life human development not just possible but probable.

A Wink and a Smile

239 Midwife of Elderhood
To understand the revolutionary nature of the shahbaz, I would like to suggest *Painless Childbirth* by Fernand Lamaze. Going beyond that text, there is the whole history of the natural childbirth movement. It is a good historical analogue to what is going on with aging in the twenty-first century.

239 Summertime and the livin' . . . , Gershwin and Heyward.
"Summertime," 1935.

247 Research supports . . .
Advanced training . . . , Grant et al., 1996.
Permanent assisgnment . . . , Teresi et al., 1993.
Involvement in decision making . . . , Waxman et al., 1984.
Self-managed work teams . . . , Yeatts and Seward, 2000.
Better pay . . . , Yamada, 2002.

248 The First Shahbaz
During the time I was preparing the ideas and arguments that make up this book, one issue was raised repeatedly by thoughtful readers

of early versions of the manuscript. Why? Why, they asked have you
sabotaged your argument for a new profession dedicated to late-life
development by giving it the foreign-sounding name *shahbaz*? Most
people have demanded that I choose a term that is much more familiar (and easier on the tongue). The reason for my stubborn insistence
on *shahbaz* lies in the importance I place on creating a clear break
with the past. The problems that cripple the jobs we create for those
who choose to work with elders are inevitable given the declinist
vision of aging that these occupations are founded upon. The choice
is between modest incremental improvements in working conditions
and management techniques, and a much more radical attempt to
create something that is new and embraces its originality without
apology. This is disruptive change and therefore uncomfortable for
most of the people involved. My study of social change has led me
to conclude that such change is always made more palatable when its
rough edges are smoothed by a story. One powerful type of story is
the myth of origin. Such stories attempt to explain the emergence of
a disruptive phenomenon on the social scene. The oldest and most
powerful of these stories attempt to explain the creation of the world
and the origin of humankind. The most recent examples can be
found in the literature of the comic book superhero, from Superman
to Batman to Spiderman. These stories draw strength from society's
longing for an omnipotent force willing to protect common people.

256 <u>The Problem of Protection</u>
When I was in college, the State University of New York changed its
motto from "Let each become all he is capable of being" to "To
learn, to search, to serve." I opposed this change—without success.
The change was justified in large part by the desire to scrub away the
sexist reference to "he" that seemed to exclude the growing number
of women in the university system. While that was and remains a
noble goal, I was more concerned with the paternalistic formulation
of the new motto. In speeches and op-ed articles I asked, "Whom are
we to serve and to what purpose?" Looking back on this little academic tempest, I can see the conflict between the hierarchical vision
of protection, with its emphasis on relative strength, and the spiritual
interpretation, with its insistence on equality. This distinction, once
it becomes apparent to the observer, is useful in many different ways.
From foreign policy to corporate human resource policies to family
law, we struggle to reconcile our conflicted visions of protection.
One of the best explorations of this topic that I know is Richard
Sennett's *Authority*. While Sennett addresses the question from the

perspective of a social psychologist, those seeking a more general examination of the workings of this conflict should read John Kenneth Galbraith's *The Anatomy of Power.*

263 Convivium

Long-term care is like one of those enchanted mirrors that show people as they truly are. When we look at nursing homes, we see the essence of American culture shorn of the frippery that suffuses life in a commercial culture. The future of our collective relationship with food is on display in a nursing home dining room near you. The main features are insipid commercially prepared food and an unending round of mealtimes shared in a room full of strangers. Marx argued that culture was derived from an underlying pattern of economic relationships. He might have argued that our culture is defined by our relationship to food. From agriculture (with its rain dances and harvest rituals), to the local patterns of food preservation and storage, to the planning and preparation of meals (including food taboos and ritually significant menus), to the ancient experience of sharing a meal with people who are important to us, our relationship to food does much to shape our shared culture. Significant changes in our relationship to food provide important clues to changes in society. The "slow food" movement offers much more than a new way to think about and enjoy food. The pursuit of locally distinctive ingredients, prepared slowly according to traditional recipes and shared intentionally and with pleasure by people who care for one another—all of these things are essential tools that can serve those who seek a better kind of culture. I suggest that those who would like to follow this line of thinking further go to a local bookstore and browse the cookbooks for works that explicitly combine recipes with a view of culture, society, and the good life. One book that does this is *If Kallimos Had a Chef* by Debra Stark.

270 The Twofold Path

The work of shahbazim is founded on the principle of reciprocity. The relationships they create with one another and the elders of the Green House are meant to be two-dimensional. A surprising number of people object to this arrangement, mainly on the basis that relationships based on the ongoing development of mutual advantage and growth are beyond the capacity of the men and women who work and live in Green Houses. I am offended by this view because I think it reeks of ageism and bigotry. In fact, the capacity to reach for and achieve mastery is all around us. We pervert humanity's intrinsic and nearly inexhaustible potential for growth and development when we confine people, young or old, to narrow, task-oriented social roles. I have been blessed with the opportunity to study and practice medicine. At every point in my education and training it was assumed that I had the potential to become a skilled and compassionate physician. The faith that was placed in me, and maintained despite my inevitable lapses in judgment and maturity, sustained me over the long years of study. There is no reason why a similar faith cannot or should not be given to the people who live and work in Green Houses. Elder and shahbaz alike, these people hold within them the seeds of greatness. The most rousing affirmation of this ideal that I am familiar with is A. S. Neill's classic work *Summerhill: A Radical Approach to Child Rearing*. In his book, Neill not only attacked the narrow, punitive, pessimistic vision of children and education that held sway in mid-twentieth-century Western societies, he went on to offer a tangible alternative to the status quo, one that demonstrated in practice what an enlightened vision of childhood learning and development could accomplish. It is an excellent book for those interested in Green Houses to read and reflect on.

THE RIPENING

277 <u>Elderhood Reborn</u>
I have been inspired and influenced by the work of Rabbi Schachter-Shalomi and his masterful book *From Age-ing to Sage-ing*. Marc Freedman's *Prime Time: How Baby Boomers Will Revolutionize Retirement and Transform America* is also very good, especially the section on leaving a legacy. I like and recommend Bertrand Russell's essay "In Praise of Idleness," which can be found with a collection of other essays in a book by the same name.

280 **An elder is a person/Who is still growing . . . ,"** Barkan, *Journal of Social Work in Long-Term Care*, 201.

286 <u>On Being an Elder</u>
How do you live as an elder? This question might seem odd coming from a writer who is still in the grip of adulthood. As of this writing, my own elderhood lies somewhere in the future. Still, there is a long tradition of writers being able to gain insight into others' ways of living, even when those lives lay outside of the lived experience of the writers. Adults can write perceptively about the difficulties of child-

hood. Certain male writers have demonstrated an acute understanding of the lives led by women. My thoughts about elders and elderhood spring from observation rather than subjective experience. It is clear to me that we are (or could be) in the process of becoming an elder from the moment we first draw a breath. Children whose lives are enriched by meaningful intergenerational relationships are actually beginning to prepare themselves for their own elderhood. Adults who become conscious of the need to take time for *being* in daily life are setting the stage for a good elderhood in the years to come. Elders who are willing to state plainly that they are no longer adults fortify themselves for the tasks that are native to living as elders even as they serve as examples to others.

The specific tasks I have named as being central to elderhood are by no means universal. In other societies, in other times, other tasks may well be paramount. What is most important is the idea that this is a time of development. Some might feel that the emphasis on development in late life is actually a rationalization of narcissism. I do not see it that way because it is possible to connect the personal development experienced by older people (gerotranscendance, for example) as an important building block for society as a whole. In other words, we are all impoverished when older people remain developmentally disabled adults, unable to grasp and make use of elderhood and all that it has to offer.

295 **The problems of aging and long-term care . . .** , Fox, *personal correspondence to author,* date unknown.

296 **"message wherefore I am sent into the world,"** Tyndale, *Webster's 1913 Dictionary.*

299 <u>Eldertopia</u>
Several early readers of this manuscript counseled me against using the term *Eldertopia.* I had coined the term to describe the specifically human pattern of deliberate and ongoing multigenerational reciprocity. Strangely enough, this system of cooperation has not had a name attached to it. My critics accepted that point but went on to warn that *Eldertopia* could be interpreted as some kind of "utopia for greedy geezers." That might be true, but I chose to embrace rather than run away from this misunderstanding. Utopian writing of any kind succeeds or fails according to the willingness of the author to be specific about the better world that is being imagined for the reader.

On one hand, those who retreat to the safety offered by a high moral ground often are not taken seriously because they refuse to engage the practical difficulties that arise immediately upon posing the question "How are we to live?" On the other hand, those who offer direct, specific, and detailed ideas and arguments risk being dismissed on the grounds of impracticality and excessive optimism. It should be remembered that Eldertopia is offered as a vision of what might be, if we are willing to change our minds about aging and longevity. I recognize that it is possible to paint a much more disturbing picture of the future, one that is based on the plague of locusts mentality, but I will leave that task for others.

The great tragedy of our time springs from the transformation of our collective longevity—and the good that the age boom can do for us all—into some frightful, impossible burden, as though it were a luxury we cannot possibly afford. The turn of this century forms the cusp of a history-making struggle. The cult of adulthood must be confronted, exposed, and dissolved before it does permanent damage to us all. As strange as it may seem, it is the elders of our time—the people who have been labeled as the least worthy, the furthest from power and influence, and the most unlikely revolutionaries the world has ever seen—who must guide us. We are being given the opportunity to create a modern Eldertopia. It is our shared success or failure in this endeavor that will shape not only our own old age but the well-being of our children, our grandchildren, and their children as well.

301 Former Colorado governor Richard Lamm . . . , Lamm, "The Moral Imperative of Limiting Elderly Health Entitlements, "199–209.

BIBLIOGRAPHY

Alexander, Christopher, Sara Ishikawa, and Murray Silverstein. *A Pattern Language: Towns, Buildings, Construction.* New York: Oxford University Press, 1977.

Amazon.com. *The Baby Boomers' Guide to Living Forever.* Customer Reviews. http://www.amazon.com/exec/obidos/tg/detail/ -/0967271207/qid=1081366431/sr=1-1/ref=s...

Amazon.com. *Look and Feel Fabulous Forever: The World's Best Supplements, Anti-Aging Techniques, and High-Tech.* Customer Reviews. http://www.amazon.com/exec/obidos/tg/detail/ -/0060988908/qid=1081438060/sr=1-1/ref=s...

Amazon. com. *RealAge: Are You as Young as You Can Be?* Editorial Reviews. http://www.amazon.com/exec/obidos/tg/detail/ -/0060930756/ref=lpr_g_2/103-7550207- 9197412?v=glance&s=books.

Amazon.com. *A Taste-Berry Teen's Guide to Setting and Achieving Goals (Taste Berries for Teens).* Editorial Reviews. http://www.amazon.com/exec/obidos/tg/detail/ -/0757300405/qid=1080155108/sr=1-4/ref=...

American Heritage Dictionary of the English Language, Fourth Edition. Boston: Houghton Mifflin Company, 2000.

Applebaum, Anne. *Gulag: A History.* New York: Doubleday, 2003.

Ariès, Philippe. *Centuries of Childhood: A Social History of Family Life.* Translated by Robert Baldick. New York: Vintage Books, 1962.

Armstrong, Karen. *Buddha.* New York: Penguin Putnam, 2001.

Barkan, Barry. "The Live Oak Definition of an Elder," in "Culture Change in Long-Term Care, Part I." Edited by Audrey S. Weiner and Judah L. Ronch. *Journal of Social Work in Long-Term Care* 2, nos. 1/2 (2003): 201.

Beauvoir, Simone de. *The Coming of Age.* Translated by Patrick O'Brian. New York: Putnam, 1972.

Bell, Virginia, and David Troxel. *The Best Friends' Approach to Alzheimer's Care.* Baltimore: Health Professions Press, 1997.

Berry, Wendell. *A Continuous Harmony: Essays Cultural and Agricultural.* Washington, DC: Shoemaker and Hoard, 2004.

————. *The Gift of Good Land: Further Essays Cultural and Agricultural.* San Francisco: North Point Press, 1981.

————. *The Unsettling of America: Culture and Agriculture.* San Francisco: Sierra Club Books, 1996.

————. *What Are People For?* Essays. San Francisco: North Point Press, 1990.

Bullfinch, Thomas. *Mythology.* New York: Dell, 1967.

Carstensen, Laura L., Monisha Pasupathi, Ulrich Mayr, and John R. Nesselroade. "Emotional Experience in Everyday Life Across the Adult Life Span." *Journal of Personality and Social Psychology* 79, no.4 (2000): 644–655.

Council on Foreign Relations. "Other Biological Agents: Botulism, Plague, Tularemia, HFVs," *Terrorism Questions & Answers.* http://cfrterrorism.org/weapons/otheragents.html.

Darwin, Charles. *The Origin of Species by Means of Natural Selection: or the Preservation of Favored Races in the Struggle for Life.* New York: Avenel Books, 1979.

de Magalhães, J. "A Vision of senescence.info," 1997–2001, http://www.senescence.info/sad.htm.

Defoe, Daniel. *Robinson Crusoe.* New York: Scholastic, 1964.

Foresman, S. *The Complete Works of William Shakespeare: Volume V.* Toronto: Bantam Books, 1980.

Freedman, Marc. *Prime Time: How Baby Boomers Will Revolutionize Retirement and Transform America.* New York: PublicAffairs, 2002.

Friedan, Betty. *The Fountain of Age.* New York: Simon & Schuster, 1995.

Galbraith, John Kenneth. *The Anatomy of Power.* Reprint, Boston: Houghton Mifflin Company, 1985.

"Gentling." *Encyclopedia Britannica,* 1979.

Gershwin, George, and DuBose Heyward. "Summertime." Warner Music, 1935.

Gesler, Wilbert M. *Healing Places.* Lanham: Rowman & Littlefield, 2003.

Goffman, Erving. *Asylums: Essays on the Social Situation of Mental Patients and Other Inmates.* Garden City: Doubleday and Company, Inc., 1961.

Golding, William. *Lord of the Flies.* New York: Riverhead, 1954.

Grant, L., R. Kane, S. Potthoff, and M. Ryden. "Staff training and turnover in Alzheimer special care units: Comparisons with non-special care units," *Geriatric Nursing* 17 (1996): 278-282.

Grimm, Brothers, and Josef Scharl. *The Complete Grimm's Fairy Tales.* New York: Pantheon Books, 1974.

Hillman, James. *The Force of Character: And the Lasting Life.* New York: Random House, 1999.

Ivins, Molly, and Lou Dubose. *Bushwhacked: Life in George W. Bush's America.* New York: Random House, 2003.

Jacobs, Jane. *The Death and Life of Great American Cities.* New York: Random House, 1961.

Johnson, Mark H. "Functional Brain Development in Humans," *Nature Reviews Neuroscience* 2, no. 7 (2001): 475–483.

Kafka, Franz. *Metamorphosis.* Translated by Albert L. Lloyd. New York: Vanguard Press, 1946.

Kleiner, Gregg. *Where River Turns to Sky.* New York: Avon Books, 1996.

Kuczynski, Alex. "In Quest for Wrinkle-Free Future, Frown Becomes Thing of the Past." *New York Times,* February 7, 2002.

Lamaze, Fernand. *Painless Childbirth: The Lamaze Method,* rev. ed. New York: McGraw-Hill, 1984.

Lamm, Richard. "The Moral Imperative of Limiting Elderly Health Entitlements," *Policies for an Aging Society.* Edited by Stuart H. Altman and David I. Shactman, Baltimore: The Johns Hopkins University Press, 2002.

Lasch, Christopher. *Haven in a Heartless World: The Family Besieged.* New York: Basic Books, 1977.

Martin, Douglas. "Obituaries." *New York Times,* January 16, 2003.

McKee, Bradford. "Scheduling In Some Dawdle Time," *New York Times,* September 25, 2003.

Mills, C. Wright. *The Sociological Imagination.* Oxford: Oxford University Press, 2000.

Neill, Alexander Sutherland. *Summerhill: A Radical Approach to Child Rearing.* UK: Penguin Books, 1968.

NewsHour with Jim Lehrer/Kaiser Family Foundation/Harvard School of Public Health. *National Survey on Nursing Homes.* September 2001.

Palmore, Erdman. *Ageism: Negative and Positive.* New York: Springer Publishing Company, 1999.

Perricone, Nicholas. *The Wrinkle Cure: Unlock the Power of Cosmeceuticals for Supple, Youthful Skin.* New York: Warner Books, 2000.

Proust, Marcel. BrainyQuote. http://www.brainyquote.com/quotes/quotes/m/marcelprou107111.html.

Putnam, Robert D. *Bowling Alone: The Collapse and Revival of American Community.* New York: Simon & Schuster, 2000.

Robbins, Christopher. *A Test of Courage: The Michel Thomas Story.* New York: Free Press, 2000.

Roizen, Michael F., and Elizabeth Anne Stephenson. *RealAge: Are You as Young as You Can Be?* New York: HarperCollins, 1999.

Roszak, Theodore. *America the Wise: The Longevity Revolution and the True Wealth of Nations.* Boston: Houghton Mifflin, 1998.

———. *The Voice of the Earth: An Exploration of Ecopsychology.* Grand Rapids: Phanes Press, 2001.

Rukeyser, Muriel. BrainyQuote. http://www.brainyquote.com/quotes/quotes/m/murielrukel131826.html.

Russell, Bertrand. "In Praise of Idleness," *In Praise of Idleness and Other Essays.* Reprint, New York: Routledge, 1994.

Sagan, Carl. *The Dragons of Eden: Speculations on the Evolution of Human Intelligence.* New York: Random House, 1977.

Schachter-Shalomi, Zalman, and Ronald S. Miller. *From Age-Ing to Sage-Ing: A Profound New Vision of Growing Older,* New York: Warner Books, 1995.

Schlesinger, Arthur M. *The Crisis of the Old Order, 1919–1933.* Boston: Houghton Mifflin, 2003.

————. *The Coming of the New Deal, 1933–1935*. Boston: Houghton Mifflin, 2003.

Schumacher, E.F. *Small Is Beautiful: Economics as if People Mattered*. New York: Harper & Row, 1973.

Scott, Walter. *Ivanhoe*. New York: Modern Library, 1997.

Sear, Rebecca, Ruth Mace, and Ian A. McGregor. "Maternal grandmothers improve nutritional status and survival of children in rural Gambia," *Proceedings of the Royal Society of London* 267 (2000): 1641–1647.

Sennett, Richard. *Authority*. Reissue, New York: W. W. Norton & Company, 1993.

Shakespeare, William. *As You Like It*. Edited by Agnes Latham. London: Methuen & Co. Ltd., 1975.

Solon. *The Ages of Man*. http://www.humanistictexts.org/grkanalec.htm.

Stark, Debra. *If Kallimos Had a Chef: Natural Recipes for a Natural World*. Acton, MA: VanderWyk & Burnham, 2001.

Strehler, Bernard, and Albert Mildvan. "General Theory of Mortality and Aging," *Science* 132, no. 3418 (Jul 1, 1960): 14–21.

Tennyson, Alfred Lord. "Ulysses," in *Committed to Memory: 100 Best Poems to Memorize*. Edited by John Hollander. New York: Academy of American Poets, 1996.

Teresi, J.A., D. Holmes, and C. Monaco. "An evaluation of the effects of commingling cognitively and non-cognitively impaired individuals in long term care facilities," *Gerontologist* 33 (1993): 350–358.

Thomas, William H. *Learning from Hannah: Secrets for a Life Worth Living*. Acton, MA: VanderWyk & Burnham,1999.

————. *Life Worth Living: How Someone You Love Can Still Enjoy Life in a Nursing Home—The Eden Alternative in Action*. Acton, MA: VanderWyk & Burnham, 1996.

————. *The Eden Alternative Handbook: Building Human Habitats*. Sherburne, NY: Self-published by author, 2001.

Tornstam, Lars. "Gerotranscendence: The Contemplative Dimension of Aging," *Journal of Aging Studies* 11, no. 2:143–154.

Turnbull, Colin M. *The Human Cycle*. New York: Simon & Schuster, 1983.

Tyndale, William. "Legacy," *Webster's 1913 Dictionary*. http://www.hyperdictionary.com/dictionary/legacy.

U. S. Department of Health and Human Services. Administration on Aging. *Profile of Older Americans: 2000*.

van Heteren, Cathelijne F., P. Focco Boekkooi, Henk W. Jongsma, and Jan G. Nijhuis. "Fetal learning and memory," *The Lancet* 356, no. 9236 (30 September 2000): 1169–1170.

Varecha, Vladimír, trans. *Grimms' Fairy Tales*. London: Cathay Books, 1979.

Waxman, H. M., E. A. Carner, and G. Berkenstock. "Job turnover and job satisfaction among nursing home aides," *Gerontologist* 24 (1984): 503–509.

Wilson, Fred. "Allergan Inc.'s Botox: An Opportunity for Dermatologists," *OTA: Off the Record Research*, May 16, 2002.

Wright, Robert. *Non-Zero: The Logic of Human Destiny*. New York: Pantheon, 2000.

Yamada, Yoshiko. "Profile of home care aides, nursing home aides, and hospital aides: Historical changes and data recommendations," *Gerontologist* 42, no. 2 (2002): 199–206.

Yeatts, Dale, and Rudy Seward. "Reducing turnover and improving health care in nursing homes: The potential effects of self-managed work teams," *Gerontologist* 40, no. 3 (2000): 358–363.

INDEX

Printed in the United States
202826BV00003B/1-75/P